THE TAROT THER

By STEVE HOUI

THE TAROT THERAPY DECK

ISBN 978-1899878468

ACKNOWLEDGEMENTS

This work is dedicated to the Spirit of the Tarot, that body of energy that exists in and of itself having been thus formed across the years by all those who contribute to it by offering their motivations, thoughts, feelings and actions in pursuit of their love of the Tarot, which includes you.

My deep gratitude and admiration also to the following –

Amy Clayton for unswerving belief and support in this, and many other endeavours.

Diane Smurthwaite for willing acceptance and swift execution of the unenviable task of proof reading my stunted efforts.

Angie Lilley for the image for Five of Water – Stream

The many lovely souls who have offered encouragement, comments, feedback and questions in the last two years of the creation of this project.

May the light of the Hermit shine on you all.

Contents

INTRODUCTION – MY SEEKERS QUEST 1

BACKGROUND - THE TAROT STRIPPED BARE 5

   THE NATURE OF ENERGY – THE ENERGY OF NATURE 10

   THE NATURE OF THE DECK – THE DECK OF NATURE 11

STRUCTURE OF THE DECK..14

   MAJOR ARCANA – SOUL CARDS 14

   MINOR ARCANA – ELEMENT CARDS...............................15

   NUMBER CARDS 18

   COMPOUND CARDS 20

PRACTICALITIES OF TAROT THERAPY...................................25

   YOU DON'T HAVE TO BE PSYCHIC TO READ THE TAROT –
   BUT IT HELPS! 25

   TAROT IS JUST A TOOL...27

   REVERSED CARDS 28

   DEFINING THE READING AND THE PSYCHIC GAME 30

   READING WITHOUT SPREADS.....................................32

   ENERGY BALANCING 35

   MAKING IT UP AS YOU GO ALONG!...............................41

THE CARDS 44

0 – THE CANYON..45

1 – TORNADO 52

2 - WATERFALL 60

3 - RAINFOREST 68

4 - DESERT 75

5 - ECLIPSE 83

6 - TSUNAMI 90

7 - AVALANCHE 98

8 - EARTHQUAKE 105

9 - AURORA..111

10 - HURRICANE 117

11 - MOUNTAIN 123

12 - GLACIER 130

13 - DROUGHT 136

14 - RAINBOW 142

15 - INFERNO 149

16 - VOLCANO...157

17 - FIRMAMENT 164

18 - MOON 171

19 - SUN..177

20 - METEOR 183

21 - EARTH 190

THE MINOR ARCANA 196

   COMPOUND CARDS.......................................199

EARTH ELEMENT..204

   1 - SEED...206

   2 - ROOT 209

   3 - SHOOT 213

   4 - LEAF 216

   5 - BUD..220

   6 - FLOWER 223

   7 - POLLEN 226

   8 - FRUIT 229

   9 - HARVEST..233

10 - COMPOST 237

EARTH OF EARTH - BEDROCK 241

EARTH OF FIRE - CHARCOAL 245

EARTH OF WATER – QUICKSAND 248

EARTH OF AIR – DUST STORM 252

WATER ELEMENT 256

1 - DROP 258

2 - RAIN 262

3 - SPRING 266

4 - POND 270

5 - STREAM 274

6 - RIVER 278

7 - LAKE 282

8 - SEA 286

9 - OCEAN 290

10 - VAPOUR 294

WATER OF EARTH – MARSH 298

WATER OF FIRE – GEYSER 301

WATER OF WATER – WHIRLPOOL 305

WATER OF AIR – SNOW 308

AIR ELEMENT 312

1 - ATMOSPHERE 314

2 – CONVERGENCE 318

3 – PRESSURE 322

4 – DOLDRUMS 326

5 – GUST 329

6 – FRONT 333

7 – TRADE WIND 337

8 – GALE 341

9 – JET STREAM 344

10 – ZEPHYR 348

AIR OF EARTH – DUST DEVIL 352

AIR OF FIRE – HEAT HAZE 356

AIR OF WATER – FOG 360

AIR OF AIR – GAS 364

FIRE ELEMENT 368

ONE – SPARK 370

2 – FLAME 374

3 – FLARE 378

4 – FIRE WHIRLS 382

5 – LIGHTNING 386

6 – BRUSH FIRE 390

7 – WILDFIRE 394

8 - FIRESTORM 398

9 - HEATWAVE 402

10 - EMBERS 406

FIRE OF EARTH – CINDER 410

FIRE OF FIRE – PLASMA 413

FIRE OF WATER – MAGMA 417

FIRE OF AIR - SMOKE 421

CARD BACKS 424

CONCLUSION 427

FURTHER READING 429

TAROT THERAPY PRODUCTS 430

THE TAROT THERAPY DECK

INTRODUCTION – MY SEEKERS QUEST

I began my journey with the Tarot when as a schoolboy I would do readings for my friends – I never was a normal kind of child! These 'readings' consisted of laying out the cards in the ubiquitous Celtic Cross Spread and looking up the meanings in the book that came with the cards. This was with the Morgan Greer deck, which I still have over 30 years later and is now wonderfully dog-eared and loved.

This process continued, with my adding further books and cards to my arsenal. As I did so I found myself struggling to relate what the books told me with what I was seeing on the cards. It was only when I gained the confidence to say what It was I was seeing on the cards that my 'clients' started to tell me it made real sense to them and that they were amazed.

Not as much as me however, but it was enough to spur me on a voyage of discovery, that continues to this day. This has led me through a great many decks, even more books, as well as teaching courses, writing my own books and exploring every aspect of the Tarot I can lay my hands on. This deck is the culmination of that journey so far.

Along the way I made a study of the symbolism and all manner of applications the Tarot can be put to. My conclusion has been that the Tarot is a great many things and has the ability to be all things to all people. I have often described it as the central spine on my spiritual path, which is really the only purpose of our life.

What started out as a fascination with the occult found its home in the Tarot and is now a deep admiration, love, passion, awe and probably a little obsession! By applying these things I came up with the term 'Tarot Therapy' as an apt

1

summary of how I came to view and try to use the cards. This is not unique to me of course and it is not a new kind of therapy or system I have devised – I'm not that clever!

What it is though, is what I consider to be a deeper application and use of the vast body of wisdom and knowledge that the Tarot encapsulates. As I progressed on my Quest I found myself wondering what the purpose of predicting the future was. We are clearly able to make accurate predictions of the future and have done so for many a long year, through various oracular means, from the flight of birds, the fall of sticks or stones, gazing at clouds, fire and sand, the lines on our palms and the deal of cards. Over the years of my quest I have seen far too many undeniably accurate predictions made, to astonishing detail, by many talented 'readers' to tell me other than that we can predict our future.

But if we do have the ability to tell the future, as it seems we do, what good does it do us, of itself? The answer to this can only be that it allows us to attempt to make changes if we wish and as we see and feel it appropriate to do so. We read a great deal these days about the nature of 'creating our own reality' and it is here that Tarot Therapy can come into its own.

As I worked professionally as a 'fortune-teller', I could not escape a nagging sensation that I was not really helping my clients, which along with my love of the Tarot, was my prime motivation. It was when I began to apply a more therapeutic approach to my readings that I began to feel I was reaching the requisite level of effectiveness and purpose to what I was doing.

This led me to work all the more with the Tarot and ultimately to the creation of this deck. The idea behind this was to equip the client to take the lead in the creation of their reality by focussing more on the present time than the future. With knowledge of the esoteric reality of this gained from my additional studies along the way, I came to see how the Tarot could be used as a tool to examine and explore the underlying influences and energies causal to what we experience in ourselves and lives.

By helping the client to understand these processes and energies I came to see my readings as a form of self-empowerment - helping the client to help themselves, as I often term it. What is vital to realise here is the nature of energy and how it exists at a deeper and as said, causal level, of our reality. It is at this level that the energies of the Tarot can really be applied to their best therapeutic use and purpose.

By investigation of the cards at this underlying structural level of life we can determine something of the why and wherefore of what we are experiencing. In effect we act as interpreter of the energies of the cards on behalf of our client. To this end, using the energies of the Tarot can show the relationship between the impulse, thought, feeling and action, as we shall see in the next section.

We need to realise here that although we can peer expectantly into the future by using the Tarot (and many other methods) this does not mean it is fixed. I have found in fact, quite the opposite. We are indeed the prime architect of our reality – or if not the architect at least the Master Mason. By seeing the possible or likely trends that are affecting us at this energetic, causal level and the use of active responses to these things, we can realise the great possibilities open to ourselves, at all levels of our individual being and the life we can experience.

On my Quest I have been lucky enough to have been able to produce three previous works on the Tarot (see 'Further

Reading' at the back of the book) and there I have tried to explain the ideas and working practices of Tarot Therapy, along with some explanation of the cards at this level. All this came out of an ongoing programme of study of esoteric and spiritual subjects, with a number of different tutors and organisations, each of which have played their part in the realisation of this Tarot deck and to whom I owe a great debt of gratitude.

As I enjoyed working with a number of different Tarot decks on my Quest and marvelled at their creation, as well as the adaptability and evolution of the Tarot, I eventually realised that what was needed was a Tarot deck that expressed these energies I had become so intrigued and enthralled by. It was this that led to the creation of this deck.

The Tarot Therapy Deck is then an attempt at depicting the energy of the cards. This book is a vital accompaniment to those cards, explaining as it does the nature and expression of those energies and hopefully, how the whole thing works!

BACKGROUND - THE TAROT STRIPPED BARE

The subject matter and nature of this deck is the end product of something that has evolved over many years. What began as a simple desire to create a Tarot deck on my own went through various twists, turns and metamorphoses until it arrived at its present and final format.

As my understanding of what the Tarot truly is evolved and hopefully grew, so my ideas behind producing a Tarot deck went with it. Eventually I came to realise that what I wanted to apply with my deck was the expression of what I saw the Tarot to be – energy.

As quoted in my previous book on Tarot Therapy (Vol.2 – The Seekers Quest), an enterprising student of mine defined the Tarot by stating simply 'Tarot Is'. This perfect dictum led me to realise that there is a core truth behind every card in the deck. Moreover, I saw this truth as a depiction of energy.

We hear and read a good deal about this thing called energy in 'New Age' circles – how many times have we heard the expression 'there's a good energy in here' or 'your energy is lovely' and such like. But what do these noble folk mean when they make these declarations (and do they know themselves)?

If we turn to the field of quantum physics we can find many an explanation of this sub-atomic world, wherein we can discover nothing less than the creation and nature of the Universe. This Universe we are of course a part of, and so it is that we share this energy we speak of. Indeed we ourselves are a part of and expression of that energy, as indeed are all things within and without us.

Many of us know this energy through various definitions from spiritual traditions across the world. This may be 'chi' or 'ki', 'prana', 'Reiki', 'nwyfre', 'ether' and more besides. These spiritual traditions, such as Yoga and the art of Healing in various forms, have been part of our existence and the human experience for thousands of years. Whilst the scientific community may continue to point towards a lack of proven or measurable evidence of such a force, the fact that it has such an established longevity must count for something. Just because a thing cannot be quantified or experimented upon successfully does not mean it does not exist.

So if we take it as accepted that this 'life-force' or energy is a part of our reality, albeit at this causal or subtle level I have referred to previously, we need then to understand how it works. For this we can turn to nothing less than the 'Big Bang', the moment of the creation of the Universe. This was essentially a massive outpouring and movement of this same energy we are speaking of. As we know, this is still going on, as that energy continues to move.

So this energy then is the 'stuff of life'. Rather like our DNA is the physical 'building blocks' of our body, this life-force is the equivalent at an energetic level. So it is we can call it 'causal' to our reality, since for something to exist in a physical or measurable form, it must first exist at and as, an energy level.

Put simply, energy causes our reality. It is a blueprint for who we are and what we experience, both inwardly and outwardly. We exist and have our being in this level of reality. The physical and material world around us and in which we operate is but one aspect of it.

The personal or human vehicle for this energy is what is known as the 'subtle body' and which has again been recognised by ancient esoteric traditions and is still widely practised and used today. In the human body this consists of the Aura, being the totality of the human being at this level. Within this are the Chakra system, together with the meridian lines, on which are structured the physical body.

From this viewpoint and to quote a well-known maxim, we are 'spiritual beings having a human experience'. This being the case, this energy and life-force is the vehicle and method by which that spiritual being has its human experience. For me, I have come to understand the structure of the Tarot as an expression of the nature and working of that energy and those forces. As such we are then able to utilise it to help guide us on our human experience as spiritual beings, if we see and come to know this energy as a spiritual, esoteric, inner, and subtle or quantum reality. In this way the Tarot becomes a therapy, since it is able to depict the nature and working of that energy, both within and without the human being.

In other words, it shows us the causes of what we experience. When we have the understanding of why things are happening, we are much more able to make informed choices and determine the future path we would like. We can make the options we wish to make and in so doing, go a long way to creating our reality; to making the life we want to have and that is right for our growth and development.

As we shall see when we examine the structure of this deck shortly, this energy finds its' outworking and expression at the different levels of the human being. This is reflected outwardly in the elements of the natural world of which we are an intrinsic and vital part and on which we depend for life.

In order to create the Tarot deck I wanted then, I needed to consider how it could depict all this. As I have said before, in my formative years of working with the Tarot I found I had difficulty equating what a figure such as the Magician or Hanged Man had to do with what was printed in a book.

Somehow, the characters themselves seemed a little superfluous, much as I love all of them. Any worthwhile study of the Tarot will also study symbolism and its use and undoubted power. As I progressed with the Tarot, I came to understand these symbols and the characters that populated the cards as an outer expression of what the card meant.

I asked myself then what would happen if I removed all the people from the cards and the symbols that went with them. I had seen that these people and symbols were all an expression of the one theme or concept of each card they were on and that this is what the card 'meant'. If we stripped the cards down to that inner concept or theme what we are left with is its pure energy. The Tarot Therapy Deck is an expression of that energy.

My goal had by now become to get down to the nitty, gritty of what the Tarot is all about – to express its vital energy. I had come to know the nature of this energy for myself through a number of healing, spiritual and magical disciplines and arts. In order to show this through a Tarot deck I realised that the characters and the symbols were not required. They were and remain a means of showing what the cards are all about and how they can be interpreted and in this they are of course invaluable.

In a quest to show the energetic nature and reality of the Tarot, I had also come to realise that the outer interpretations and meanings did not apply. The nature of this energy and life-force simply is, rather like our earlier definition of the Tarot itself. As such it does not 'mean' anything, it simply exists and its nature is to move and flow; no more and no less. If we understand that the cards are a depiction of the structure and nature of the movement of this energy then we can see that they do not need to mean anything. We need only to know what the energy is and how it may be affecting us at that causal, subtle and inner level that we know it exists at.

From here we can see the manner of the Tarot as therapy. If we accept that energy or life-force is the stuff that gives rise to, guides, directs or shapes both ourselves and our lives, both within and without our being, we can realise that if we can see the nature and direction of its flow and how it may be affecting us, we can also learn to utilise this to help create, shape, guide and direct our own beings and lives for ourselves. The Tarot is the perfect expression to do just that and why its very nature is not predictive but therapeutic.

THE NATURE OF ENERGY – THE ENERGY OF NATURE

As 'spiritual beings having a human experience' we need to realise that we exist entirely of this same energy, our physical beings being just one short formation of it for the purposes of the lifetime we live. What is needed now is to understand how we receive that energy, as spiritual beings, and how it becomes part of our human experience.

If we are indeed spiritual beings the implication here is that we are, in essence and in part, divine, whatever we may conceive this to be. If energy is something that exists in all things and at all levels of our existence, we can see how we receive this first from a divine level, then to our individual consciousness, through to our body. This can then be translated to the Tarot.

We are able, through a variety of techniques and practises, such as trance, ritual, meditation and the like, to experience something of a level of consciousness that we can describe as 'pure energy'. This is pure in the sense that it is as yet untainted or influenced by our individual, human instinct, thought, desire or action. We can see this as the level of the Soul; what we see in this deck and experience as the energy of the Major Arcana cards.

From this 'higher', divine or collective level, we receive a down flow or outworking of energy into our individual consciousness. Here we gain an instinct; a motivation that creates our belief. This gives us an impulse to 'be' a certain way. This is the level of the Fire cards, the individual 'spiritual' nature of our reality and experience.

As we respond to these impulses and drives, we are then required and need to come to understand what they are for and why they are so, for us. It is then that we engage our brains and we seek to come to an understanding, both of ourselves and why we are experiencing what we are. Here we process what is going on in our minds. This is the mental level of the human being, what in the Tarot Therapy Deck are the Air cards.

Next the energy descends, slower and heavier in its vibrational form, as each successive level or layer is, as it moves into our hearts. This gives us our desires and promotes our feelings. Here we need to learn to come to terms with and process what is happening in our hearts. This is the emotional level of the human being and in the deck, the Water cards.

Lastly comes the outworking of the energy, as it takes on is densest formation. It is this that prompts our actions and what we do, hopefully as a reflection of that higher energy and reality we first sensed instinctively. This is where we need to determine a course of action that reflects our true self. This is the physical level of the human being and the Earth cards of the deck.

THE NATURE OF THE DECK – THE DECK OF NATURE

We can in effect, then reverse the above procedure. As we seek the fulfilment of our souls we follow our quest in life to find and experience wholeness, individuation and enlightenment. The Tarot Therapy Deck uses the fact of our intrinsic connection to the natural world for the understanding and outworking of this, since we share the same energetic connection with the planet on which we live and are a part.

Over the years of working with it, I have come to see the Tarot as being alive of itself – something I call the Spirit of the Tarot. Just as we know the planet Earth it(her)self is alive and evolving, so it is we are the same. We have come to classify the constituent parts of the human being by relating to what we see and experience in the natural world around us.

We are beings that are Physical, Emotional, Mental and Spiritual, producing the collective result in combination as the Soul. These are expressed in the natural world of this planet as the four Elements of Earth, Water, Air and Fire respectively. The construction of the Tarot deck is based on this same 'philosophy'. The four suits of what are traditionally called Pentacles, Cups, Swords and Wands form the Minor Arcana, the Major Arcana being the Soul level.

To express the energy of ourselves in this way, this deck applies these elements directly, in the following way. The table below shows you the correspondences from traditional Tarot to Tarot Therapy and its level of the human being.

TRADITIONAL TAROT	TAROT THERAPY ELEMENT	HUMAN LEVEL
PENTACLES	EARTH	PHYSICAL
CUPS	WATER	EMOTIONAL
SWORDS	AIR	MENTAL
WANDS	FIRE	SPIRITUAL
MAJOR ARCANA	SOUL	SOUL

In the reverse of the above descent of energy, we can see how, in order to find the fulfilment of which we speak, we need to raise the energy back up to blend with our Soul's purpose. By following what is right for us to do, we can transcend the lower, selfish emotional desires. This in turn can grant us understanding of why we are the way we are, which in turn allows or permits understanding in our mind of who and what we are and need to be. From here we tune our instinctive selves into a more sacred, or spiritual, way of being. It is this that automatically results in the fulfilment of our Soul, the ability to fulfil our destiny and reach the highest level we can and be the best we can be.

STRUCTURE OF THE DECK

We come now to the deck itself. First we will look at its structure, as an expression of the energy of the human being and the natural world. Second we will look at how it can be used and the particulars of working with the Tarot as a therapeutic tool. This will include techniques unique to this approach and how to respond to the cards.

Initially however we should state here that this deck consists of 78 cards, being the accepted norm for Tarot decks (although variations do exist in some decks). These are divided into two 'halves' just as traditional Tarot decks are, known as the Major and Minor Arcana. We should stress here also that this does not imply that the energy of the Major Arcana cards is in any way greater or stronger than those of the Minor Arcana cards. It simply operates at a different level. Its reach may be greater, deeper or higher, but it should not be viewed as bigger or better, or more important in anyway. Following the holistic paradigm, they are each parts that create a greater whole in combination.

Just as with 'traditional' Tarot decks, the four suits of the Minor Arcana consist of fourteen cards each. These are numbered One through to Ten, with the remaining four cards, usually the 'Court' cards of the Tarot, here renamed as 'Compound' cards, which are explained below. The twenty-two cards of the Major Arcana follow the traditional structure of the Tarot, as we shall see.

MAJOR ARCANA – SOUL CARDS

For the purposes of the Tarot Therapy deck the Major Arcana cards are classed as energies depicting the Soul of the human being. In this way they are depictions of energies as they effect and operate upon us at the level of our Soul. This is distinct from our individual spirit, this being the Fire level of the Minor Arcana which is covered below.

14

The Soul level can be looked upon as the whole human being. This is a composite of the four separate but interlinked elemental levels that the Minor Arcana suits represent. When combined, these four elements produce or result in the complete human being. In this way the Major Arcana cards are the energies of the Soul, the whole self.

Just as with traditional Tarot decks, the Major Arcana is really the journey that each of us must travel through on our way to enlightenment, realisation or individuation. This is the method, or in this case, the energies, which we need to integrate in order to be more whole and complete. These energies and cards are the means by which we learn what we are here to learn and assimilate into our beings in this lifetime, the way in which we fulfil our destiny, if you will.

Given that the Major Arcana depict the energies of the person or client, as a whole, it follows that the images used are those at a more collective, or 'greater' level from the natural world. As can be seen from each of the cards, their scope is greater, wider or more dramatic in their effect, just as it is with those things that seem to affect our whole self and life. These can then be pivotal moments of realisation, decision or choice when we can make or create a profound impact on the direction and shape of our life path and self. These are the energies of the Major Arcana.

MINOR ARCANA – ELEMENT CARDS

In working with the Tarot Therapy Deck one of the primary ingredients to realise is that the structure of the deck is the same as that of the human being and indeed of the world around us. To quantify that, we can look at the human being as a composite of four fundamental states, or if you will, elements.

The science of physics - the study of matter and energy - tells us that there are four fundamental states of matter, known as solid, liquid, gas and plasma. Classical philosophy and many worldviews also tell us that there are four elements that reflect the fundamental parts on which anything can consist and on which the fundamental powers of everything are based. These are earth, water, air and fire.

It is a simple step to look at these two systems of classification, one scientific the other philosophical, as very closely aligned to and representative of the other. For the purposes of the Tarot, this allows us to provide a system of classification for the Minor Arcana. The four suits of the deck, which as we can see from the table below, in turn allow us to place a level of the human being on each suit and thereby its outworking, or energy.

ELEMENT / SUIT	MATTER	HUMAN LEVEL	ENERGY / FUNCTION
EARTH	SOLID	PHYSICAL	PRACTICAL / ACTION
WATER	LIQUID	EMOTIONAL	FEELING
AIR	GAS	MENTAL	THINKING
FIRE	PLASMA	SPIRITUAL	BELIEVING / BEING

As can be seen from just a cursory look at the cards, the images within each suit reflect the workings of that suit. One of the ways in which the Elements are traditionally depicted are in the colours attributed to them. In the Tarot Therapy Deck these are used in the colouring of the lettering of the name of each card, together with the border around the image. These are shown in the following table.

ELEMENT	COLOUR
EARTH	GREEN
WATER	BLUE
AIR	YELLOW
FIRE	RED
SOUL (MAJOR ARCANA)	BLACK

So it is the Earth cards trace the workings of (at least one aspect of) the element of Earth in Nature. This begins with a Seed, from which all natural things grow, and follows its course of growth, bloom, harvest and decay, then back to Seed again. Similarly the element of Water cards begin with a Drop which creates Rain, forming a Spring and ever onwards until we reach the great expanse of the Ocean, which returns to the sky as Vapour. Air begins in our Atmosphere, travels to the Convergence Zone which creates pressure and so on until the Gale blows itself out, rises to the Jet Stream and out as a Zephyr. Fire begins with a Spark to form a Flame which continues to grow in its power until it produces a Heatwave and dies out as Embers.

In this way each suit effectively traces the evolution of the Element from its origins to the realisation of the fullness of its power or energy. This leads to its final release and from here it returns to its beginnings once again. This same cyclical process is repeated in the Natural world and indeed human life cycles and so it is appropriate it is used here. As we shall see now this is also the case with the numbered aspect of the Minor Arcana cards.

So we have the four suits, or really Elements, as the expression of the Minor Arcana. What we must now do is further divide those four energies into ten energies, for the Number Cards and then a combination or 'Compound' of two elements to give the energies of what are the traditional Court cards.

NUMBER CARDS

The numbering system of the Tarot Therapy Deck does not deviate from the norm in any way from the accepted numerological applications. Indeed it applies these perhaps more directly than is usual with Tarot decks, since the Number Cards are seen as a simple combination of the energy of the Element of its suit, together with the energy of the number of the card. These two factors conjoin to give the essential energy and theme of each card. As will be seen when we examine how to use this deck, this is then modified intuitively to account and allow for the cards that appear alongside it in a reading.

Esoteric numerologists tell us that the entire workings of the Universe and its formation can be attributed to the energy of the ten digits that exist. This is of course, One to Nine, plus Zero. This system shows us -

Out of the primordial origins of matter there was the potential (Zero) for matter.
Then came the point of manifestation (One), emergence into matter.
This gave rise to the Duality inherent in matter Two), with its masculine and feminine polarities. When combined this creation (Three) produces growth.
This established security and a foundation (Four) on which to

18

build.

Changes then took place (Five), allowing for adaptation and interference.

Which resulted in progression once harmony and order (Six) had been restored.

This gave rise to purpose and direction (Seven) and a sense of meaning.

The advancement then resulted with a sense of rhythm and direction (Eight).

Culminating in the peak of attainment (Nine) and achievement.

Lastly the cycle ends and dissolves (Ten) and we return to the Zero of the 10 once more.

This highly simplified take on the numerological workings of all things does serve to give us the essential and central energy for each number. I have covered this in more detail in my previous workings on Tarot Therapy (see Further Reading) so I will not repeat those here.

What is vital to realise, as said above, is that we arrive at the energy of each of the Number Cards by combining the energy of the Element with the energy of the Number. In essence this is simple. For example, if we take the One of Earth we can see easily how its energy gives us a potential for practical action, an impulse for taking the first step with a project and a need to act on what we may have thought, planned, felt and desired about previously.

Similarly, the Nine of Water promotes an emotional energy of abundance, being the highest numerical energy. This may give us the possibility of highs and lows emotionally and a need to balance our feelings, with appropriate expression.

These also highly simplified examples show us the way in which the Number Cards operate in Tarot Therapy. What should be noted here is that the energy of the cards do not dictate but act at that causal level referred to before. They promote opportunity for choice and options; they inform and suggest rather than command or govern.

COMPOUND CARDS

Lastly we come to the traditional Court Cards of the Minor Arcana, here called Compound Cards. To clarify, a Compound in the science of Chemistry - the science of matter - is a 'whole or substance formed from the union of two or more elements or parts'. For example the Element Water as many know is known in chemistry as H20, i.e. two parts Hydrogen, one part Oxygen The two ingredients which we combine, or Compound, are two of the four Elements of the four states of matter, as Earth, Water, Air and Fire.

Traditionally speaking the Court Cards are seen as representing the involvement or presence of people involved in the client's life or the subject of the reading in some form or another. The type, appearance, age and some character aspects are defined by which court card appears in the reading. In Tarot Therapy, this changes. As we take the cards directly from what we have come to know as their energy, we see them directly in their elemental form and expression.

For those familiar with traditional Tarot, it is simply a matter of allocating an element to each of the Court cards, most commonly called Page, Knight Queen and King. These are as follows, in tabular form.

COURT CARD	ELEMENT
PAGE	EARTH
KNIGHT	FIRE
QUEEN	WATER

In the Tarot Therapy Deck the Element of the suit is the first or prime energy we encounter or receive from each Compound Card. This is the first, instinctive response we have to its energy. Because of this, each of the Earth cards are Earth of . . ., the Water cards called Water of . . . and so on. So each of the Earth Compound cards respond first in a practical way, the Water cards in an emotional way and so on.

This is then modified by the element of the card itself, which is the manner in which the energy is expressed. So the Page of Cups becomes Earth of Water. The practical nature is expressed as a love of what is done. The Queen of Wands becomes Water of Fire. Here the energy is first emotional and of a feeling nature, expressed instinctively, according to the beliefs.

Of course this does not necessarily mean that someone of this type is bound to appear when these cards appear in your reading. In Tarot Therapy it tells us that there is an energy active within us that may cause or require us to be any of these aspects – i.e. cautious and slow-moving for Earth, feel our way with Water, think and plan with Air and follow instinct and belief with Fire!

For the sake of ease of reference, the traditional Court Cards are shown again in tabular form, alongside their therapeutic equivalents, together with the quality in them and the response to this.

COURT CARD	COMPOUND CARD	QUALITY	RESPONSE
PAGE OF	EARTH OF	PRACTICAL	ACTION

PENTACLES	EARTH		
KNIGHT OF PENTACLES	EARTH OF FIRE	PRACTICAL	BELIEF
QUEEN OF PENTACLES	EARTH OF WATER	PRACTICAL	FEELING
KING OF PENTACLES	EARTH OF AIR	PRACTICAL	THINKING
PAGE OF CUPS	WATER OF EARTH	EMOTIONAL	ACTION
KNIGHT OF CUPS	WATER OF FIRE	EMOTIONAL	BELIEF
QUEEN OF CUPS	WATER OF WATER	EMOTIONAL	FEELING
KING OF CUPS	WATER OF AIR	EMOTIONAL	THINKING
PAGE OF SWORDS	AIR OF EARTH	MENTAL	ACTION
KNIGHT OF SWORDS	AIR OF FIRE	MENTAL	BELIEF
QUEEN OF SWORDS	AIR OF WATER	MENTAL	FEELING
KING OF SWORDS	AIR OF AIR	MENTAL	THINKING

PAGE OF WANDS	FIRE OF EARTH	SPIRITUAL	ACTION
KNIGHT OF WANDS	FIRE OF FIRE	SPIRITUAL	BELIEF
QUEEN OF WANDS	FIRE OF WATER	SPIRITUAL	FEELING
KING OF WANDS	FIRE OF AIR	SPIRITUAL	THINKING

We should remind ourselves here that cards are energies, nothing more. Therefore, this does not necessarily mean they will represent people. That said, it is most common that these energies are expressed either through ourselves (or the client), or people in our lives. What is important is that we understand that the energy we are receiving when Compound Cards appear in our readings we may experience in a number of ways. This is what the Compound Cards will show us.

I have illustrated the nature of the Compound Cards in Tarot Therapy as these twin energies and shown a basic sample of how they would be seen in people, in order to help you adjust to the way in which they are used in Tarot Therapy. This does not mean however that they are limited to this in Tarot Therapy. What we must now do is to expand our understanding of the energy of the Compound cards to realise that they, as with all cards, are energies and energy simply is.

Your job as Tarot Therapist is really to describe the nature of that energy and, using the cards that also appear in the reading, determine how it might be experienced in the client and their life. This may, or may not be through a person, whether themselves or another. It is about understanding the nature of the Elements and their workings, both within us as human beings and the natural world. As mentioned above, we are part of the world and so it is hoped that study and use of the Minor Arcana cards here will establish and aid this understanding.

It may be that at the beginning of a reading we see the Fire of Fire card. This will bring an energy of impatience, motivational 'get up and go', perhaps rashness and even hot-headedness. Somewhere near the end of the cards selected we see however the Fire of Air card. This brings an energy where the urge to rush forwards towards the target is tempered with a more reflective, thoughtful approach. Perhaps it is then that the client is needing to shift from the Fire of Fire state to Fire of Air. The cards between the two will indicate how this can be achieved, what obstacles, challenges and opportunities they will face and find along the way. Any cards after this will indicate how this newly acquired energy can be used.

PRACTICALITIES OF TAROT THERAPY

Now that we are familiar with the deck itself we need to turn our attention to how to use it. As we shall see there are some vital differences in the way that the deck can be used for therapeutic purposes rather than the usual predictive means. What follows is a suggestion only and you are of course quite free to utilise the deck in any way that seems fit for you. As with all things Tarot there are no hard and fast rules that one must stick by, since there is no written original rule book we can turn to for an authoritative statement. The sections below take you through the process of a Tarot Therapy consultation in the hope that by the end you will have at your disposal a means whereby to use the cards in this manner successfully.

YOU DON'T HAVE TO BE PSYCHIC TO READ THE TAROT – BUT IT HELPS!

Even in these supposedly enlightened days of tolerance and acceptance, I still come across people who are suspicious and even fearful of the Tarot. Such people tell me that this because it is all part of the occult (whatever they believe that to be) and that there is 'something evil' about it. As I have said elsewhere, that is not a bad achievement for some pieces of laminated card!

The Tarot has become labelled in some peoples' minds as something only understood by the select or (god forbid) 'chosen' few. Whilst it certainly requires some familiarity to be used for readings between friends and definitely full study if one is to read for others; given these essentials it can be used by anyone.

There is a popular conception that to use the Tarot – to give readings with it – one has to possess some special ability or have inherited a 'psychic gift' from one's elder relatives. Whilst this can happen, it is absolutely not a necessity. Firstly,

I have long held the view that being psychic is not a 'gift' or even an ability possible only for some of us,

Whilst it may be true that, just as with musical ability, sporting prowess and so on, some of us may be born with a genetic disposition towards psychic subjects and abilities, every one of us has at least a latent psychic ability. My view here is that being psychic, or if you prefer, intuitive, is a natural part of the human condition and a normal functioning process of our body, heart and mind system.

Again, just as with musical and sporting ability, it can take time and practise to perfect one's psychic skills and attain a high level of achievement. This may require hours of meditation, development exercises, visualisations, and in the case of the Tarot, more study and further meditation. None of this requires an already existing or proven psychic ability.

In fact, one of the 'side-effects' of working with the Tarot is that it will naturally develop and enhance that aspect of our psyche and functioning. As you will discover when you work with the cards, it is in part an intuitive art as much as it is a study.

To achieve this level of 'knowing' we must first read about the cards and get to know them on a conscious, mental level. The more you can read and write notes about your thoughts and knowledge of the cards at this stage, the better. By a clear focus on such information the brain is able to absorb a body of information that can then be accessed intuitively when we then come to give readings. It is this that is the intuitive process used during a reading.

This takes time and confidence. What is required here is a good study of the cards, thereby allowing the essential information as we see it to be committed to memory. When we then see the cards in a reading the intuitive, 'sensing', right hemisphere of our brain supplies us with the information we know logically but may have forgotten consciously. It is for this reason that I instruct my students to read all they can about the cards, make notes as they go, then forget them.

With that knowledge nestled happily in your brain and by working with the symbolism, colour and so on, of the cards, you will find that a natural process of psychic development will occur. This is simply the natural outworking and expression of what already exists within you. This is just the same as if you lift a weight repeatedly, the muscles involved in doing so will get bigger. It is in this way that you do not have to be psychic to use the Tarot – but it will help.

TAROT IS JUST A TOOL

One other topic to cover here regards something that I hear uttered all too often by those who I usually find do not have much knowledge of the Tarot. This is the adage that the Tarot, like any other psychic method, is really just a tool to allow for the 'slightly more advanced', or 'higher' ability of Mediumship.

Mediumship is communication to and from the spirit world, whether this is receiving and passing messages on from loved ones who have passed on to this realm or giving information from spirit guides and such like from that level of existence. This is quite different from reading the Tarot, especially so when it comes to the modem of Tarot Therapy.

Mediumship ability may also be a natural part of the human condition, just like in my view, psychic ability is. This is not the place to debate this issue, for it is a different subject. However, its inherent demotion of the Tarot to being 'just a tool', and therefore having no real value or role of itself, is.

If this is the case, then the simple response is that we should not need to use the Tarot. If we are at a sufficient level of ability as to be able to charge people money for passing on messages and information from the spirit world, then we should not require any such tool or aid to do so. If we choose to do so, then we should recognise that we are providing a psychic based reading as well as a Mediumship consultation.

Equally, if the Tarot has no real value other than being just a tool for the spirit world to communicate with us through, then how come we have not evolved beyond its use? What was it created for and why is it so widespread and popular? It has to be because it can do a whole lot more than just serving as a tool or link to the world of Spirit.

In Tarot Therapy we concern ourselves with the energy that the cards represent, as a 'map' of the client at this level of their existence at the time the reading takes place. If we then choose to involve the spirit world as part of our reading then we are, literally, adding another dimension to what we are offering and we should be clear about that distinction.

With such a rich depository of knowledge, wisdom, information and all that the energy level of our reality contains and that is expressed in the Tarot, it seems to me somewhat disrespectful, if not downright insulting, to label it as 'just a tool'. I'm reminded of the proverb that a 'bad workman always blames his tools'.

REVERSED CARDS

The accepted use of Tarot has come to identify two 'meanings' or interpretations for each card, depending on which way up the card is dealt in a reading. These two meanings give a positive response if the cards appears in its upright position and the negative for the reverse.

In Tarot Therapy however, no use is made of reversed cards. Should a card appear upside down in a reading when it is dealt, it is simply placed in the correct position. The reason for this takes us back to an awareness of cards being energy, and only energy. As we have seen, energy simply is. It may be that our response can turn it into a seemingly positive or negative thing, but that is our choice. How we choose to respond to the energy of each card we are dealt is what matters. Of itself, the energy of the card is neither 'good' or 'bad' – what matters is what we do in response to it.

This approach seems more logical to me, quite apart from the energetic reasoning given above. Any Tarot card is designed quite specifically to look the way it does and if it is turned upside down, we cease to make use of this use of imagery and symbolism. Of course the best example to turn to here is that of the Hanged Man in traditional Tarot decks. The Hanged Man is shown quite deliberately hanging upside down and of course if he is reversed he is turned the right way up and so loses his symbolic effect and power. Somehow it always seems to me a little insulting to the designer of the deck to turn their beautiful creation upside down!

If in Tarot Therapy we are working with the card as energies as an inner reflection or map of the causal level of our reality, we can express this another way. This is that a Tarot Therapy 'reading' consults the cards to determine the natural forces and tides of our life and their flow, so that we may best divine how to adapt to and live in accordance with that flow. In this way Tarot Therapy becomes a Taoist approach to the cards, which in essence is all about knowing and following the Way, as the word Tao means, that is right for each of us.

To then manually adjust a card so it is upside down suggests to me a human interference with this natural way, and so should be avoided. It is like going against the natural order of things, which is precisely what these cards show us, so it would be wrong to manipulate this.

DEFINING THE READING AND THE PSYCHIC GAME

The process of a Tarot Therapy reading is more specific, even without a limitation of this kind and is much more client led. First it can help to set the parameters of what the reading is about. This means asking the client if they have any questions or a subject they would like to look at. Many clients more used to the traditional approach with Tarot may then ask whether they will meet someone for a new relationship or if they will get a new job soon and so on. For the purposes of Tarot Therapy it is preferable to re-define this predictive approach to suggesting that the dynamics of the clients' relationship situation in general is examined or the situation around their work. Taking the lead is vital in this approach to working with the cards and the client will feel more secure if you do so.

The vast majority of clients come for a Tarot reading because they have a problem or feel the need of some guidance and information to help them. Whether they tell you this or not (and some may not even be aware of it on a conscious level) may be another matter. Many play what I call 'The Psychic Game'. This is where they do indeed have a burning issue they want to look at but prefer to see if you will 'pick it up' or if it comes out in the cards. The suggestion behind this is that they will then know you are genuine and can trust what you are saying.

Whilst there is certainly no requirement to feed the reader with information, the Tarot Therapy approach works better for the client if they help us to help them. This they can do by simply stating why they have come for a reading and what they would like the reading to be about. This may be something as clear and simple as 'I want to look at my relationship' or 'a reading on my career'. With this clarity we can then respond to the energy of the cards more specifically than might otherwise be the case and so better 'help the client to help themselves', as I often describe this way of using the Tarot.

If we walk into a baker, for instance and ask for some bread, we will be asked what type of bread we would like - white, wholemeal, crusty, sliced and so on. If we go to an estate agent and declare we want to buy a house, they will want to know what type of house, how many bedrooms, town or country and so forth. So it is, or should be, with Tarot reading. It makes much more sense to tell the reader what we would like them to look at and get stuck in!

I have found it necessary and helpful to explain to the client that if they have something in mind they want to 'come out' in the reading that it may do, or it may not. Equally if it does appear it may be only after other more surface or immediate issues have been discussed and it may leave little time and energy to be explored fully in the reading. For those with a greater spiritual understanding, it can be useful to explain that by asking the Tarot to tell us what it wants to say, which in effect is what we are doing if we are do not set a question or subject – the infamous 'general reading' – then what we will receive (for which we may be truly thankful!) may be what the spirit world wants us to know. This again, may or may not be what we want to know about.

There is one of those rare things that can help illustrate our point here – a spiritual joke! This is of the man who kept asking 'God' to let him win the lottery. He promised God all manner of servitude and good works if he granted him this one wish. The weeks wore on and the man's prayers and requests became more fervent, seeing him declaring unceasing charitable deeds, chastity and obedience and anything else he could think of that might please God. Eventually God tired of all this and appeared to the man, and said 'Look, help me out here . . . buy a ticket'!!

READING WITHOUT SPREADS

The approach of Tarot Therapy differs from the accepted style of Tarot reading in one important regard. This is that it works to its best advantage if readings are done without using a 'spread'. For the uninitiated, this is a specific pattern or layout of cards wherein the placing of a card relates to a specific area in relation to the question asked. This might be the client's past, present, future, attitude to the question, influence of those around, likely outcome and so on.

Because we are working with the cards as energies, and energy, as we have seen, simply is, it works to better effect if we remove any restrictive influence upon that energy. If we impinge the placing in a spread upon a card and therefore its interpretation, we do, by virtue of this structure, limit what we must say about it. Energy is unlimited and therefore it goes against the grain to restrict it when we use it in this way - the way being Tarot Therapy.

This may seem to those established with readings with spreads rather like working without the aid of a safety net, but I ask you to consider making this leap of faith. If you consider the Tarot deck to be a vast repository of wisdom, knowledge and guidance, it seems sensible to avail ourselves of all that is available, rather than restricting ourselves to a peak at only one chapter of such a book. By not placing a restriction on the number of cards used in a reading it is rather like asking the Tarot deck what we need to know or what it wishes to say or tell us. We should be clear at this stage that this is not an excuse to keep putting more and more cards down during a reading and spurting out the little nuggets of knowledge we have memorised about them, hoping it will make sense to the client.

Rather what we do is concentrate on the cards that have been selected and work with those in whatever depth is required, instead of skimming a little off the top and settling for that. The nature of Tarot Therapy is to delve deep and seek to uncover and address the root cause of whatever issue the client presents with.

Just as with the vast majority of matters concerning the Tarot, there are no hard and fast rules we 'must' follow. We have determined the subject matter of the reading and what follows is to simply make the entire deck available to the client to choose from.

On a slightly separate note here, if the practicalities allow, I usually opt for the client to sit at the side of the table we are working from. This allows for easy and direct eye-contact to be made both ways and avoids the slightly confrontational 'interview-style' of having them sit opposite me. This also makes it easier for both parties to view the cards without straining.

So it is also easy to sweep the deck in an arc, face–down, across the table and for them all to be within relatively easy reach of the client. Prior to this I have taken the time, while we are discussing the nature of the reading, to shuffle the cards several times to ensure random choice of them. Shuffling the cards is again, rather like ensuring they are in alignment with the Tao, the Way that is for that client at that time. To ensure maximum flow through your cards in this sense, it is best to shuffle the deck seven times.

When, after practice, you have gained confidence and smoothness of the technique of 'sweeping the cards' they will usually emerge in an attractive rainbow shape across your table. Something requisite for this to happen is two cloths - one to cover your table and one on which to lay out your cards. Just one cloth inevitably slides under your sweep of the cards.

Once this is done I invite the client to pick as many cards as they wish. This usually brings a response to ask how many, and I repeat however many they wish. This may elicit the response of how many is usual or how many most people pick and again I encourage them to be an individual and go for how many they feel is right. Those who are naturally more intuitive will respond to this, whilst those who may not be will make a decision, which is in itself, informed from an intuitive level.

It can also be good to observe the manner in which cards are chosen as this can tell us something about the clients' energetic state of being at the time of the reading. This may be basic psychology but it can be surprising how effective and useful this can be. As well as telling you about the client at the time, it can also help to put them at their ease and lets them know you are paying attention to and focussing on them.

Should they select their cards very swiftly this can indicate a certain amount of impatience about them, disliking having to wait. If they go to select a card then put it back and change their mind, this can point towards indecision and perhaps a lack of surety and confidence. If the client prefers to pass their hand over the top of the cards (which are of course face down) then we can see they are of a more intuitive or sensitive nature. It should be noted that these traits will apply in relation to the subject matter of the reading or question posed, which you have previously established.

We then come to observation of what they do with the cards as this can also say something that may be relevant. Clients that keep hold of all the cards, piling them in one hand, may like to be in control, or need to in the situation you are looking at. Those that flick the cards out of the deck with a finger not really paying attention to where they go may be uncaring in their approach or not focussed on the outcome. There are many more possibilities to both the manner in which cards are selected as well as their placing. With thoughtful observation you can ascertain a surprising amount of accurate information that can help to begin the process of interaction with the client, even at this stage.

You will also find that many clients will arrange the cards in their own spread, usually unconsciously. When you point out to them what they have done they will normally not be aware of this. This may be that they have placed two cards in one row, three below that and one more beneath that. Again, there are many more possibilities here of course. These 'spreads' or perhaps better called 'arrangements' of cards should be noted and followed, simply turning the cards over in the place the client arranged them, telling them you are doing this as it may become relevant when it comes to responding to the cards, which it usually will. Again, this unconscious process can help to add a very useful dimension to the overall reading.

ENERGY BALANCING

Next we come to a general observation or analysis of the cards chosen by the client for the reading. This is what I call 'Energy Balancing' and it serves to give an overall indication of what is being dealt with and the general relevant factors affecting the reading. It is rather like looking at the chapter headings in the Contents page of a book before you begin reading the individual pages.

We begin this process by looking at the number of cards the client has chosen for their reading. Any student of the Tarot will know that the influence of Numerology is a significant one on the cards. Here we explore the numbers as energies, just as we do with the cards. This means that the energy of the number of cards chosen will indicate the general energy that the client is dealing with or 'working', at the time of the reading.

I have written in my previous works on Tarot Therapy on the numbers and there are a good many books available on this ancient practice that you can refer to. Rather than repeat them inadequately here I will give you the following information to work with.

In Numerology there are really only ten numbers, or energies, with which to deal. These are of course, One to Nine, plus Zero. Since we cannot do a reading with no cards that does not apply here! What can be done, should the client select more than Nine cards, is to bring the numerical energy back to a single digit by simply adding the digits of the number chosen together i.e. 12 cards = 1 + 2 = 3 and so on.

That said we should also take note of a selection of cards between 10 and 22, since with the Tarot we have 22 cards in the Major Arcana. This means that the energy of that cards' number will be significant in at least some general way i.e. should the client choose 15 cards then the energy of the Inferno (Devil) may be at work somewhere. We should specify here that this is only in a very general way – rather like picking up clues to follow a trail – unless of course the Inferno appears in their chosen cards, when it takes on more significance.

This Energy Balancing exercise is rather like a process of finding clues amidst the map that the cards of a Tarot Therapy reading present. Next on this Trail of the Tarot comes the search and identification of the cards chosen in a section we can call 'The Balance of Cards'. Here we see where in the pack the cards have come from and take note of the following factors –

- Major Arcana Cards – These make up (very) broadly speaking one third of the total cards in a Tarot deck. We can therefore take this as a reasonable, general ratio of the percentage of Major cards that should be chosen in a reading. Remembering that the Major Arcana cards show us the energies at the Soul or total level of the client in a reading, it follows that there needs to be at least one Major card in their selection, even if that selection is just two cards. We all need a connection to our soul to be healthy and whole and so it is we need to see this reflected in the cards chosen. The ratio of Major cards needs essentially to be 'not too few and not too many'. Too few can point towards a weak connection to the soul at that time, manifesting in a lack of sense of purpose and meaning in the clients life. Too many can indicate a tendency towards obsessive behaviour and a time of intense activity; a search for deep meaning and pivotal directional decisions.

  We can also note the placing in the cards of the Major cards. Should they all be gathered together this can indicate a coming together at a specific time - an intense period as described above - a focal point. Should they be more evenly placed apart this can indicate a move from one cards' energy to the next in a more progressive sense, but equally one that requires that the client respond to each card as they encounter its' energy.

- Elements Present - The Balance of Cards continues then by looking at the suits, or here Elements, of the

37

Minor Arcana. First we look to see if each of these is present. Just as with the Major Arcana cards, there ought to be at least one card from each of the four suits, to show a connection to this level in the client at the time of the reading. Remember here that the Elements correspond to the four levels of the human being – physical, emotional, mental and spiritual.

We can of course note the prevalence of any one suit, indicating a focus energetically on that level and therefore a need to work there first and foremost. Should any suit be absent, this can indicate that the client may be lacking energy at this level and need to work to bring this in to themselves at this time, or that they are avoiding doing so for some reason.

- Compound Cards – here we can look to see the significance of any Compound Cards in the reading. Whilst the above factors can apply equally here, the placing of Compound Cards can often show a move from one elemental state to another, through the process and scope of the reading. This may indicate a stage of development that the client may go through as they deal with whatever issues are being looked at in the reading. If there are more than two then there may be several processes or stages to encounter and absorb, or attitudes to adopt as they progress. If there is just one then this approach will most likely be the one required to resolve their dilemma.

Next we look at the numbering of the actual cards chosen. Here we can gain further clues on the 'Tarot Trail' into our clients self and life. Look at each card chosen and note its number (apart from Compound Cards obviously, which do not have a number). From this overview of the numerical energies affecting the reading we then need to look for the following –

- Multiples of numbers - more than one card of the same number (whether Major or Minor Arcana). The more duplicities, the great the influence of that number.
- Progressions of numbers – This can be any sequence of numbers in order that seems to appear significant. This will be as they apply in the order of cards chosen – i.e. the first card may be a Two, followed by a Three and later a Four and so on. Take note especially of the progression of Three, Six and Nine as this can be very powerful energetically, giving the client a strong creative, driving urge for progression that if not responded to will create equally strong frustration.
- Tens and Ones – As you will see from the energy of numbers, Tens can indicate a time of dissolution and a need to let go, embracing the end of a phase at some level. It follows then that we need to look for where the beginning that will inevitably follow it comes. If there is a Ten chosen in the cards, look then for a One appearing to show how and where this can appear.
- Addition and Subtraction – Take note too of any significant ways in which the numbers of cards chosen may be added to or subtracted from. It is the result of the mathematics here that may give us a further clue on the Tarot Trail. For example, it may be that adding the first two numbered cards chosen, together, produces the number of the third numbered card and so forth. Obviously there are myriad possibilities here and once you gain experience these things will leap out at you. Once pointed out to them clients are usually surprised, since this is not something they

tend to see – it all helps add to the effectiveness of what you say when they see such random significances occurring.

It may seem somewhat trivial or even unlikely that many of the above factors will occur in a reading but you may be quite surprised just how many in fact do and how often they can. The effectiveness of this process will reveal itself to you in the doing of it and will serve to

- allow time for the client to have a good look at the cards
- creates some faith in you and the process you are following
- allows you the chance to see what you are dealing with in the reading
- sets the general scene before going into specifics

One last piece then follows before we come to the individual response to each card. This is simply asking the client if there are any cards that 'jump out' at them for any reason or if they have any other questions before you progress. This gives the client chance to off load anything they have seen in the cards that might be worrying them at this stage and you can outline the energy of this card, thereby allaying any fears they might have. This is usually the result of pre-conditioning of names of the cards or anything they have seen they might be alarmed about. More aware or intuitive clients may also notice something you have not or see something from a different perspective that will be an aid to helping them through the reading process.

Now all the preliminaries are done we can progress to responding to individual cards. Take note that we refer here to a response to each card rather than an interpretation or meaning. This is simply because we are dealing with energy and energy as we know, simply 'is' and requires of us a response to it, rather than trying to determine what it 'means'. We could say here that what it means is the response we come up with at the time, nothing more or less. With this in mind we then proceed to examine each card.

MAKING IT UP AS YOU GO ALONG!

This is simply a matter of starting at the beginning (a very good place to start!), giving your response to the first card, moving on to the next and keeping going until you reach the end. This is over-simplifying it of course, but the basis here is sound.

It is here that the intuitive process needs to take place. This is something that is impossible to 'teach' via a book, but do not over-complicate the process. As you observe the cards is it basically a matter of allowing yourself to respond with the words and feelings that come to you, as prompted from the cards. The Tarot Therapy cards are designed to elicit such responses, rather than giving meanings or interpretations based on what you know. For certain we use what we know from a logical perspective, gained by reading the information on the cards in the book and then allowing a deeper communication to take place.

This stems from the intuitive, 'right-brain' working that every human being naturally has. In this way, by using the information you have already gleaned from the Energy Balancing process you can be confident in knowing the basic subject matter. The energy of the cards as expressed in the images then facilitates an intuitive or natural response that simply occurs.

Confidence comes from practice, familiarity of the cards and a certain sense of diving in. Once you have this, you can be free to respond to the cards in the manner described here. It is in this sense that you 'make it up as you go along'. Not in the sense that you come out with any sort of nonsense of course, but in the way that intuition bypasses logical thinking. The more you do this, the easier it becomes.

This reading style is one that will prove itself the more you do it, rather than reading about it 'dry' here. In this way, you will find that every reading is unique, just as every person you read for is a unique person. No two readings will ever be the same, even should you find that the same selection of cards is chosen in the same order. Your response, stemming from your intuitive faculty, means that it is tailored to that unique individual.

Another important aspect to be aware of is that a Tarot Therapy reading is a two-way process and does not involve the reader talking 'at' the client. One of the advantages of having the images of the Tarot Therapy deck is that no prior knowledge of the Tarot is required to respond to them.

The deck celebrates the intrinsic connection we all have as human beings with the natural world around us and the planet on which we live and are part of. It is easy then to ask a client what the image causes them to feel as they look at it and how it seems to them. In this way the process of a Tarot Therapy reading becomes something of a discovery or unravelling of what energies are affecting the client at the time and how they can best be responded to.

Rather than dictating what the client must do, Tarot Therapy works with the client to offer them information they might not otherwise have access to, creates an opportunity for detached observation of themselves and their life and gives them choices and options they can used to empower themselves. In this sense I often describe Tarot Therapy readings to clients as 'helping you to help yourself'.

Once you have then worked your way through all the cards you will usually find a natural ending occurs. It can be easy to pick another card, but try to avoid falling prey to this temptation. Whilst you may occasionally find that this is suitable to do, it is far more often the case that the cards chosen initially are the right and only ones needed. Additional cards often just have a way of saying the same thing again.

Of course it is good to offer the client the chance to ask any further questions they may have at the end of the reading but you will usually find that these can be answered without recourse to further cards, but looking again at what you already have, unless of course it is a different subject entirely. This may require a different reading and you should not be hesitant in suggesting this if so required, at a later date.

How long a reading takes can be a difficult issue. For the purposes of Tarot Therapy it is good to allow a goodly amount of time, rather than thinking that it can all be rushed through in 30 minutes. I recommend allowing at least an hour, with perhaps a limit of 75 minutes. There is only so much information that anyone can retain, without losing the gems that can be gained in a mountain or avalanche of knowledge.

It is also good if readings can be recorded and then given to clients, so they can make their own notes afterwards – although I also recommend supplying them with pen and paper for the reading itself. I have written elsewhere of the many issues that can come up on the practicalities of giving readings so again I will not repeat them here, but refer you to Volume One of the preceding 'Tarot Therapy books (see Further Reading).

THE CARDS

As you will see, there are three sections presented for each card, to give you all the knowledge and information you need to understand what they are trying to convey, in terms of the energy of each one. These are as follows –

BACKGROUND – This shows you the reason why each card is as it is, its basis in 'traditional Tarot' as I term it and how this aspect of nature relates to the use and working of Tarot Therapy.

DESCRIPTION – This is a description of what you are looking at on each card, together with any relevant information you may need as to its specific design and working.

ENERGY – This is an explanation of what the energy of each card is about, how it can affect us and suggested responses to that energy.

0 – THE CANYON

BACKGROUND

In traditional Tarot, card 0 or the unnumbered, first card of the Major Arcana is The Fool. Here we see a depiction of the human spirit personified, portrayed as a free spirit, lost in the wonder of the moment, untainted by guilt, pessimism or any of the ills that beset our reactions and responses to human experience as we live our lives. Retaining that positive, instinctive way of living with a loving, soft heart, could be seen as the ultimate challenge for each of us and one that very few seem to have achieved when we examine our history.

It is vital to realise here that we cannot avoid the full force of human experience with all its emptiness, tragedy, grief and disappointment, alongside the love, laughter, exuberance and exhilaration we are bound to know. Much like Humpty Dumpty in the nursery rhyme, what matters more is our reaction to it, and whether we can put ourselves back together again. However, we can all be said to be destined to have our full taste of the range of human experience in our time.

So as it is, the traditional Fool is set upon the edge of a cliff, unknowingly about to head right on over! In our therapeutic approach we can see the cliff as a canyon and for this I have chosen the most famous of them all, the Grand Canyon in Arizona, in the United States. As I have mentioned previously, nature has to me always been a source of beauty, wonder, awe and inspiration and when I visited the Grand Canyon, all these and so much more, were brought into one moment, as I caught my breath and looked out over the edge.

The Grand Canyon, although not the deepest, widest or longest in the world, is the best known and arguably the most dramatic. It was formed over 17 million years ago, as the Colorado River sliced its way through layer after layer of rock along with the uplift of the Colorado Plateau in which it lies. The Canyon has been home to Native American peoples, known as the Pueblo People, since at least 1200 BC. They have also been called the Anasazi, which is Navajo for 'Ancient Ones'. The first Europeans to see the Canyon were Spaniards in 1540, then a series of white Americans on expeditions throughout the 1800's. The Canyon became an official national monument in 1908 and a national park in 1919.

Fittingly, for our purposes the Canyon supports a huge variety of life forms, with over 1700 plant species alone. This is due to the vast height differences inherent in the Canyon. It can be almost arid at times but receive high rainfall at others. It is known that to journey into the Canyon contains some risk and so it fits our image well here, since it acts as a symbol for the Seekers Quest, in which we literally take our life, all of it, into our hands.

Just as I have said, each of us sees different things in nature and responds differently to different scenarios and places, each finding something different in what we see and why we see it. It is that difference that makes us who we are. So what comes to you when you stand on the edge of the canyon?

DESCRIPTION

Here we see the vast, almost bottomless cliff plunging away beneath our feet, disappearing into the shadows created by the sunrise. In the image on the card it is as if we have become the Fool and are seeing the world before us through his eyes, in this case stood at the edge of the canyon. The Canyon symbolises nothing less than all of life and all that awaits us within.

We see the vast expanse stretching out before us as the sun rises, taken in fact, from the South Rim of the Grand Canyon. This symbolises for us the beginning of our life and our Quest. The journey ahead is akin to the journey one can take nowadays down into the Canyon. As we step, or in some cases fall, over the edge of the Canyon, so we must descend into the morass of anonymity that is now the seething spectacle of humanity.

Just as a new dawn creates within us a new energy, giving us an essential rebirth each day, so too does it bring new shadows in its wake. Our Quest must take us through the shadows that we see. We know even now that our Quest will take us to dark places, the depths within our soul into which we must allow light to shine. Deep as the Canyon is, vast and wide, so we must endure all that we encounter with the promise that we shall emerge out the other side, still the same but somehow changed.

Both spiritual and biological teachings tell us that we are born anew each day and with each dawn there can be fresh hope, new wonder and awe at what the day may bring, what we may experience, discover and achieve, should we choose to see it that way. The rising Sun reminds us of these possibilities and creates that emotional and psychological lift within us, which we all experience when the Sun comes out. It is like that smile within our beings reflected here in the sunlight and the first light of dawn.

Close to us in the bottom right corner of the card we see the top of the edge of the Canyon, just next to where we stand. The Sun illuminates this for us, showing us that what we already know is clear and within our reach and understanding. Just as the child grows and comes to learn through experimentation, or trial and error, so do we through our lives. It can be argued that we are given what will be an obstacle so that we learn what we do not need in order to learn and gain what we do.

The skies above us are illuminated by the rising Sun, a reminder of the spiritual and energetic realm from whence all originate and will return. Prior to our descent into the Canyon our consciousness is still aware of what we need to know, instinctively. In actuality this remains the case throughout the Quest if we but knew it, it is just that the shadows grow around us and symbolically blot out the light of clarity. However if they did not do that there would be no Quest and no purpose to life.

In the distance the landscape is not clear, hazy perhaps from the rising heat of the Sun and it is hard to determine where the Canyon ends. We see the Colorado River, coursing its powerful way ahead of us and disappearing from view ahead. This is the path of our life and Quest. This tells us we do not know how long our journey may be and where it will take us. We know only that we must traverse what we see before us. As the saying goes we are 'spiritual beings having a human experience' and this card shows us that in full measure.

ENERGY

The energy of this card can be something of a shock, in the sense that it can occur out of the blue and hit us in an instant, rather like the Big Bang that we are told heralded the beginning of the Universe. This 'eureka moment' usually occurs when we are not expecting it and certainly we cannot force or try to seek out and find this energy. It simply comes to us, or perhaps more accurately, we open ourselves to it.

Rather like that sacred explosion, we find that this energy opens us up and we are transmuted into an almost continual experience of ecstasy. We can find ourselves somehow fully in the moment, pleased to see anyone and everyone, going with the flow and taking delight in whatever comes our way. There is no judgement within us while experiencing this energy, just a trusting disposition that some may call naïve but in that flow we find natural and necessary. There is a total openness to the flow of life's processes. We live simply and eat when we want, sleep when we want and do just as it seems right to do. The energy of this card brings us an instinctual urge to naturally be who we are, in essence and free from strife, guilt, worry, dishonesty or pretty much any motivation other than 'because' – it is rather like the perennial and only answer to the question why – why not! We can also turn here to the author E M Forster when he said in 'A Room with a View' that 'alongside the everlasting why, there's a yes'! ('And a yes and a yes' to quote Denholm Elliot in the film version!).

Another way of putting this is that we experience the essential love that is the strongest force in the Universe - or our bit of it anyway. We find ourselves being the 'pointless optimist'. There is logically no reason to be optimistic when we look at the history and state of the world and everything in it, but we cannot go about miserable and downcast the whole of our lives – where's the point of existence and life if that's the case? So we make a choice to be optimistic without reason, the perennial joker as the Fool in traditional Tarot can be termed. We see the good in people, the potential in all.

It is that potential that is reflected in the numerological association of this card, each card's number being a further expression of its energy. The non-number or energy of 0 here tells us that anything can and may happen, depending perhaps on whether we are brave enough to take that leap over the Canyon. It also tells us that, like the glyph of 0, eventually we will find our way back home to the goal of our Seekers Quest. So it is we must brace and throw ourselves on the mercy of the energy of the Universe and commit willingly, if fearfully, to our unknown fate.

49

Of course as we absorb this energy it can leave us open to all kinds of deceit and deception but if we remain tuned into our instincts, we will find that we are given due warning from within when this is likely to occur. This is one reason why the personification of this energy, the Fool, is also known as the wisest Fool. His infinite wisdom comes in his ability to accept all things as they are, do what he knows it is right to do with a good and positive intent and keep moving on. This is how we can and need to find ourselves when this card turns up for us; the attitude we need to have is that of seeing the opportunity of learning and adapting.

The love that can be the expression of this energy is unconditional, just like our 'pointless optimist'. The Sun that rises in the card does not discriminate and choose who to shine on, it just does and we all feel the benefit and uplift of its warmth and power. The unknown that lies ahead of us is the reason for living and the challenge of what we may discover and experience. The joy that we can feel is in the experience of it, whatever 'it' may be, for each one of us. Just as in the film 'City Slickers' where we are told that life is all about just one thing – the trick being that this is an individual thing, different and unique to each of us and all we have to do is discover what this is for us. The energy of this card is that one thing!

A good maxim we can take with the energy of this card is 'carpe diem', first expounded by Byron in his work 'Letters' of 1818 and popularised more recently in the wonderful film 'Dead Poets Society' starring Robin Williams . The extended use of this phrase is in fact translated as 'seize the day – put no trust in the future'. The energy we feel from this card exhorts us to do just that, being fully awake and alive in the moment and throwing ourselves bodily over into the Canyon, knowing all will be well, but not knowing how or why. Life is indeed a mystery and here we are challenged to embrace it.

It is when we experience the Canyon energy that we are challenged to go against the grain, to act without reason, logic or even understanding and do whatever it is, just for the hell of it, or what I have come to know and love as the 'Fuck it' principle, from John Parkin's wonderful book of that title. It is the urge to resign our boring jobs and live the dream we have always had, follow the good life, even if it takes us to poverty and despair at times. We are more alive and more ourselves, since we are being true to ourselves and that is more valuable than any bank account.

We feel the urge now to exceed our limits, to push ourselves to go that bit further, force just a little more effort from within, to face our fears and know that there is nothing to fear but fear itself. The challenge we feel within cannot be destroyed, only avoided and if we can rise to this we can excel, in the game we call life and so avoid the dull normality of existence.

This challenge and energy can seem impossible to maintain as we are all beset by personal tragedy and malady within our being. Such is the human condition. When the Canyon looms in front of us by appearing in our reading, we are being challenged to find the ability to laugh at our disasters and pain and when we do, we are backed and supported by an unstoppable force called the Universe. The challenge here is to look at logic, but see that it is, in the words of the great Spock in Star Trek, only the beginning of wisdom, and then apply our instincts and act anyway.

1 – TORNADO

BACKGROUND

In traditional Tarot, the first character the Fool encounters when he lands from his leap over the cliff is the Magician. In his quest for wholeness of experience and personality, this is the part of him and of course ourselves, that can be defined as the outer male aspects of the human being and condition. Here we must learn the full ability control and correct function of our senses, expressed here as awareness, thought, feeling and action. There are many other ways these can be depicted, from the above psychological Jungian functions, through the elemental attributions of fire, air, water and earth to their symbols of rod, sword, cup and pentacles. It is in the Magician himself that these all combine. Here we learn to incorporate the Yang, active, outer energy of life and of ourselves.

The result of this elemental combination is the human being and we need to realise and respond to this truth for our most effective self to be expressed. In short, it is in the combination of these four forces that we find and can use our full power. For our therapeutic purposes with the Tarot, it is power with which we are concerned when we see this card. There is often a question that can arise of whether a client, or ourselves of course, is 'in our power' in a certain situation or in life generally.

We are continually challenged and required to live, move and have our being in the fullness of our power, if we are to develop and progress, not just spiritually, but psychologically, emotionally and physically too. It is only when we can operate from this rounded and integrated place that we can expect to move toward the fulfilment of our potential. This is the challenge presented to us with the power of the Tornado.

Most Tornadoes have wind speeds of up to 177 kilometres per hour and are about 250 feet across and travel several kilometres before they dissipate. The largest known however, reached speeds in excess of 438 kph, were 3.2 kilometres wide and travelled dozens of miles. Although they have been detected on every continent except Antarctica, the majority occur in North America in a region known predictably as Tornado Alley, essentially a band down the middle of the continent. The name Tornado comes originally from the Latin 'to thunder' and can also be called twister or cyclone. A feature of the Tornado is the funnel cloud that forms as the conduit for its force or power, linking it clearly with the focus and purpose of the Magician in the Tarot.

Tornados are basically formed from the interplay between cool air descending below the cloud and warm air being drawn upwards. The Magician in the Tarot stands as a conduit between the energies of what we can call 'Heaven and Earth' or the energetic and material realms. This is why we see him pointing upwards with one hand and down with the other. Here the Tornado does that for us.

The numerical energy brought, or offered to us here is that of identity. The number 1 is the 'I' perhaps obviously, and this speaks of the self. As we see, this is the adjustment to the soul becoming fully aware of its human incarnation as it lands below the Canyon's edge and on solid ground; the metaphor for the material, everyday world we must now learn to operate and function in. This is the realm of the senses as depicted by the symbols of the four suits and elemental powers which of themselves represent the human being. So it is the challenge and energy here that is to become who we are, a soul or spirit in human form learning to discover and express its power.

We can each respond differently when challenged with our power. The sense of responsibility that can come with it can be too much for some, and we turn and run. Others head onwards and upwards, into the storm, taking delight in 'testing their mettle'. In truth it is neither a fight or flight response that is required, rather a blending with the power: opening to it then merging with it which allows us to access its full force. It is then we become a conduit for the energy on offer here and in this way we can truly become a more conscious part of the Universe.

DESCRIPTION

Having picked ourselves up and dusted ourselves down from the leap over the Canyon, we find ourselves at the source of a vast landscape that opens out onto the plains before us. We catch our breath, and check that no lasting damage has been done, no broken bones or evidence of further injury apparent, just perhaps an ego slightly more aware of itself than before, through its bruising.

With this ego fluttering in the breeze that seems to be blowing, we cast our eyes forwards and find we can see something in the distance and perhaps even sense within ourselves the storm that is brewing. We could perhaps see this as the storm that is the rest of our lives. However, here we take a look at the scene we are presented with. Just like we human beings, Tornados come in many shapes and sizes and often take the shape of a funnel, the wider opening at the top connecting with cumuli nimbus cloud, with its distinctive anvil shaped, or flat-topped, mushroom-like appearance. The formation of these clouds often herald severe weather and thunderstorms and in the image here, this is most certainly the case.

The foot of the tornado we see, which is particular to all tornados, cyclones or twisters, in contact with the ground and is encircled by its resultant cloud of debris and dust. Indeed for a 'vortex of violently rotating column of air' to be classified as a tornado it must be seen to be in contact with both ground and cloud, the significance of which we shall see shortly and which lends itself to its perfect placing in the Tarot Therapy Deck'.

As we can see in our image here, the river that was beneath the Canyon is now the path, making its way through the landscape that awaits us on our quest. The path beckons us forward along the road upon which we must travel through our lives. It is true and straight, in juxtaposition with the Tornado we see whirling overhead. A short way ahead of us spins the mighty Tornado. It is surrounded at its foot by dust and debris forming the dark cloud we see having its effect of great energy on the immediate environment. It grows in girth as it rises and spins and we can see its connection with the cloud at its top, from where it expands out to merge and blend with the stormy sky it has created. All are connected in this image, the one flowing into the other and in its centre is the vortex of the Tornado, forming a focal point to which we are inextricably drawn.

Interestingly, Tornados rotate anti-clockwise in the Northern hemisphere (when seen from above) , and clockwise in the Southern hemisphere. In our image here we can see the curvature of the funnel cloud of the Tornado; such is its force and power. This may remind us of the 'lemniscate' symbol of infinity that occurs in many Magician cards in Tarot. It is like a figure 8, to illustrate the flow of life and energy itself, which the Magician and ourselves, are called to create and then flow with. Many of us are familiar with the adage to 'go with the flow' but more than this we need to first learn to create that flow for ourselves, whatever that is for each individual, then 'go with it'. This is the magic of the Magician and the gift the Tornado brings.

We can see the bright expanse beyond this, appearing as if the Sun has now risen over and into the Canyon. This to, beckons us forward, seeming to entice us on and representing the goal of our Quest, the centre of this Solar System and symbolic spiritual home to which we long to return. We shall meet this again of course, later on our Quest but for now it is enough to recognise its brightness and be drawn to its radiance and warmth.

ENERGY

The energy and challenge when we experience this card is, as we have already seen, that of becoming more in tune with the energy of the Universe and our place and part in it. This energy calls us to be a conscious part of the land and wider cosmos of which we are an intrinsic part. With the Canyon we may have known this instinctively, but now with the Tornado upon us, we find a need to lift our awareness and make conscious that which was known only instinctively before.

Here we need to connect every level of our being and raise its vibration to become in harmony and in tune with what is around us. It is as if, in traditional Tarot, the Magician sounds the 'Om', the note that vibrates in accordance with that of the Earth and the Universe. As we open our throats and let this vibration sound through our whole beings, so we begin to resonate in accordance with our environment and we join with what is above, below and around us. It is for this reason that the Magician is depicted with one arm raised towards the heavens and one pointing down to the Earth, just as with the Tornado it makes a connection to the Universe and to the Earth and to ground and sky. The challenge we face now to adapt to this power and make full use of it, is to become like the Tornado; the conduit between heaven and earth, if you will.

This is done by becoming conscious of every level of our being; to realise our holistic reality. We must become conscious of our spiritual, mental, emotional and physical levels and do what is required at each of these levels to achieve this. This can be different for each individual and the pull we may feel now can come at any, and all of these levels in order to express itself. As we learn to give this expression, so it is we raise the level of our self and our being and learn to become in balance and harmony, within and without.

By this we achieve the embodiment of this energy, the realisation and conscious living that all is 'as above, so below' or 'as within, so without'. As we absorb this energy, so we realise that our power flows not from within, but from above, below and all around. It is known that the human brain consists of two hemispheres, the right side governing our unconscious, intuitive faculties and the left side the conscious and logical. By letting the energy here flow through us and learning to consciously and actively create and then go with the flow of our life, so we create the synapses from this awareness, thought, feeling and action that bridge the gap that divides these two hemispheres. In this way we can become a more fully realised and conscious human being as we allow ourselves to experience this energy.

We also know that the right hemisphere of the brain governs the left side of the body and the left brain the right side of the body. It is easy to imagine then a figure of eight forming, as this energy flow through us. This in turn reminds us of the DNA spiral shape that science has been identified as being our 'building blocks'. We also connect here with the Magician in traditional Tarot, which features the lemniscate symbol (a figure of eight lying on its side), as described above.

As we become more conscious, so it is we can see a little more of the journey ahead of us, just as we see the path on the card stretching off into the distance. It is as if we can visualise the journey ahead of us, with its trials and tribulations, joy and wonder. We adapt to the situation in which we find ourselves and can now exert our will, from a holistic awareness, to create what we require to best equip us for the journey ahead. We feel the responsibility of being alive, the requirement to live as we should, and make the correct application of our will, mind, desire and action.

In some ways we can see the Tornado as the force within us that sustains us on our Quest. As we shall see over the course of the coming cards, this Quest is to find what was lost. It is to spend our lives seeking a reunion with the awareness or consciousness of what we once were. A union with our soul if you will, of which we had awareness of before we leapt, or fell, over the Canyon. Just as with the scientifically measurable energy detectable in the Universe, this force cannot be killed or destroyed. It can however be manipulated and enhanced to fuel us on our Quest. The challenge of the Tornado then is to achieve a balance of that force within us and something of a blending with it, which will then be reflected without us to create the experiences we need to guide us to the conscious awareness of our soul once more.

It is as if in order to reclaim our lost soul we must release it completely and immerse ourselves fully, with all our senses, at the four levels listed above, into the World. We must become part of the world, even if a part of us, however small and wobbly, knows that we are not really of it. In this we can rise above our lower ego and not fall prey to worldly matters and desires, since the goal of our quest does not belong there. We sense that these things are futile, and so our need, as the Tornado comes to us, and is not to be tricked by the world and its illusions or our own baser desires and way to live.

As we learn to balance the force of the Tornado and adapt to it, recognising we cannot control or dominate it but blend with it, so it is we become more consciously aware of the purpose of our quest, this being to perfect ourselves so as to serve the world better. It is a matter of raising our consciousness and energetic vibration to the highest level we are capable of for this purpose. So we must ask ourselves, or our clients, what we need to do to achieve this. As we do so, we fulfil the traditional purpose of this card, becoming the transmitter or mediator of divine will on Earth, expressing our divine motivation. As we know, we are spiritual beings having a human experience, not the other way around. A grand target perhaps, but no less real for all that.

The energy of this card presents us with opportunities to learn to act with integrity and honour in all things and do what we instinctively know is right. As we recall the four symbols that represent the four levels of the self, so we know we have the full potential within us to be the stuff of our sacred existence in reality. As a result we may find a manifestation from the energy here in a creative spurt, or a spontaneous outpouring of ideas or expression in whatever form our creativity chooses to express it.

We can find great confidence to, as we absorb the energy on offer here, as we come to know that we act in accordance with the Universe. We should guard against our ego as we have said but we can employ great surety where it may be lacking. With this comes responsibility, not just to do the right thing but to ensure we maintain whatever practises we deem necessary to sustain the balance of ourselves with what is above and what is below.

2 - WATERFALL

BACKGROUND

Following his meeting with the Magician, the next character the Fool meets on his long journey or quest through the Major Arcana is the High Priestess. Robed in deep blue and sat atop her throne, she guards the inner feminine mysteries of intuition and our natural, instinctive feel for what is right. The High Priestess is the personification of these things, sitting as she does between the twin dark and light pillars that form the entrance to this enchanted world.

These pillars could be seen as the masculine and feminine, equal and opposite poles of magnetic energy that between them galvanise us into creation. Through the interplay of these energies or forces we can arrive at a sense of inner knowing, a state that simply is, that cannot be arrived at by force, coercion or struggle. When we find our sense of inner self, we just know. It is a state which is inbuilt into each and every human being and what is required to discover it, is something akin to the Buddhist 'Middle Path' approach to life, whereby we avoid extremes, but settle for calm and quiet within. When we allow ourselves to do this, a sense of inner-tuition is allowed to flourish and surface. By attuning to this, through relaxation methods (something as simple as a walk in the park or any natural place) or by deeper meditation, we can be our own guide as to the correct path in life for us, at any given moment and in any given situation.

A Waterfall is obviously a vertical drop in the course of a river, usually formed when the river is young. We can learn much from the slow, inexorable carving of the effect of the waters' flow, just as we saw with the formation of our Canyon. As the flow of the water increases towards the drop, it picks up material from the riverbed. The whirlpools from the turbulence as well as sand, stones and suchlike increase the erosion which causes the waterfall to carve itself deeper. Waterfalls can retreat up to a rate of 1.5 metres per year. The area above a waterfall can often be wider and deepen, telling us something of the nature of the energy within us here. At the base of the fall there is often a deep area, created because of the kinetic energy from the fall itself.

Waterfalls are grouped into ten categories, based on the volume of water present on the fall. The tallest waterfall in the world is Angel Falls in Venezuela, being 979 metres high. For our purposes we see the Victoria Falls that at their highest flow can contain a sheet of unbroken water flow over a mile wide.

The geological basis of the Vitoria Falls is that of basalt, which has many large cracks filled with weaker sandstone. The flow of the Zambezi river has over time, eroded these cracks to create the gorges of the fall. This symbolises again our emotional flow, which no matter how we try to stem it, will eventually wear down the hardest of surfaces and break free. Like all the Major Arcana cards, it is energy stronger than us and we are wise to learn to adapt and flow with it as best we can, lest we be swept along against our will, and thrown headlong over to who knows what eventuality.

The number 2 of this card tells us that having come to terms and grips with our identity and its resultant power, we must turn within to seek its balance, its 'complementary opposite' force and energy. We discover and realise in the Tornado that we are human, now we realise that this is a vehicle for the soul and we need to connect to and be guided by this, if we are to fulfil and succeed in that quest we accepted as we threw ourselves over the Canyon.

There is a strong emotional aspect to the High Priestess card in traditional Tarot, shown by the colouring of the card and the various showings of water that proliferate this card. This is, symbolically at least, linked to female energy and the watery tides we can all feel within. Like the tides, these can rise and fall and be anything from a serene flow to a raging torrent. The High Priestess however, remains calm and placid, regardless of what currents are pounding away beneath. So it is we come to see one of the major teachings of this card and energy; that of how we can become the master of our emotion, not by suppression but by acquiescence and therefore joining forces. Neither the will of the Magician or the emotion of the High Priestess has dominion over us. Rather it is a blend of the two that gives us, not control, but understanding and connection that gives us the peace that comes from knowing what this energy can give rise to.

DESCRIPTION

Having survived and perhaps blended with the force and power of the Tornado that swept through and became us, we find ourselves faced with another plunge. This is not over the cliff as with the Canyon, although we do see echoes of this in this image, but into the frothing, swirling mass of water we are here presented with.

The image we see here is taken from the largest waterfall in the world (not highest or widest however!), Victoria Falls on the Zambezi River in Southern Africa. In African its name translates to 'the Cloud That Thunders', in which we can see the reality from our image here. Victoria Falls are surrounded by flat plateau all around, suggesting for our purposes that there is calm after the storm that heralded the Tornado within us. Just as it seems to be in life, we negotiate our way round or through a time of trial and tribulation and then all seems calm for a time until the next challenge rises to meet us.

Like the High Priestess card of traditional Tarot which is the basis of this card, the true nature of the fall cannot be seen when it is in full flow or flood, since it is constantly shrouded in mist and spray, such is the force of the water movement. This flow, like our emotional natures, is at its most dangerous and unpredictable at this time of year (February to May for those who are interested) and animals as large as hippopotamus can be swept over, to be found swirling about in a pool known as the Boiling Pot.

The exact point we see in this card is Danger Point, known as such as it is a rocky outcrop amongst the Falls, over which, as you can imagine, it is all too easy to slip! Our image has a natural reflection of the standard High Priestess image, with the shades of blue pervading the scene and the twin pillars of the traditional card echoed in the cliffs at Danger Point, even given here dark and light shadings by the spray.

The High Priestess herself could be said to be represented here by the mist that we see rising from the fall of water. At once beautiful and mysterious this has an enticing quality that seems to beckon us forward to discover what lies behind and within. So it is with our own nature now and the only way we can satisfy that curiosity is to take a deep breath and give ourselves to the flow of the water.

Behind the twin pillars in our card we see further cliffs in the distance, shrouded further beyond the mist and from our vantage point, undefined and unclear. So it is with our inner, yin nature, which changes, flows and redefines itself according to the information it receives from our outer action and yang nature (the Tornado). These cliffs in the distance are a reminder then that there is a much greater distance we have yet to travel to fulfil our Quest, but here we learn and absorb the awareness and tools necessary to equip us for it.

So it is we come to see the Waterfall reaching deeply within us, shielding and protecting that which lies within, a calm within the storm of our emotions, calling us deeper and deeper to discover its mysteries and befriend the psyche. In this way we open to our inner-tuition.

ENERGY

The energy we learned to integrate from the Tornado allowed us some semblance of knowledge of our four senses and how to operate with them in the outer, material world. Here that energy is turned within and the energy that flows to us when we experience this card in our readings prompts us to look within, to discover what it is that we naturally know, how this affects us and how to operate in tandem with it. As we shall see, this opens us to a number of differing inner influences, all of which we can turn into resources that will guide us through the Quest we call life.

The scroll or book we see in the accepted image of the High Priestess contains the laws by which these inner tides operate and we must educate ourselves here as to our own workings from within, since these laws can vary for each individual. These are the inner mysteries the High Priestess 'guards' and to befriend these is to become our own High Priestess. The inner-tuition that she informs us of is subtle; just as is the nature of energy itself and here we are called to learn to operate from this inner, subtle level. This requires patience, diligence, calm and quiet as we have already seen.

This will give rise to an ability to see into the depths, not only of ourselves, but also others. This ability or function we can call empathy, which as we absorb it is greatly increased, meaning we can become compassionate and understanding beings, able to offer these gifts of insight to those that come to us. First however, we must learn to do these things for ourselves, before we can guide any other.

The passivity which the response to the energy of this card requires should not be mistaken for inactivity. It is simply that in order to access the flow of this energy and absorb it requires stillness, quiet and meditation. This gives rise to another natural ability we can all have should we so choose - that of clairvoyance, or inner sight. We can then become a passive channel for receiving energy itself, from which we can offer understanding and knowledge, to ourselves and others. This however, must be requested and should never be forced on someone.

Almost a by-product of this can also be a healing 'ability'. This is not something bestowed on only a worthy few as a gift, but a natural and non-technical tendency to want to help and guide others. Given that we can gain knowledge of the inner, energetic world that gives ourselves and the world we live in its form and substance, but by learning to work with these energetic tides, we can help by directing a force and flow of that energy, both within ourselves and to others, which we can simply call healing. Those wishing to pursue this further should study the energetic structure of the human being and a good deal more besides in order to become fully-fledged healers.

A further aspect of these inner realms is that of dreams and by using the naturally arising clairvoyant and 'knowing' tendencies that arise with this energy we can also gain knowledge as to the purpose or 'meaning' of dreams and with practice and patience, learn to use these to great effect . One other by-product of this energy can be simple inspiration. We may find ourselves coming up with ideas literally hitherto undreamt of and effectively becoming a creature of vision, fuelled by what may be seen as divine inspiration. It is as if we can see the need for something before it happens just as a fully flowing and operational intuition will do, since it is part of the human condition, if we allow it to be.

Once connected to and aware of this natural aspect of our working, it is important we take and make time to be still and listen to it, or attune ourselves to it. It is true to say that the more we learn to operate intuitively and instinctively the more naturally intuitive we become. However we must remember that this energy operates at that subtle level within and will not slap us around the face or between the eyes in order to be heard. It is simply there and it is up to us to do what is required to hear, see or feel it.

Should we choose not to do so we can find that this energy will turn us within ourselves to an unhealthy degree and we can become distant and aloof from others and the outside world. We need to ensure that our sensitivity does not become so great we cannot operate in the everyday world for then we are of no use to ourselves, let alone others in this state and cannot then fulfil our purpose for being here, whatever that may be. Part of this requires us to meet our own needs, which this energy can cause us to neglect if we are not disciplined and careful to obey. Again we are of no use if we do not. All that we will present to the world and those we encounter then would be coldness, distance and lack of care; quite the opposite effect from that which this energy is intended to produce.

As we experience this energy, we can discover the great lunar influence it brings with it and how that affects the tides of all waters and fluids on the Earth, including that within us. This in turn and by association, has a profound impact on our emotions and the feelings they give rise to, something that so many sensitive people struggle to not fall prey to and be controlled by.

Rather than being a 'moody bitch' which the High Priestess could be accused of to the initiated, we find that we need to learn to go with the flow of our moods. This means that we do not become downcast and gloomy at times, but rather that we naturally sense and just know when we need to withdraw a little, to turn within and seek stillness and when it is time to be more active, playful and gregarious, the beginnings of which take flower with the next cards' energy, as we shall see.

Successfully and healthily integrated however, this energy creates an inspired, creative person, full of empathy for the causes of disharmony in the self and others, who is able to serve as a link between darkness and light. What is required now is a force that turns that energy into matter, or put another way, someone to carry out those ideas and visions.

3 - RAINFOREST

BACKGROUND

The previous two cards have dealt with the inner energy of the masculine and feminine aspects of the human being, which we all naturally and instinctively possess. Having learned what these are and something of how to assimilate them, we now turn to their application in the world; how we use and what we do with these powers. First comes the expression of the feminine force with our version here of The Empress: the Rainforest.

The Empress is traditionally shown seated on her throne amidst a glorious natural setting of abundance, often surrounded by flowers, animals, and fruit and so on, or else possessing a 'cornucopia' – a horn of plenty. This is to represent the expression of her creative product, further emphasised by her apparent pregnancy; a symbol that she gives to us all. The Empress is seen as Mother Earth and this blends entirely with our purposes of depicting the natural energies of the cards.

Our amazing planet is full of so many wondrous and vital places that many could qualify and be appropriate here, but I have chosen the Amazon Rainforest to represent this energy, or at least a tiny snapshot of it. This card is partly about how we are all linked to and part of our planet and how she provides for us all. As we look about the natural world we find that this is demonstrated nowhere better than in the Rainforests of our planet and chief among these, the Amazon. Up to 75% of all living species are indigenous to the rainforests with possibly millions, of all classifications, as yet undiscovered.

The Amazon River itself is known as the life-force of the rainforest and is over 4000 miles long, its drainage area covering nearly 3 million square miles. Each minute 28 billion gallons of water flow into the Atlantic from the river and it receives 9 feet of rain per year, half of which is returned to the atmosphere through the foliage of the trees. The water level rises between 30 and 45 feet in the wettest period, between June and October. Amazonia itself is the drainage basin for the River and its' over 100 tributaries, and is shaped like a shallow dish in the northern half of the continent. The water drains into this basin creating the largest river system of the world in the largest tropical rainforest.

Much has been said concerning the destruction of the Rainforest which unbelievably still occurs and I will leave it to those more qualified to continue their good work here, and exhort you to do what you can in this regard, to halt it.

Numerically the 3 of this card brings us the energy of creativity. In terms of our quest it is as if now that we have discovered who we are and learned to operate in this world to best effect, being guided from within, the Universe is asking us what we will do - what will we create with this precious gift? It is ours now to do with what we will, but it is as the outgoing, active energy of the 3 is absorbed into our being that we begin to discover that we are all linked and each a part of a greater whole.

There are three titles the rainforests have been gifted with, which further show us how much they do for and give us – 'the lungs of the world', 'the world's largest pharmacy' and the 'jewels of the Earth'. From these we can see that the rainforests allow us to breathe, they provide for our health and well-being and are therefore of inestimable value.

DESCRIPTION

Much as humanity has sought to exploit and control the rainforests of the world and their resources, as they are seen, we can apply here the knowledge that they are not a thing to be contained or utilised in this way but for our healthy application need to be expressed and demonstrated; in other words they are a symbol here of how we learn to deal with and appropriately express the full force and energy of our emotions and feeling nature.

The traditional Tarot image of the Empress card is a symbolic expression of the active, female, maternal power and energy. The deeper, darker colouring of the Waterfall is here replaced with a vibrant green, the lushness and life of the outpouring of the Rainforest apparent in this. We have already seen how the Rainforest (and the Empress) gives to us all and here we see something of her life-blood, symbolically flowing in the river. The maternal nature of the feminine energy of this card is displayed in the protective canopy of trees and leaves. Above this the bright expanse of sky seems to beckon us on and forward, down the river and further on our Quest.

The trees and their canopy and the lower plants in the Rainforest trap the sunlight and covert this into energy for themselves and those that eat them. Again from this we see the life-sustaining role Amazonia provides. It is significant that the rainforest is usually seen as having four layers or communities, each inter-dependent on the other for their life - just like the construction of the human being. These are classified as the emergent and tallest layer, then the canopy, the understory and the forest floor. All this creates the most efficient ecosystem in nature. To destroy or even interfere with one of these is to destroy all. So it is we see the integration and inter-dependence of the natural world and ourselves as part of this.

A further notable factor here is that the undergrowth in the rainforest is restricted by the poor penetration of sunlight to ground level. This means we can move about with ease from the protection offered us by our bounteous parent. Should this canopy become too thinned or damaged, the rainforest swiftly becomes a jungle – impenetrable, tangled, full of unknown dangers and threat – a very different kind of energy.

This is symbolised in our image by the depth of the river and its colouring. This reflects what grows above it but also ensures we can see far into it. Just like mothers, there are hidden depths and deeper levels and an inherent, instinctive protective layer and demonstrate that there is more than may at first be apparent. Just as we abuse the rainforest and the symbolic heart of Mother Earth so it is we abuse and destroy ourselves.

So our image shows us the vitality of this ecosystem and expresses its function, protection and life-giving nature and instinct. As we are moving outward for the expression of this energy so it is we find we need to look deep within our hearts, see what is there and act for the good of ourselves as life-bearer and the good of all as life-giver.

ENERGY

Here the inner secrets of intuition so well protected and preserved by the mystery and power of the Waterfall are open and presented to the world. We find that the instinct we receive from the appearance of this card and so the energy that it brings to us, is one of caring. This is firstly for ourselves, since if we are not whole and healthy, we are of no use in caring and providing for others. This simple basic principle is one that can in fact allow us to become jealous, bitter and cold in our motives and action if we ignore or avoid it.

The energy here is intended to produce an open and loving heart, full of an unceasing abundance that comes from what can be termed maternal instinct, irrespective of our physical gender. The key to this and perhaps the biggest and strongest

71

learning that this energy brings is that of love. The more we come to love ourselves, the more that loving and creative energy can flow and so the more we can love others, as well as care and provide for them. It can be all very well to have a heart full of love, compassion and empathy for others but this is really worth nothing if we do not act on it. Following numerological principles it is worth remembering that this card is numbered 3, the number of the creative principle and energy and this means we need to respond to what we feel within and do something. Much as The Beatles may have been right when they proclaimed that 'All You Need is Love' you also need to know where your next meal is coming from. This energy can cause us to be both nurturer and cook!

This expression of love is in reality an aspect of our journey of spiritual growth. If we are to fully transcend this physical life and ascend to greater heights, whatever these may be, we have to have a full experience of it. The energy here then is that of love, in all its forms. This can include sacrificial love, the production and care of children, love and passion for another and the sensuality this brings and a great deal else besides. These are all fuelled by what we feel within our hearts, and the energy here connects us to this in a deep and powerful fashion.

Just as the 'complementary opposite' principles and energies of the male, yang Tornado and female, yin, Waterfall are contained within each of those cards, here we see the result of their union as the outer expression of the creative principle. This energy can therefore connect us to our creative inspiration in a powerful way, in whatever outlet we may be inspired to follow. In the spiritual path that is Druidry, this is recognised as the 'Awen', defined sometimes as 'flowing spirit' and can be seen to produce a kind of reverie that can be seen in the best of performers in their chosen art.

This same energy can also be sensed in the interchange between performer and audience and is why live music, theatre, opera etc. is always best. As the performer presents their art the audience responds and in turn the performer 'feeds' from this, not to fuel their ego, but to raise their performance to greater heights, to which the audience is raised and so on. This wonderful occurrence also illustrates for us the basic creative principle and energy of the Universe of which we are a part and is why the creative arts are at their best, a spiritual force and language.

Just as in the animal kingdom we know that the fiercest creature of all is a mother when she feels her offspring are threatened, there is a certain toughness that this energy can also bring to us with this cards appearance. In keeping with what we saw of the need to act on the love we feel ,so it is we need to nurture and develop, not just to survive but to rise to the greatest heights we can as we respond to this energy, whether this be in what we create (music, poetry, meals, children etc.) or in the manner in which we live and express who we are. In this the Bible can actually give us much sage guidance, exhorting us to 'love your neighbour as yourself' and to 'do unto others as you would have them do to you'. Laudable principles yes, but here this energy directly challenges and offers you an opportunity not just to smile, nod and agree but to actually do it!

As Mother Earth this energy also brings with it an awareness of the sanctity of life; all life. In this regard we can learn that life is a sacred thing and to abuse, waste and neglect it flows against the natural force of energy that indeed is life. We are pushed to live in the full awareness of this and to act with this mindful intention at all times. This can be a great challenge but we can find that we soon acquire a habit (psychologically it takes three week to make, or break, habits) so this can soon be done – and undone, so we cannot relax. However nothing

73

great was ever achieved by sitting back and letting life drift by and here the energy brings us onwards and upwards in our development as a conscious human being and expression of the love that (should) motivate it.

The Mother has to not only feed her young, she must also create and provide shelter and protection and as such this can give us a strong 'homing instinct' as we experience the energy here. This can manifest itself in a number of ways, either to find and establish one of our own, to change what we have, to open it to others or seek out and help those who do not have one. Matters of the home as well as the heart are brought to the fore with this energy in all their myriad forms.

With the positive expression of this energy we can find ourselves becoming a person full of love with all its wonderfulness, engaged in selfless acts simply because we can and have a desire to. We must ensure this does not turn in on itself so that we become selfish and self-obsessed as the always possible negative side takes over. When we allow ourselves to fully love and be loved, as this energy can cause us to do if we can be open to it, we find ourselves becoming like the Goddess of old, the queen of our lives and hearts.

4 - DESERT

BACKGROUND

From the abundant fertility of the Rainforest we come now to the dry, sandy expanse of the Desert. The fertility we find here is of an altogether different nature and it is in the extremes we can see in each of these cards where their relationship and dynamic lies. The Rainforest image gives expression to the feminine force within nature and of course within us. Here the Desert does the same for the masculine principle and energy within our earthly realm. It is in that dynamic that between them these two cards show us the twin equal and opposite or complementary forces within each of us and all around us.

So we find that we need to look deep within our being, firstly to find that source of love and compassion in the Rainforest, and informed by this, come to act and step into our full power of self-knowledge and awareness in the Desert. Put another way, we can learn here to become our own Emperor. We act for our own good and when we know who we truly are we recognise that this serves us all. We must be careful not to forget or lose the love within and fall prey to our ego but if we remember that the Major Arcana cards show us the journey of our soul, we see the progression as we absorb each energy, moving from one on to the next, compiling and adding as we go, on our path to individuation and completion.

The Desert replaces the Emperor here, the apparent barrenness we are confronted with hiding much we can learn from. Living conditions are hostile in a desert of course, but about one third of all the Earth's land has this aridity, inclusive of the polar caps, sometimes called 'cold deserts'. The dryness of this card is in juxtaposition to the Rainforests wetness, the difference between the essential masculine force and the feminine flow. Both need each other.

Deserts are formed by big variations in temperature between day and night causing stress on rocks which then break into pieces. The rare flash floods that can occur can also break rocks, which are then further eroded by wind. The desert is then arranged according to the whim of the wind. A desert is classified as such by its extremely low level of precipitation, usually identified as less than 400 millimetres annually – the Sahara has just 25mm per year. It is also one of the hottest regions of the world, with temperatures that can exceed 130 Fahrenheit (55 centigrade). Due to the heat the majority of the water is lost as evaporation.

We take the Sahara for our image partly because it is the largest (non-polar) desert in the world, covering an area of 3.5 million square miles, roughly 10% of its continent, Africa. Despite this size there is only very sparse vegetation and animal life. Despite this and with typical tenacity, the Sahara has been home to humanity for over 8000 years. Interestingly the majority of these have always been nomadic. This seems to bring to mind the idea of 'shifting sands' and tells us that change is inevitable, and we must always be on the move in terms of our growth and development, but that this must be gradual and natural for it to be lasting and effective.

The symbols we see in the traditional Emperor card are often those of authority and rule, the sword, the sceptre and orb, the eagle and, most applicable to our therapeutic purposes here, the heat of the Sun. It is worth noting here that the eagle is able to look directly at the Sun, which would of course, blind us. We can do this metaphorically, experiencing the heat of the Desert, the dryness in our own being, needing to find what inspires and fires us to be the very best we can be.

We can discover a force of determination within us that is rooted not in our own self and being, as we shall see, but in our sense and awareness of the sacred. The energy here connects us to our actions and lets us know that what we will creates our reality. The Emperor is a wise ruler, full of power, ability and confidence and so behind the seemingly barren desert we can locate and literally, divine, an unending power to determine to use that will in the manner of our own choosing.

DESCRIPTION

With the Emperor in traditional Tarot, the Desert removes him from the setting we are used to seeing him in and allows us instead to relate what we see, directly. Whilst most of us will be attracted to and even inspired by the wonder of the Rainforest with all its lushness and abundance, here we may be repelled or, ironically, left in the cold, by the hot, dry, sandy landscape that we see before us.

The Emperor is shown sitting on a throne in a high place to indicate his lofty position of dominion over all things worldly and material. Here the hills are the sand dunes that we see. The Sahara Desert, from which our image is taken, does have several mountain ranges (some volcanic, to note for a later card) reaching a height of over eleven thousand feet at their peak. Equally and significantly, its lowest point is below sea level in an area of Egypt known as the Qattara Depression. Water is also found in the Sahara in the form of seasonal steams and aquifers (an area of water beneath the surface) and where these can reach the surface we find oases.

The significance here is that the traditional image for this card shows a small river flowing, almost hidden, at the foot of the card. This symbolises that despite all the harshness and immovability we see, there is something of an awareness of emotional needs, of the need for flow, change and adaptation. If he wants to remain Emperor he must understand and allow for these things. So it is with the Desert.

If we look deeply enough we can find water and the presence here in this form, i.e. underground as it were, tells us something of that relationship and dynamic between the male and female energies – there is always something of one within the other, one cannot exist without the other and life is created by the interplay between them. So we may not be able to see the water in our image here, but it is there, perhaps nestling quietly but powerfully in our subconscious, occasionally bubbling up to the surface to take its due and necessary influence.

We can 'see' something of a heat haze in the background of the image. In terms of the energy we receive now, this brings an intensity and an encounter of a force within ourselves that demands we stand up and be counted and rise to the challenge of our potential, to begin recognising who we truly are and establishing that in our life and world; a tall challenge indeed.

Beyond the ridge of sand we find ourselves standing on as we look into the image, ahead of us we see further dunes. Here our journey may be hard, requiring an unrelenting quality, determination and steely rigidity, just as we must sometimes in life. It is perhaps only as we look more intently at the hills we can realise their size and the difficulty of the harsh climb ahead of us. It is time to get tough and get going. We can see tracks of those who have gone before us, telling us we are not alone and are dependent on others, just as they may depend on us; we are all linked.

We can also see areas of shadow or shade created by the lie of the dunes. Whilst quite beautiful and even relaxing in their gentleness, we can see they offer but little and brief respite from the heat of the day and the progression of the Sun. Intensity, by its very nature, rarely lets up and as Emperors of ourselves and lives, we must be ever vigilant, determined and strong.

The Sahara is subject to winds resulting from the hot air conditions, which are most commonly known as Sirocco. At their strongest these can create sandstorms lasting four days – blending nicely for us with the numerology of this card. The symbolism here is that the change that we have already seen is necessary, cannot be predicted, none of us truly knows our future and the result of our actions and how things will pan out. Despite this we must make decisions we believe are the correct ones in the here and now and adapt to the outcomes and results as we go. Despite whatever sandstorms may blow, we need to keep our focus on the now.

ENERGY

As with all Major Arcana cards the energy we are given here presents us with a challenge. It is easy to see that challenge as how to survive the desert, the dryness, the heat, the search for life giving water and an oasis, mirage, visions and madness. Indeed there can be times deep within our beings that we may wonder if we are being brought to the edge of madness, such can be the pressure and intensity of life and what is presents to us.

So it is with the energy that the Desert brings. There are times of intensity in our life and times of calm and peace. This is an intense time, of focus, concentration and control. Here we can learn to fully step into our power, find our place in the world, our vocation if you will; what we are here to do and to begin to do it. This is a time for carefully thought out, structured action. Stay in the same place in the Desert and you will die. Change, as the good Emperor knows, is necessary for survival, but that change should be gradual and so not traumatic.

Numerically the number 4 is steadfast and strong, unmoving, like the Desert, or at least moving very slowly. Change is gradual, like the proverbial 'shifting sands' we see here. Evolution is a necessity most certainly and we must ensure we absorb this into our being, but slowly and as it suits us to move with, lest we lose the control and stability so preciously on offer to us here. Once we have established this we can seek to move on and embrace the change that shall surely come, as we cannot become stuck in one place forever. Should we do that here, we will shrivel and die, just like our spirits do in life if the status quo is sought to be maintained throughout.

The energy brought to us here we can undoubtedly classify as masculine in its call to arms and action. We may find a deep need to look to the source of our security, to what is established, known and safe. The adage that 'no man is an island' rings true here as we recognise that despite needing to source our own security, we also need a little water to ensure we do not become totally dry and unfeeling. So it is we arrive at that dynamic fusion of energies that sparks the male, female creation.

As we delve deep within our beings with this energy, so we can create an order, structure and foundation for who we are and who we will become. This may be found differently in each individual of course, owing to their genetic make-up, karmic requirements and much more besides. The energy here stands for and offers to us sensibility, self-awareness and commandment over the self. It offers to us a chance, sometimes through pressure and persistence, pushing us to the limit, to discover who we really are and find out 'what we are made of'. It could be said that this energy sorts the men from the boys.

What we are made of, is 'star-stuff', the same material that exists throughout our Universe, showing us that we are intrinsically a part of it and each connected to the other and to all things. At perhaps its deepest level then, this energy can allow and guide us to discover the sacred within us. It can bring us to a self-realisation that we are spiritual or sacred beings having a human experience, not the other way round. Once we learn and know that this is the true source of our security, our real foundation and the building blocks of our being and identity, we have something that is unshakeable, eternal and infinite.

The energy here is an awareness of the sacred presence that exists in all living things, even in the harshest, hottest, driest Desert. Even here, that certain sacred something resides and gives life and so it is within each of us, no matter how close to the edge we may become. Our sacredness never leaves us; it cannot for it is interwoven into us, it is us, from our facial expression down to our DNA. Here we can make the major revelation that we are the Emperor of our own life.

Once we know this we are empowered to do what is necessary to fulfil our destiny. As we absorb the energy here so it is we know what we must do and we do it, without pause, without delay, in sure and certain knowledge of its rightness. Such power can be a rare thing and does indeed need careful management and we would always do well to remember that we always need that water, even if we cannot see it, to keep us flowing the right way. This energy can lead to egotism, causing us to think we are invincible, something we see all too prevalent in today's world, even in the so-called spiritual or 'new-age' community. Power, as we know from history, corrupts, and we need to ensure we continually recognise and acknowledge the source of our power, and it is not us. Whatever term we choose to use, it is the Divine and we are but a grain of sand in this particular desert in comparison with its energy and vastness.

Each grain of sand is a vital and equal component of the Desert however and so it is we can absorb this energy by the construction of our life's plan based on that sacredness, safety and power we have come to know. We can discover the Universal laws we must obey and live by and if we apply these to ourselves and lives, so we can step into the full and awesome energy of who we are, doing what is right with our life. Almost magically, we find that nature and the Universe supports us in our efforts, for when we follow such a plan we are literally going with the very flow of creation and the Universe and we cannot fail; it is simply not a possibility.

Just as the Rainforest brought out any maternal issues we may have to deal with, so the Desert can do the same, but paternally. More mundanely, this may manifest in highlighting our relationship with our Father, this being one of the many Jungian archetypes we encounter in the Tarot. Again, the more we can be who we truly are, hopefully guided and strengthened by our father, the 'better', more complete and fulfilled we become.

We can surmise the energy here as the force behind the knowledge accessible to us when we know that if we apply our minds and determine to act, we can achieve anything at all. It is time to ask yourself what you will achieve.

5 - ECLIPSE

BACKGROUND

From the dazzling brightness of the desert landscape we move now to the darkened skies of the Eclipse. Strewn with suspicion and significance throughout history, an eclipse has always been a momentous event. Those of us who were present during the total eclipse of the Sun in 1999 in our home land of the UK and across much of Europe and Asia can attest to the impact it can have upon us.

The traditional fifth card of the Major Arcana, the Hierophant, has to do largely with our belief and tradition and here we see this as both an internal and external energy. What we choose to believe in by way of faith or religion, or equally a belief in nothing, can have a profound impact upon ourselves and lives and the way in which we are motivated to act, the decisions we make, relationships we form, our morality and much more besides. In short our beliefs are central to our character and our actions – again internal and external factors. We shall see some of the beliefs regarding a solar Eclipse shortly, and how these affected people, but for now we can content ourselves with that sense of awe and wonder as we stare at the disappearing Sun and the ensuing darkness that descends.

A good way to summarise the effect of an eclipse upon the Earth and its inhabitants, of all kinds, is to imagine living without the Sun – which of course we could not for we depend upon it for life. Imagine however that the Sun did not rise one morning, and the gloom and darkness were permanent. This can give us something of an idea of the impact of a solar eclipse and explain why it was so feared in ancient times. Indeed the word eclipse is of Greek origin meaning 'abandonment'. This tells us a little more of the sense induced by the event and why we see the energy of the card as requiring us to examine and explore our sense of belief, faith and trust in a higher force (or not).

If we look at the history of eclipses, we can trace accounts of their occurrences back 4000 years in China and Babylonia and a further 500 years before that in ancient Egypt. The Chinese believed an eclipse foretold the future of their Emperor, and that a celestial dragon ate the Sun, this same being devouring the Moon during lunar eclipses. People there would emerge to bang pots and drums during an eclipse to frighten the dragon away. Indians however would immerse themselves in water during an eclipse to help the Sun in its struggle against the dragon. The Egyptian mythical snake Apep attacking the boat of the Sun god is thought to refer to eclipses.

An eclipse that occurred during the lifetime of the prophet Mohammed coincided with the death of his son. Mohammed stated that eclipses are cosmic spectacles that demonstrate the might and knowledge of Allah the Great. Muslims now perform the 'eclipse prayer' during eclipses because of this.

Astronomy was widely practised in Mesopotamia, enabling eclipses to be predicted with high accuracy, with known dates of 3rd May 1375 BC and 31 July 1036BC which "turned day into night". The ancient Greeks were also astronomers, their work remaining influential until the Renaissance. It was Zeus "father of the Olympians" who was seen as responsible for "hiding the light of the shining Sun and sore fear came upon men".

The element of Helium was discovered during an eclipse in 1868, by the French astronomer Jules Janssen, as he observed the spectrum of the Sun. Helium is now known to be the second most abundant chemical in the Universe. The eclipse of 29 May 1919 was also known to confirm some of Einstein's theories regarding relativity, the Hubble Space Telescope since confirming pictorially that gravity bends light rays.

Eclipses seem to have knack of appearing at pivotal times in our history, this last popping up to herald the new Millennium, heralded by some as the fabled Aquarian Age of spirituality and peace.

DESCRIPTION

The term 'eclipse' itself refers to the astronomical event when an object is obscured from view by passing into the shadow of another body or by having another body pass between it and the viewer. The term most commonly describes a solar eclipse when the Moon's shadow crosses the Earth's surface, blocking out sunlight completely or partially, depending on what is called the 'totality' of the Eclipse. When totality occurs the Sun disappears from view completely, along with its light and subsequent effect on all things.

The image we have here is immediately prior to the moment of totality. There are actually five stages of a solar eclipse, one of the reasons it is placed as card number five in our Major Arcana. The first stage, helpfully known as 'eclipse begins' occurs at the start of what is called 'tangency' between the Moon and Sun, when we first see the Sun beginning to be obscured as the Moon takes a 'bite' out of it. The second stage, which takes about an hour, is the beginning of the total eclipse itself, followed by 'maximum eclipse', the point at which our image is taken on the card.

The temperature drops at this point and the skies grow dark and the Moon's 'umbra', its dark shadow, gathers on the western horizon, encroaching upon you. Plants and animals react as if night has come now. Flowers close, birds stop signing, cows and chickens come home and nocturnal life comes out! It is a reversal of the norm. Just before totality itself the last of the Sun's rays are distorted by the Earth's turbulent atmosphere, producing wavy patterns of light and dark bands moving across the ground. Just ten seconds before the moment of totality we can see bright rosary-like beads of light, called Baily's Beads after the astronomer who first recorded them, as the sunlight streams through the valleys along the Moon's edge.

Then the magnificence of the Sun's corona appears as the Moon blocks its path to Earth, as we see on the card here. For just a few minutes you stand in the shadow of the Moon surrounded by what can be described as a 360 degree sunset. It is as if the Universe has pressed its own pause button and everything becomes still and silent in breathless homage to the sustainer of life, the Sun.

Then the Western edge of the corona begins to brighten and the chromosphere, the Sun's atmosphere, becomes visible again as the Moon moves on. The eclipse is effectively repeated in reverse order over the next hour, the first two stages forming the fourth and fifth. The Universe turns its dimmer switch back up to full as daylight returns and everything breathes a collective sigh of relief.

Although somewhat dark and mysterious, allowing us to see and sense something of the awe and suspicion with which our ancestors viewed an Eclipse. Fully understandable when you don't know it's coming and everything suddenly goes dark. There is also a majestic beauty as we see the visibility of the Sun's corona streaming and rippling out beyond the confines of the Moon.

ENERGY

As we have seen, eclipses are littered with awe, fear, superstition and belief and it is these things to which we must turn when this card appears in our readings. We have seen that the energy of this card affects us on both an internal and external level and this is symbolised by the interplay here between the Sun and Moon that creates an eclipse.

The Moon reaches within us and shines its reflected sun light in our darkness. As we shall see when we deal with the Moon card itself, this creates all kinds of weird and wonderful reactions, but for now it is enough to know that the light cast within us to light up our dark shadows, means we need to question ourselves and what motivates us. It is a generally held view that there are really only two motivational factors in the human being – love or fear. The energy with this card asks us to question which we are driven by.

The Sun is the giver of life and without it we would of course all perish. We shall again explore its energy more closely in its own card but symbolically speaking here we can see and feel its energy as the outer counterpart and projection of what the Moon has illuminated within us. Here we can observe the impact our fears, motives and beliefs have upon our lives and the direction they take.

What happens during an eclipse is that the Sun, along with the force or energy we get from it, disappears. We are plunged into darkness and chaos and all that we take for granted - light, warmth and logic, are gone. So it is we must trust to something deeper and higher and hope or pray for its safe return. If the source of our life, the Sun, is removed what then are we left with? We are required to have something to believe in and the appearance of this card heralds an influx of energy at this level. Who or what do you believe in and what do you do about it?

The energy here takes us to the core of our being and asks what motivates us – again, love or fear. We are challenged now to learn to apply a love, even in the face of ridicule or worse for our beliefs, for they are our beliefs and 'lest it harm none' as the creed goes, we can believe and do what we wish. This energy asks us to examine whether our belief and motivation allows for a flow of love into our lives and if this is projected all around us. This is not in an idealistic 'love and peace' hippy way, but a down to earth love, grounded in solid reality that prompts us to do the right thing each and every time, in every moment and action. If we are open to this, our conscience will guide us. Deeper than our conscience are our motives, which are often fuelled by belief.

Sometimes our motivations and beliefs are handed down to us as traditions that we are taught we 'should' do and we follow like sheep along with the rest of the flock. Certainly we have a pull to gather, especially at momentous times such as an eclipse, but it is the awareness and knowledge of why we do this that matters here. The energy of this card causes us to look at what we might be doing blindly and without full consideration and knowledge of why. Consider now if there are things within you and your life that you do because those around you or perhaps your family has always done and so you do too. This is not to suggest they are wrong and should stop, only that the energy available can help you to understand why you do what you do and open you to new possibilities or at the least a greater awareness.

Very often our pre-conditioning comes from our family and schooling and here we can experience a force that compels us to look at ourselves and the world around us, literally here, in a new light. The trappings of unquestioned tradition can become apparent and we can seek a deeper motivation based on our own truths, knowledge and instinct. We are given the opportunity through the energy of this card to become more at peace with ourselves by examining our deepest inner motives and beliefs and coming to terms with these things, whatever they may be.

With the removal of the Sun so symbolically, and perhaps literally with the energy of the card, is our logic removed. Here the Sun represents for us what is safe, known, trusted and logical, for it is there before us. Suddenly however it goes dark and so we need to turn inward and allow a deeper force to guide us. This we can call our instinct and so it is good when we experience the energy of the Eclipse to consider to what we turn when all that we trust and know is removed. What do our instincts tell us about ourselves and life? Now is the time to consider these things and perhaps consider seeking the guidance and literally with the eclipse, the 'enlightenment' of a wise teacher or guide.

When Eclipse comes along in your cards then its energy challenges you to lift yourself above and beyond yourself and your limitations, to question what motivates you and what you believe in, not just religiously or spiritually but in yourself and life. It is a reminder that there is a world beyond that which we see, observe and take part in and we have a need to acknowledge this and do something in response to it.

6 - TSUNAMI

BACKGROUND

The card of choice, the Lovers in traditional Tarot may seem an unlikely transition to make to a tsunami, but as we shall see the symbolism fits and the energy is much like the energy we need to respond to both within and without. As the result of the choices we make changes are created within, in this case beneath the sea bed, and these have their effect and opposite above ground too. As we will see, this is much like the creation and effect of a tsunami.

Until the tsunami that occurred in the Indian Ocean in 2004 we seemed not to see that word much and knew less of what is was all about. In fact the word is from the Japanese and translates as 'harbour wave'. Only few languages have a native word for this since they occur in only a few areas of the world. A tsunami is a wave or series of waves caused by the displacement of a large volume of water, usually an ocean. This is turn can be caused by an earthquake, volcanic eruption or underwater explosion.

The vibrations created by the earthquake or other event on the ocean bed can travel thousands of kilometres. Tsunamis occur mostly in the Pacific Ocean near Asia, due to the position of the tectonic plates and topography of the ocean floor, but could happen anywhere. Although the Greek historian Thucydides suggested in 426 BC that tsunamis were related to submarine activity it was not until the 20th Century we began to fully understand their nature and causes. Now much study and research takes place into tsunamis and the prediction of their possible occurrence.

The Tsunami that occurred at Christmas in 2004 killed at least 250,000 people across fourteen countries and was the deadliest ever recorded in human history. This was caused by a massive earthquake in Sumatra, reaching a huge 9.2 on the Richter scale. The largest tsunami ever recorded was at Lituya Bay in Alaska in 1958. This reached heights of 524 meters but it is possible for waves to be far larger even than this. Other massive tsunamis occurred in Chile in 1960 and in 1964 where the water hit the coasts of Japan and Hawaii, caused by an earthquake in Alaska.

Apart from the cost in human life, there is of course massive destruction to land and buildings over a huge area. The impact of all this upon humanity in that area can last a generation. The force contained within the waters of a tsunami is massive and no structure can withstand it. Once the water does retreat, this is plain for all to see, and then follows the risk of disease from stagnant and contaminated water.

Numerologically speaking, as card number 6, this speaks of the flow of forward movement, which seems a gross understatement given the magnitude of a tsunami. However this reminds us we are dealing with the Major Arcana and the major forces that our amazing planet contains, as do our own souls at which level we are located with these cards. In numerology we arrive at 6 by 2 x 3; 3 being the number of creativity. These twin forces tell us that change is not only possible, but inevitable, just like the tsunami once created.

I often explain to clients during readings that the Major Arcana cards contain an energy that is bigger and stronger than we are and their effects will sweep through us whether we like it or not. The trick lays in 'fore-warned is fore-armed', hence the beauty and effectiveness of Tarot Therapy as this is what it can give the client. Although clearly applicable to all the Major Arcana cards, this inevitability and sheer power seems perhaps, nowhere better illustrated than here. Once created, nothing can stop a tsunami.

DESCRIPTION

The waves of a tsunami are unlike 'normal' sea waves that we may be used to. To start with their length is far greater, reaching hundreds of kilometres. They begin as a rapidly rising tide, like a tidal wave, but much, much bigger. They can be hard to observe further out in the ocean where they may start, rising to a height of just 30 cm. Some of the water displaced moves further out to the ocean, some towards land, echoing the different directions we can choose to take in our path in life at this stage and time of choice, from this cards energy.

Curiously the water reaches greater heights in more shallow water. The 'wave train', the series of waves in a tsunami, arrives over a period of minutes or hours. Amazingly tsunamis can travel at around 800 kilometres per hour, reducing to approximately 80 kilometres per hour in shallow water. The power within that has built up however, is enormous.

Prior to the waves hitting land, the water actually recedes in what is called a 'drawback'. This phenomenon drags the water back, almost as if the tsunami is taking one large inhalation before it expels its watery breath. If seen, this is decision time for anyone within range, basically to move and move quickly. This is the warning sign of the impending tsunami breaking free.

What we see here is very different from the Lovers Tarot image, of a Cupid figure firing his arrow to the 'star-crossed lovers' below. However the symbolism is similar. The shift of the tectonic plates is below rather than above but just as with the unexpected nature of love when it strikes, we do not see it coming and it is still such a shock, like Cupid's arrow. There are two choices open to the Lovers, symbolised by the two directions in which the water flows at the tsunamis 'epicentre' or point of creation point, some towards land, some to the ocean. The image captures an enormous wave just as it builds to its point of release. We can see the light shining through the top of the waves, reminiscent of the 'higher force' of Cupid's arrow in the traditional card. The sense of power is almost palpable as we look at the wave and understand the enormity of its height and width. It is clear this energy is somewhat bigger and stronger than we are and there is something of a feeling of our choices not all being of our own choosing.

The drawback described above is the last chance we have, if we have not heeded the warnings signs of change and the need for choice, which this card is concerned with, to take charge of ourselves and lives and do something. If we don't, we will surely drown. The symbolism here is clear but will be explored further below. However for now we can speak in analogous terms of the depths of the ocean floor being our deepest feelings, needing to emerge from the murky depths to find expression, this being seen in the white water breaking of the waves from the tumult below; the never-ending pounding we receive of the inner tides we feel from the 'wave-train' the tsunami contains; the great heights we can reach if we choose to from the wave height; the far-reach of our stretch and release once done in the coverage of scale of water, the warnings, signs and prompts we can detect if we choose in the 'drawback' the destruction and pollution resulting if we ignore all this and do nothing and so on.

All these have in common the nature of choice and change which are the traditional interpretations of the Lovers card – 'the choice card' as it is often known. As we shall see now, when we explore this at an energetic level it offers us great potential if we can 'embrace and face' it and so avoid the terrible results if we do not. It's up to each of us.

ENERGY

93

At this stage of our souls' development, we come to learn about the power and need for choice. Along with this comes a certain sense of responsibility, since we must account for the results of the choices we make. As mentioned, the Lovers card of traditional Tarot is referred to as the 'choice card'. As such on the outer level, this card is about the choices we make and on the inner level our level of recognition of their need and our willingness to do so, coupled with the ensuing consequences we must accept, learn and grow form, whatever they be. So as we can see from this, there is more to it than just making a choice.

Some Lovers depict choice as the moment at which a son must choose between his Mother and a young lover or wife. This represents for us a choice between the safety of familiarity and the thrill of what may be discovered; between the known and the unknown. We should remind ourselves here that the energy that comes with each and every Major Arcana card and perhaps every Minor Arcana card too, heralds a time of change, at some level. As we know this occurs within and is then reflected out, into our lives, usually in some dramatic, potent or significant form. This card is no exception.

Change, it has been said, is the only evidence of life and so it is the Major Arcana energies do all they can to help us stay alive by being causal to that change. As also previously mentioned, the Major Arcana energies are bigger and more powerful than one individual - the level exceeds that of our individual human will. So if the energy of the Tsunami here is greater than you or I, it makes sense to, quite literally in this case, 'go with the flow' of that inevitable and inexorable change.

At different stages in our lives we can find a niche, whether this be partner, job, house etc. that we feel we would like to 'settle down' with, stick with and that may see us through our days. Like our favourite clothing, it is comfortable, safe and adapted to us. We can relax a little and perhaps not quite put the effort in that we once used to. However that is not what we were built for, not really. For certain we are here to have a good time and find contentment but these are only truly achieved at a spiritual or inner level (which these cards operate at), by making an effort of will and continually reviewing any need for change, avoiding becoming stale and bored, life becoming all too easy and having the bravery to enter into the unknown.

What we must also realise at this stage, is that life, the Universe or in our case here, the energies of the cards, will continue to buffet and cajole us if we do not recognise and respond to their existence. We know that earthquakes will happen but we never know when or where and to what degree they will affect us. The result of an earthquake under the ocean floor may be a tsunami entering our world. If we do not pay attention to and heed those inner tides and energies and learn to recognise the warning signs, we can become submerged and drown in whatever our drug of choice may be – over-familiarity causing boredom, ease of life causing automation and so on. When the Tsunami wells up in your cards, it is time to consider what is happening deep within you, at your own sea bed, the base layer of yourself and life, and consider what may need shaking up; what choices and decisions must be made.

Just as the beginning of the Tsunami springs forth from beneath but can be hard to recognise, so it is we must work hard at delving within to spot the signs of potential flood and ruin. In our quest, we may wish to set everything just as we would wish it, but that is very rarely a possibility. More commonly we find that we can take some steps towards our goal at this stage but must let other things go. In this we remember the way in which some of the tidal flow of the Tsunami flows towards our shore, some flows away.

What is important to recognise here is that once we have opened this particular 'Pandora's Box', it cannot be stopped. As soon as the inner quake has happened the outer shift is inevitable. The warning signs are there in the drawback of the Tsunami. These may present themselves in different ways in our lives, such as hesitancy on our part to do what we know we must in our hearts or instinct. We may feel a certain pull away from particular people, places, and work and so on, as if the Tsunami energy is drawing back out to expose what is no longer right for us. They may be scary and painful to an alarming, even seemingly life-threatening degree, but these energies are ultimately helpful.

Of course we can also see from the after effects of the Tsunami that if we just leave things, hang on for dear life or simply run away and hide and hope for the best, there is a high degree of pollution, contamination and disease. The message again here is that if we do not heed the tides that flow and respond to them, we become stagnant and both ourselves and lives become infected and polluted.

So it is that we return to the need for choice, the necessity of not backing off and allowing ourselves to be drowned. Rather we must embrace that which we do not yet know, learn about it and love it. Keeping ourselves focused on what we love, what we have passion for in life, whether in the form of where and how we live, who with and what we do, and more besides, is perhaps the only way to avoid being submerged beneath the inevitable waves that will surge over us at some stage if we do not.

The energy here simply asks you what you need to do, what and whom do you love and where is the passion in your life.

Are you living or existing and what must you do to rise above the mire and stay there?

7 - AVALANCHE
BACKGROUND

An Avalanche can be triggered by either natural or man-made forces. It is when such a trigger occurs that these twin forces come together to result in the onrushing cavalcade that is the avalanche or snow slide, as they can also be known. This is rather like the two horses we see depicted as pulling the Chariot of the Tarot card on which we are based here. It is when these horses (or other variations) are united in their destination and destiny that the Chariot is pulled.

Once it is set in motion, like the Avalanche, there is no stopping it. The direction, speed, power and the resultant effects of the Avalanche are dependent on several factors, including terrain, slope steepness, temperature, weather conditions and the formation of the snowpack held in 'suspended animation' until it is released. It is often the force of gravity on the accumulated weight of newly fallen, uncompacted snow or older, thawing snow that heralds the beginning of the avalanche.

Though they are most common during the months between December and April, Avalanches have been known to cause fatalities in every calendar month. Along with the conglomeration of influences listed above, an avalanche can mix air, water and earth to produce it's somewhat fiery result, giving us a further link to the Chariot and its pure, elemental 'force of nature'; that terminology applying equally here. Remembering that the human being, the Fool, or for our purposes the Seeker, that is each and every one of us is a combination of these four elemental energies, it would seem we each have the capacity to manifest our own personal Avalanche in our lives.

Avalanches are not random events, requiring that mixture of forces plus a trigger point to manifest. Just like we find with the Chariot card, it is only when we create that focus and concentration of different forces in ourselves and lives that we can expect to experience that onrushing force described here. A further link is given in the sheer amount of snow that is displaced extremely rapidly and over a large distance, by the avalanche. This equates to the force released by the Chariot in our lives, its natural force and power creating the effect rather like we see in cartoons where the snowball gathers speed, pace and size as it careers down the hill, taking everything in its path.

Avalanches are classified by their morphological characteristics – their form and structure. There are five categories of avalanche, classified by mass and destructive potential. Included here are the type of snow involved, the nature of the cause, and the slope of the surface beneath it, its elevation and its trigger. A large avalanche might release 230,000 cubic metres of snow – roughly equivalent to 20 football fields filled three metres deep with snow.

Factors such as a rapid change in temperature, wind speed and direction can all bring about an avalanche. Snowfall of greater than 30 cm is considered extremely hazardous and prone to the formation of an avalanche, with 90% of all of them occurring during snowstorms, the same percentage being those caused by human triggers, highlighting what can happen when we interfere with natural forces. So it is that we can learn one of the messages from the energy of this card, that if we seek to interfere with the natural order of things, that natural tide, ebb and flow in our own lives, we risk creating destruction and chaos, leaving ourselves submerged and choking from our own fury and loss.

DESCRIPTION

Avalanches have three main parts. The starting zone is its most volatile area where the unstable snow can fracture from the surrounding snow cover and start to slide. The avalanche track that results is the path or channel that the snow follows as it descends. These can be indicated by the absence of trees or other objects following a course down a slope. Lastly the run out zone is the area where all finally comes to rest. This is where the snow and resultant debris will pile highest, strewn by the force and magnitude of the snow the avalanche brought with it. Those people unfortunate enough to be caught up in an avalanche will usually end up in the run-out zone, tossed there by the snow like a child's toy.

Our image depicts this in full-flight and we can see for ourselves the very creation of the avalanche track and easily imagine the power and volume of the snow being displaced, along with its effect. The scope and height of the snowfall is instantly awe-inspiring in both these aspects. The most common type of avalanche is known as a Full-Depth Avalanche, which we see here, so-called when the entire snow cover slides across the ground. There is something of a blur in our image, (how long would you wait around to take a picture like this!), showing us the speed of movement and force created by the Avalanche. Similarly, we can see something of the height and the power the snow generates as it cascades downhill.

The different type of snow that can fall also has a high-bearing on the likelihood of an avalanche. Snow known as 'depth hoar' which is rather like dry sand, coarse and grainy, does not bond well with other snow particles or crystals. This snow most commonly occurs in early winter, meaning its weaker form becomes buried beneath heavier snow in later months causing the 'slough' or loose snow slide of the avalanche we see here.

As can be imagined by the image, avalanches can move at speeds of over one hundred miles per hour. A speed of up to eighty miles per hour can be reached within five seconds of the time of fracture that marks the start of the avalanche. In other words we are seeing here a huge release of kinetic energy that is unstoppable and will follow its own path as it wills, sweeping all before it and stopping only when it is spent.

Whilst outlying rock formations and trees can cause a small and temporary break-up of the path and pace the snow takes, it would take a great force to have any perceivable effect upon it. This we can see from our image, as the snow is funnelled in our direction and we realise we are helpless in the face of such might.

ENERGY

When we see the card of The Chariot from the Tarot, we often see our erstwhile reader predicting much good that is to come, of progress and rapid development. We can immediately take this within and see that the energy that underlies this progress is just that: energy. Of itself it does not create that progress and development – it is our response to it that does or does not manifest in this or any other way. Energy simply is and in this respect it is neutral. It is our response that can give it the label of positive or negative.

When we examine what we have seen of the nature of an avalanche there is much we can learn from the energy offered to us when this card appears in our readings. The Chariot or Avalanche heralds the opportunity of galvanising what is within ourselves and without in our lives into one focussed and onrushing force, power or energy, that can propel us forward.

We have seen that it is a combination of natural forces that result in the occurrence of the avalanche. So it is in our lives that we find we need more than one thing to take advantage of this type of natural energy. Perhaps most significantly we have seen that it is what is underneath the surface that creates the potential avalanche. So it is that we need to look within now to our deepest motivations, seeing the result created within us by the decisions and choices we made with the Tsunami before. Where are we in our lives and what comes next?

These things can only come from within and this energy does not give us a time to rest on our laurels. It is a reminder that energy cannot remain static and is bound to move at some point. The energy within us must move outward and onward and the key now is to move with it. By aligning ourselves through effort of will and determination and if necessary pulling ourselves up by our bootstraps, we can make full use of this energy of inevitability and avoid the destruction that we could experience if we allow it to go unheeded.

We should note also that avalanches are not random; they are triggered by this combination of factors and forces, often released by one 'tipping point'. Similarly we now need to get to a point when we cannot resist the urge to move forward in our lives. This energy or card highlights the need we have to avoid the status quo, the settling down and the static viewpoint. This is rather like the sports person who will just not give up the fight, race or match and refuses to keel over, give up or accept defeat. This human spirit, much like Tim Robbins brilliant portrayal of the wrongly-imprisoned character of 'Andy Dufresne' in the film 'The Shaw shank Redemption,' who never loses his spirit and hope, even after

40 years of brutality and abuse, can be threatened but never extinguished completely.

This is rather like energy itself. It cannot be destroyed and what we must realise is that we are this same energy. When we allow ourselves the hope and freedom it brings; to imagine or even just fantasise, pretty much anything is possible and we are capable of great feats. This is a time to ask yourself what you are capable of and whether you can step up to the mark to create it.

We can be aware now of the immense and immediate speed and power within the avalanche. As soon as it is released, the avalanche reaches almost its top speed in five seconds. This shows us that once we have tapped into the unending well of energy we each have within us, acceleration happens in our lives. Have you ever noticed that when you take a step forward with bravery and belief in yourself how you seem to 'get on a roll'? This is the energy the Universe brings to us here.

If we also look at the three zones of the avalanche we can learn from these. We have seen that the most volatile is the first 'starting' zone. Here the point of release summons that speed and power spoken of above. When we look at the nature of our life-events, it is when we allow ourselves to fall into that effortless flow of not struggling but fixed on our desired outcome with a steely determination and knowledge of success, that we can see the greatest effect and these are not limited by time. Life and the Universe are truly gifts waiting for us to unwrap them.

Next is the 'avalanche track', which is the main flow of the snow that we see on the card. This is where we must learn that we cannot force or control by power the direction and outcome of all events in our lives, no matter how clever, perceptive, psychic or strong we think we are. We must adapt to where the natural flow goes, and if need be, get out of the way, lest we get swallowed up and submerged.

Lastly we have the 'run-out' zone. It is the nature of things that there are times of concerted effort which this energy brings us. For a time things are intense and we must maintain what is required to keep up with it. Then we are wise to learn to adapt and go with the flow and then to relax and observe where we have ended up, where this particular phase of our life's path has taken us. At the close of the experience of this energy we can look around us and let the dust, or in this case, snow, settle.

Then we can see a new landscape around and ahead of us and all may seem stable and calm for a while. If we have gathered our forces and maximised on what is on offer here, our life may have taken a dramatic leap forward or equally forced us down a certain track. Either way, we are the architect of our own manifestation, so when this card appears for you, consider what you need to do to move forward in yourself and your life and go for it! If you don't, it will go for you!

8 - EARTHQUAKE

BACKGROUND

Here the traditional image of 'the lady and the lion', her wild beast within, turns into the Earthquake, which as we shall see, is something of a wild beast within the Earth. We should remind ourselves here that part of the premise for this Tarot deck is that we are part of and intrinsically and energetically connected to the planet on which we live and therefore part of what happens in, on and around it.

Earthquakes are recognised as one of the most powerful natural forces on Earth and they can occur at any time and almost anywhere. Their consequences can take effect and be felt far and wide. It is only comparatively recently that we have come to understand what causes them but there is still precious little we can do about them.

The earliest recorded earthquake was as early as 1831 BC in China. Earthquakes have been a part of myth and legend too with the Greek god of the sea Poseidon (or Neptune in Roman myth) being seen as 'earth shaker' and causing earthquakes. This seems to fit since a tsunami can be a result of an earthquake. Aristotle was known to have studied earthquakes, attributing them to heavy winds. After a massive quake hit London in the mid 1700's more comprehensive study began, the field being called seismology, the Chinese being recognised as the pioneers in this field. Work continued and we came to understand what is called plate tectonics and their causal role in Earthquakes.

Earthquakes are defined as a vibration of the earth's surface that occurs after a release of energy in the earth's crust. The Earth's crust consists of numerous segments, or 'plates' that are in constant, though slow, motion. Earthquakes happen when these plates slide past each other or collide, releasing energy in the form of the quake. As they do so fractures in the Earth's crust are created with Earthquakes being more commonly located on these. These are known as faults and are divided into three types.

A 'normal' fault is nearly vertical and occurs where Earth's plates are pulled apart. A 'reverse' fault is created when the Earth's crust is compressed when two plates collide. A 'strike-slip' fault is a horizontal fault where the rock plates slide past one another and it is these with which we are most familiar.

The most powerful, and damaging, earthquakes occur when the rock plates become locked together and continue trying to move until enough pressure or energy is released to enable them to be released, creating the Earthquake. The point of release is called the epicentre, with the focal depth being the depth beneath the Earth surface of the point of energy release. Once released this energy radiates out in rings, like ripples in water.

This rippling effect is known as 'waves', not unnaturally. Body Waves are those that move underground and can then break onto the Earth's surface, where they become known indeed as 'Surface Waves'. Body waves move faster than surface waves and can be felt a second or two before the surface wave. As they continue to move out they become weaker, their effect also being influenced by the rock and soil formation at their location.

The Earthquake itself can be preceded by foreshocks and followed up by aftershocks. These represent a build up to the 'main event' as it and the consequences following the release and shake of energy and as the crust realigns. The effects of an earthquake are felt over a huge area around its epicentre and can create tsunamis, landslides, avalanches, fires and all manner of destruction.

DESCRIPTION

The image we see here is that of arguably the best known fault-line in the world; that of the San Andreas Fault. This rose to prominence, if that is the right term, in 1906 when a massive Earthquake occurred along it causing the death of over 700 people. The San Andreas Fault is at the point where two tectonic plates, the North American and Pacific, touch. There are other fault-lines of course and especially so in California, such as the San Jacinto Fault, which is the most active, plus the Hayward and Calaveras. California is one of the most geologically complex places on Earth.

The San Andreas Fault is approximately 800 miles long and 10 miles deep and has been dated to be about 28 million years old. Its formation was by a process known as subduction. This occurs when one huge earth plate is pushed beneath another, in this case those known as the East Pacific Rise sub ducted under the North American plate near what is now Los Angeles. The San Andreas Fault grew gradually as a result of this Earth movement and it is still growing, at a measured rate of 2.5 inches per year.

The San Andreas Fault is distinctive, apart from its size and proximity to habitation, in that it occurs on land, the majority of fault lines occurring in the ocean. Whilst we can see it as something quite beautiful, with its spine-like curves and vertebrae protruding from its snake-like crawl across the Earth, we should also be continually mindful of its potential, which rather like the lion of the traditional Strength card lies in wait ready to pounce when it is right to do so, to claim its victims. We should be aware as we look at this image of the size of the fault and we can gain something of this perspective when we remember our image is taken from above and we note there is no end to what we can see, the line seeming to become smaller as it stretches off into the distance.

In this distance we see a heat-haze, a reminder of the intensity of the energy we can experience from this card and the equal intensity we must find within ourselves as we absorb it. This heat is further indicated by the deep blue of the cloudless sky we see ahead of us.

It can be easy to imagine a fault line as a big and deep crack in the ground. This however is not usually the case. Time and erosion do their job across a fault-line, along with our own activity. Natural features that can be seen on the San Andreas Fault include stream and water channels flowing from it, grotesquely twisted rock formations, fault gouges in the rock, different rocks either side of the fault itself and sag ponds.

ENERGY

The Strength that of which the traditional card speaks , is widely documented in Tarot books as being an inner one, closely aligned with the virtues of courage and fortitude, as qualities required to summon the aforementioned strength. For our more therapeutic purposes it is again to the inner processes that we turn to utilise the energy given to us when this card appears.

We have seen that the nature of Earthquakes and more specifically their cause, is unpredictable. Just as in our lives we can be meandering along its curves and bends when all of a sudden we encounter something that indeed shakes us to our foundations, just of course, like an Earthquake. We know that the accepted image for this card has the lion as symbolic of our wild, more masculine temperament and shows us our untamed, potentially destructive force, this being tempered by the lady on the card. In our image the potential for a personal Earthquake lies within each of us at any time. We all have our faults, as depicted in our image.

So the energy here encourages us to look within at our own faults and consider where we get things wrong, where we fall prey to letting loose our wild nature to destructive effect. This is not to say that we should forever bury that wild side, but learn to befriend and work with it, so it can be directed and focussed in a positive aggrandisement.

We have seen that it is not the friction between Earth plates that create the Earthquake itself but the release of the pressure and energy they build up by doing so. This tells us here that when we encounter Earthquake in our cards we need to consider where the pressure is in ourselves and lives. This may be caused by events around us, but it is our inner reaction that matters now.

We can expect to be experiencing a build-up of pressure somewhere in ourselves and lives when we experience the energy here, just like the fore-shocks that can pre-determine an imminent Earthquake. We are all intuitive and instinctive beings if we allow ourselves to be, and if we have the courage to be honest with ourselves we can always know the cause of our pressure and what we need to do. Too often we back off and it is then that the Earthquake may strike to detrimental effect within and around us. It is then that we can only admit that we 'saw it coming' and watch as the after-shocks ripple out to do as they will in our lives and those involved in them.

So it is that honesty and bravery are required to accept and admit that we may not be the architects of the pressure we are experiencing but we can make every effort to address the faults that we know exist. It takes those courageous aspects to do so, but here we have the energy provided for the task. We must act according to our truth even though we may be shaking to our very core, just like the Earth does now.

Earthquakes can be triggered by the burial of one plate beneath another. This reminds us that whilst it is perfectly possible to bury our own consequences, feelings, thoughts and motivations (at each of the four levels of our being) the act of doing so only increases the effect and impact when they do, as they inevitably will, rise to the surface.

Once we can turn to our own epicentre and face it, whatever 'it' may be within us, our own failings, faults and potential disaster-areas, we can then allow a controlled and sustained release of pressure as the ripple effect moves in a more measured way through our beings and our lives. We can also be reminded of the inter-locking nature of all life now, since the effects of the Earthquake reach far and wide physically speaking. It may not just be ourselves and our loved ones we can effect positively now, but those in turn attached to them and so on, farther out, spreading the intention and action of the 'right thing'.

What that right thing may be is of course individual and requires all the power we can muster not to be shaken off our true course, which is wholeness and enlightenment; to be the most true and complete being we can, living an exemplary life full of achievement, significance and above all, love. The energy of this card can enable us to move a good and sizeable step closer to these goals, gaining a force or indeed strength from the power of truth and honesty that lets us know we can face anything life may try and shake us up with, to our very core and foundation.

9 - AURORA

BACKGROUND

Here we depict the Hermit from the Tarot as the dazzling Aurora Borealis, his lamp-light subsumed into the stunning display available to us in the heavens around the North Pole. The nature and formation of the 'northern lights' as they are usually known have much in common with the form and function of the Hermit, offering us an energy we can utilise on our Quest to wholeness.

The aurorae (plural) actually occur at both poles, the southern equivalent being called the Aurora Australis. The northern lights were named in 1621 by the French philosopher and astronomer Pierre Gassendi, after Aurora, the Greek goddess of dawn and Boreas being the Greek name for the north wind. The Cree Native American nation, poetically call them the 'Dance of the Spirits' and in the religiously superstitious Middle Ages they were seen as a sign from God. Whatever they may be called people the world over are drawn to them like the proverbial moths to flame, to partake of their beauty.

The lights occur when the highly charged electrons from the solar wind interact with elements in the Earth's atmosphere. These solar winds move at speeds of approximately 1 million miles per hour, which is quite fast. About 40 hours later they reach the Earth and are then travelling at a paltry 250 miles per hour, and follow the lines of magnetic force generated by the Earth's core and flow through the magnetosphere, the oval-shaped area of space around the Earth controlled by those magnetic forces.

As these electrons enter the Earth's upper atmosphere they encounter atoms of oxygen and nitrogen between 20 and 200 miles above the Earth's surface, which produce the fantastic colours we can see in the night sky. These may actually be there all the time, albeit occurring sporadically, but the brightness of the sky in the day renders them invisible to the naked human eye.

The reaction between these magnetic and electrical forces in their continually shifting combinations create the light and colour display of the auroras, with forces that can reach 20,000,000 amps at 50,000 volts, which is quite strong. House circuit breakers cut the flow out if it exceeds 15-30 amps).

As many know, the auroras occur around the magnetic rather than geographical) poles, which of course correspond with the Arctic and Antarctic circles. It is the interaction between the magnetic fields of the solar winds and the Earth that causes the electrons to be trapped and accelerated, which is what we see.

DESCRIPTION

There are generally two aspects to the aurora. A diffuse aurora is a featureless glow in the sky that defines the extent of the auroral zone but may not be visible to the eye. The discrete aurora is sharply defined features within the area of the diffuse aurora which varies in brightness from being just visible to too bright to read by. The colours we see in the aurora depend on which atom is struck and the altitude of this heavenly interaction.

Green is formed from oxygen atoms and electrons up to 150 miles in altitude, with Red being formed also from oxygen but above this altitude. Purple or violet forms from nitrogen atoms and electrons above 60 miles altitude and below this, also from nitrogen, we see Blue. Orange is produced very rarely, from neon. Oxygen can take three-quarters of a second to emit green light but up to two minutes to produce red.

It is worth noting here that it is the Sun that is the ultimate source of our cosmic firework display here, since it is solar winds that bring these atoms our way, themselves generated by the million-degree heat of the Sun, which is quite warm. Also noteworthy, is that the lower in our atmosphere the particles penetrate, the brighter the colour, since they pick up speed. This means that collisions are more frequent and so the brighter colours are produced.

In the image on our card we are lucky enough to be able to see the full colour spectrum. From the silhouetted trees in the foreground with the deep sunset red amongst them to the stars just visible, dotted amongst the inspiring violet and green, it is worth remembering that we are seeing an expanse easily over 150 miles in height. Although sun spots can be predicted which increase aurora activity, we do not know exactly what we will see and when, when it comes to the auroras.

What we do know however is the quite literal magnetic beauty they possess which we can get just a glimpse of here. Shimmering lights, rarely seen but full of awe inspiring beauty remind us of the Hermit's light imparting that which we need to know, at just the right time. Appearing aloft and following its own path, the way upwards and onwards is lit for us.

ENERGY

There are many clues common to both the Hermit and the Aurora that tell us about the energy of this card. Both appear at altitude, and at night, the Hermit being depicted atop a mountain in the dark. In that darkness they both give us light, sometimes referred to as the 'Light of Knowledge'. To see that light we must journey, to a place that few are able and willing to go, but those that do can be pulled by some inner force. Once there we must wait patiently for the light to appear, not knowing when it will do so, but determined to find its source and what it can give us.

The fact of the altitude of the lights of the Aurora is akin to our quest. We must seek, ever onwards and upwards, to find the knowledge that we need. It is only when we can rise above the common goals of most folk; that of material attainment and comfort, that we can see our way clear to what we need. That this appears only in the night is related to a need to turn within, for it is there that we can find the wisdom that we need. Only then can the true beauty be seen and the truth embraced.

These are the lights of the Aurora and the lamp the Hermit holds aloft to guide us forwards. Seen symbolically these lights, historically seen as 'signs of God', can be seen to contain the full spectrum of knowledge and wisdom that is available to us from the spiritual truth of existence. This is often expressed in the maxim 'as above, so below,' meaning that what is real here in our material, everyday world is reflected and true in the 'unseen' world of spirit and vice-versa. This is demonstrated to us in the energy of this card by the Aurora being visible around both poles, north and south.

We know that these poles are magnetic and we have also seen that the display of light and colour is created by a magnetic reaction and response to what is happening. This equates to our sacred quest that is the true purpose of life. For those with the will to do so, when we look within, as this cards appearance beckons us to do, we can sense and feel an equally magnetic pull to learn more, of ourselves and the truth, knowledge and wisdom of our existence. The appearance of Aurora challenges and requests you to discover what you know of yourself, what is your truth and how do you express and live by this wisdom in your life? This can be felt as an irresistible flow of energy to always learn more, not for knowledge's sake itself, but for the pearls of wisdom that can be revealed that act as guide and way-showers both on our own Quest and those of others we may encounter.

The full spectrum of light being potentially visible in the Aurora tells us that all knowledge lies within. Some of this is more easily seen than others, some may be seen more immediately whilst other requires greater patience and may come as fleeting moments, glimpsed in one moment in time and seen only briefly before disappearing once more. However once seen the beauty of that knowledge is never forgotten. It becomes more conscious and is now known to be real and true. We may never be able to explain its revelatory meaning to others, for it is an inner, personal thing, but we can find ourselves, through the experience of the energy of this card, guiding others to find this for themselves.

To find all this we must turn within, we must 'harken to the spirit within', as is demonstrated for us by the appearance of the Aurora at night, to the naked, natural eye. It is always there but the brightness and immediacy of the everyday things of the world obscure inner truth and wisdom until we look to what we know within ourselves. The energy here advises you to do just that, in whatever situation you may find yourself or question you have posed. So often we find in life that if we can just get honest and rise above the failings of our hearts and fears, we know what to do and what is ultimately right for us.

Once we have accepted this wisdom, it is then that we can find its true source and origin, physically here that of the Sun from which the Aurora begins its journey. In traditional Tarot the Sun appears in different guises and symbolises the goal of the Quest, the home to which we are following our journey back, the light of the Spirit, if you will, seen here in a wondrous way. The Solar origins here remind us that we seek

115

the light in the darkness within. It is the only way to true wisdom, self-awareness and self-knowledge. So it is the energy here can reveal pearls of great wonder and wisdom.

We cannot uncover these things by force however and we have mentioned the need for quiet patience and inner contemplation to do so. This is again shown for us in the Aurora, this time in its titles, those of 'diffuse' and 'discrete'. Knowledge, as is often said is power and power, as we know from our history, corrupts. This is also true of spiritual or sacred truth and with their awareness comes a responsibility. This is why we must take this inner quest on a solitary basis and seek out the knowledge ourselves. First we may see the diffuse 'blankets' of light in the aura, but if we remain steadfast to the truth, the full display is revealed, although 'discreetly', in this sense. This energy then, is not for all, not in its truest form, but if you have eyes to see, it is there.

Like the nature of our self-awareness, knowledge and wisdom, it can come to us in glimpses, as a revelation that makes us gape in awe and wonder, just as we observe the Aurora. And so we must ask ourselves, what do you see?

10 - HURRICANE

BACKGROUND

Here we move on to our energetic version of the traditional Wheel of Fortune. This title suggests something of what we need to know in terms of how to respond to the energy this card brings, along with something of what is required to deal with it! The word hurricane itself comes from the West Indian word, meaning appropriately enough 'big wind'. There is also a Native American word 'hurucane' meaning the 'evil spirit of wind'.

Like we have seen with other massive natural phenomena, there is a classification system of the forces that gather to create a hurricane, cyclone or typhoon as they are known in different geographical areas. It is when the wind speed exceeds 74 miles per hour that it becomes an official hurricane and is given a name. The five stages of classification progress according to the maximum wind speed as well as its potential for damage, the highest being winds greater than 155 miles per hour.

A hurricane is a giant, spiralling tropical storm with potential wind speeds in excess of the above figure and able to unleash an incredible 2.4 trillion gallons (or 9 trillion litres) of rain per day. They begin as a disturbance in warm ocean waters with a surface temperature of at least 80 degrees Fahrenheit, such low pressure systems being fed by energy from the warm sea. Once the resulting storm reaches a wind speed of 38 miles it becomes known as a tropical depression. When this increases to 74 miles per hour it gets christened as a hurricane. The naming process begins with the first Hurricane of the year being a name starting with A, the second a B and so on, with gender now alternating.

117

Perhaps most significantly to our purposes, a hurricane is an enormous heat engine that generates energy on a simply staggering scale which is released in its storms. The hurricane spins to generate and propel this energy, in an anti-clockwise direction in the Northern hemisphere and clockwise in the Southern Hemisphere. This effect is caused by what is known as the Coriolis Force, in physics this being the deflection of moving objects.

In the centre of the hurricane there is 'the eye'. This can be a 20 to 30 mile wide area of low-pressure, which is free of cloud, where the sinking air creates a space of calm, the significance of which we shall see for our therapeutic response to this energy. The eye is surrounded by an 'eye-wall' which contains the hurricanes strongest winds and rain. It is generally only when a hurricane reaches land that its destructive power takes effect, producing a storm surge extending up to 100 miles.

DESCRIPTION

In this card we have subverted the accepted image of this card of a spinning wheel with accoutrements to the Hurricane. What we must realise as we observe this image and allow ourselves to respond to it from within, is the enormity of what we are seeing. To put this into context, we can remember that the eye of the hurricane which we can clearly see at the centre of the storm here can be up to 30 miles wide. Given that this appears to be small in relation to the total area and size of the complete hurricane, we must be aware that we are looking at something hundreds of miles in diameter here.

We can then translate that in our minds to realise the sheer power and force of the thing, with which we are concerned in terms of the energy of the card. Whilst our eye (excuse unavoidable pun!) may be inextricably and naturally drawn to the eye of the storm, it is interesting to note the significance of this at the same time – this is the area of calm and peace that we always long for amidst any storm.

Equally we know that the sea around this area can be extremely turbulent and violent, giving us a further message. This area of cloud above it, the eyeball, features and outward curving, seen usually in mature and powerful hurricanes. This is often called the stadium effect since its slope creates the effect of a football or sports stadium. We should also be aware here that the eyeball contains many strong thunderstorms and all that they bring and it is these, with their combination of potential floods from their rain and destruction from winds that cause the most destruction, this being a further note for us to take.

Beneath the expanse of the hurricane itself in the dramatic and strangely beautiful cloud-scape that is depicted, we are able to see that this scene occurs just at the point of landfall. The blue expanse at the bottom half of the image is sea and the green at the top half is land. As we have seen above it is at this point of landfall that the power and full force of the hurricane is able to be released; all that it has gathered and held on to explodes in a cataclysmic display of nature's power.

This moment of landfall, dividing the card as it does in halves of blue and green, reminds us of the spiritual or esoteric maxim 'as above, so below'. This tells us that our human lives are a reflection of the spiritual, the energetic realm mirrored in the physical and that what we experience on the inner is manifest on the outer. This being the case here, we need to reflect on how to weather this particular storm and find that peace and calm at the centre, that place in us that always exists within, and so can also be found in our physical lives.

We can also observe from the spiralling motion of the hurricane how it appears to gather in its full force, as if the spiral motion allows it to inhale, holding its enormous breath until it is jolted out when it hits land and a massive exhalation happens. If our amazing planet has lungs, this is it taking one hell of a deep breath.

ENERGY

Something I have often mentioned to students on my Tarot Therapy courses is that 'life teaches you about the Tarot and the Tarot teaches you about life'. The one is a reflection of the other and we are reminded of this maxim too, in the energy of this card.

Most of us know that we seem to experience life in stages, just like the stages of the hurricane and other natural phenomena we see in our Major Arcana. With a sometimes supernal effort we can create something of a level playing field for ourselves and then rest on our laurels a while. However the Universe and the forces active within it, do not allow such latitude for long. As we know, the nature of energy is to move and flow and the result of this is change. If we resist that change all that happens is that the pressure builds up and continues to do so until it must inevitably explode.

That intensity is akin to the energy we are offered with this card. In order to stay ahead of the game and above the bullshit of mundane, everyday existence, we require all our guile, pluckiness and perhaps a little luck as we go. If we can respond in a welcoming way rather than resistance we can utilise what is on offer here. Though it may be uncomfortable, one truth we know, as is pointed out directly with this energy, is that nothing lasts forever and all things will change.

Any wheel, in this case that of fortune's whim, spins more on the outer rim, that is in its centre, and this is demonstrated all too ably by the eye of the storm where we have that blessed calmness. This tells us that in order to embrace and progress from the inevitability of certain change and yet still find a security, we must look within to our own centre. Here there is always a place of balance, peace and rest if we but look, breathe and are still.

From this stillness we can become more self-aware and objective and we can learn to see the spiral of the storm forming in ourselves and lives and adapt accordingly. Of course just as the temperature rises to create the storm, so the heat is turned up in us as the going gets tough. If we back off we place ourselves in danger of being swept along by the winds that gather force as we go. If however we can face what we are scared of and frightens us, whatever this may be, and push on through, we can find that sweet place of peace. Following the analogy if we can look fear in the eye we can find the truth that 'you are like a hurricane, there's calm in your eye', from the exhilarating song of Neil Young's.

Once we have begun this journey into the storm, there is no going back. If we do, we find ourselves in the eye-wall, buffeted mercilessly this way and that as we flail about, the plaything of fate. Soon we hit landfall and chaos ensues. This is where the storm releases itself, to powerful destructive effect as can be the case in our lives. If we try and head away from the chaos, by whatever means, we only make things worse.

It is notable here that hurricanes produce both incredibly strong winds and huge volumes of water. As we know, the four elements of Earth, Water, Air and Fire relate to the four levels of the human being, the physical, emotional, mental and spiritual respectively. Our emotions are symbolised by water and our thoughts by air. In terms of dealing with the times of intensity, the storms that gather in our lives, it is

121

either in our minds where we struggle to understand what is going on or in our hearts where we cannot accept what happens, that blockages occur. These are shown for us in the huge winds and massive rainfall the hurricane brings.

The energy of this card then manifests in order to sweep away those blockages. If we 'break on through to the other side' (the doors this time), we can reach the calm at its centre. There is always that place of balance, rest and peace at the centre of our beings that truly passes all understanding. With this card we are challenged and requested to place ourselves there, no matter what. If we do this we can observe the chaos that may be erupting around us, largely untroubled by the questions in our minds and fear in our hearts.

Once we have weathered the storms of change, the ups and downs, and ebb and flow that life will bring us, we know then that we can face anything that life and the Universe may throw at us. We have the inner knowledge that we contain, at all times, and an unassailable peace that cannot be destroyed, no matter what we may encounter or experience.

11 - MOUNTAIN

BACKGROUND

Many of us are familiar with Mountains in a way we are perhaps not with many of the other natural phenomena featured in our Major Arcana. This may be by direct experience or from films, TV and other images. However when we look at them more closely we can see how they fit neatly amongst our other energies.

Here the Mountain serves as the centre-point of our Quest, replacing the Justice card and sitting as it does at the central point of the Major Arcana. From its vantage point, towering above all it has encountered and has yet to deal with, we are granted an overview, a meeting point where at the centre of our Quest we meet ourselves.

Mountains make up one-fifth of the Earth's landscape as well as providing homes to 12 per cent of our population. Approximately 2 billion people depend on their ecosystems for food, hydroelectricity, timber and minerals. Further than this, about 80 per cent of the planet's fresh water originates in the mountains of the world with all the major rivers starting on a mountain. There are mountains on every continent of the world and in 75 per cent of countries.

The fresh water we get via our Mountains is received as rainfall and the mountain ranges of the world vary from very-wet to very dry. In the space of a few minutes a severe thunderstorm can roll in to what was a perfectly clear and sunny day. Temperatures can drop from high to below freezing in just a few hours.

A particular feature of the mountain environment is that they are all subject to rapid changes in altitude, climate, soil, vegetation and weather conditions. The higher the elevation, the colder the climate and the less oxygen and carbon dioxide there is. In one mountain range alone, California's Sierra Nevada, there are between 10 and 15 thousand different animal and plant species living, due in the main to elevation changes. At the highest altitudes the tallest mountains can be completely devoid of plant and animal life, above what is known as the 'timber-line' – the point at which there are no more trees or notable vegetation.

Mountains are formed as the Earth's crust collides, cracks, crumbles and folds, spewing out these dramatic and inspiring formations, dominating the surroundings with their height and presence. They normally feature steep slopes and either shard or rounded edges. A mountain is usually classified by rising at least one thousand feet above its surrounding area. Mountains then erode slowly through the actions of rivers, weather conditions and glaciers.

There are different types of mountain, classified by their formation. Volcanic mountains form when molten rock from deep within the Earth erupts through the crust and piles up on itself. When this magma pushes the crust up but hardens before it reaches the surface, Dome Mountains, such as the Black Hills of South Dakota are formed with their sculpted peaks and valleys. When colliding tectonic plates push the land up without folding or faulting then Plateau Mountains are formed, which are then shaped by weathering and erosion. Stresses within and between the tectonic plates lead to cracking and faulting of the Earth's surface, forcing blocks of Earth up and down, to form fault-block mountains' such as the Harz Mountains in Germany.

DESCRIPTION

The Himalayas in Asia, which contains 90 of the world's tallest 109 peaks, were formed about 55 million years ago by the plate tectonic process causing a massive collision resulting in the tallest range in the world. The highest peak above sea-level is Everest at just over 29 thousand feet. We should however be aware that mountains can begin in the seas and oceans too and if we take this into account then the tallest on Earth is Mount Kea in the Pacific Ocean in Hawaii. Measured from its watery base this stands at a total of 33,474 feet. If we were to measure from the centre of the Earth however, then the tallest mountain is known as Chimborazo in Ecuador and stand at over 3,900 miles. The longest mountain range on the planet is actually under the Atlantic Ocean, called the Mid-Atlantic Ocean Ridge and stretches over 40 thousand miles.

Mountains usually occur in ranges and the words longest range on land is the Andes, at over 4,900 miles. However, for reasons that we shall see below, we are focussing here on the peaks and so what we see are the stunning Himalayan peaks, the 'roof of the world' so to speak. We can also bear in mind that its famous tallest peak grows by about 4 mm per year, due to the movement of the tectonic plates, way beneath.

Our image here is appropriately that of Everest. This is chosen since, as we shall see below, at this stage on the Quest we find ourselves at the very centre of ourselves and everything. This is rather like climbing to the highest point we can and above the Earth there is nowhere higher - we can go no further.

In the foreground we can gain a sense of the remoteness and inaccessibility of the place (although this is perhaps sadly becoming less so now with advancement in climbing techniques and technology). Further on the climb we can see it is steep and fraught with danger and trepidation. The Quest of life is just like that however, the closer we get to things, the harder they can seem to stomach and accept.

The Sun reaches out to us from behind the peak of Everest, reminding us that we have to be the best we can be, be true to who we are and live a life that is marked by 'doing the right thing; by being honourable and upholding all that we hold sacred in each and every moment. The Sun is ever the symbol for that wholeness and the goal of our Quest. Here it may seem unreachable but we must strive forever onwards and upwards.

Far above us the goal of our Quest remains, shining its light even amongst or above the clouds. Sometimes it may be obscured by those clouds, lost in the mists of confusion and storms that come our way as we seek to progress on our Quest and climb. At the peak however, all is clear and calm and from here we can quite literally see everything. Nothing is higher than we are and there is nothing to distort the view. From here we can see things like never before, whether we look outward or inward. The question is more whether we like what we see.

ENERGY

The Tarot card Justice, which we are dealing with here, lies at the midway point of the Major Arcana. As such it is the point on our Quest where we are at the very heart of all things and from where we can see things exactly as they are, in total clarity and truth – just as if we are standing atop a Mountain viewing everything clearly from above for the first time.

Justice acts by reflecting us back to ourselves. In the Tarot she is a mirror image of who we really are, at a soul level. The key to working with the energy of this card lies in the acceptance of this view of self – raw, naked, vulnerable and powerful, all at once.

Here we make the analogy of climbing a mountain to afford ourselves the best view of life - from above. We have a need to detach ourselves from the manic meanderings of our head and more specifically the workings of the left hemisphere of our brain. This governs the logical and commonly negative programming we seem to inherit – traditional thinking such as 'I'm not good enough', 'Nobody loves me', 'I must do more', 'I must get this, that and the other done' and finally 'I'll be happy if . . . ' (you can fill in the blanks here).

If we can learn to extract ourselves from this inner and quite compulsive mode of thought, by climbing our analogous Mountain, we can find that we can see things much more clearly. By using any one of a variety of techniques, such as simple relaxation, breathing, meditation, Chi Kung and such like, we can find that we can switch from where we operate in our heads to the right brain. This governs our more intuitive and instinctive functioning and here, once you get used to it, you can find a sense that all is well; that feeling of calm, peace and stillness. This is a part of our being that is actually always there, despite whatever traumas, dilemmas, pain and betrayal we might be encountering and which we have been guided to find and establish by our encounter with the Hurricane.

This is what lies at our very hearts or more accurately, our centres. If we can do this on an energetic level, which this card offers us – a way to our true selves – we can access this lovely awareness and feeling easily. By grounding our energy, then becoming aware of our connection above to the Universe (or whatever you wish to call it/him/her), those twin energies naturally blend and balance at your centre and so you come to stillness. To begin with this may take a little time but can soon be easily developed so as to be done with a few breaths and an attitude of 'letting go'. I have described the full, detailed process in my previous book 'Practical Meditation' and it is excellently summarised in a different way by John Parkin in his seminal book 'Fuck It'. This is the energy that Mountain can bring into ourselves and lives, if we let it.

The key then is how we respond to what we find at this very centre and whether we love it or not. You can assess this yourself by standing naked in front of a mirror and seeing how you feel – do you love what you see – not just physically, but look deeper and see the person you truly are. We can remind ourselves here of the apparent stillness and solidity of the Mountain. However most of our planets' water – akin to our emotions – begins here, so beyond the tumult, twist and turns of the raging rivers of our feelings, there is stillness and peace at the source, and at the centre of ourselves.

We know that climates can change all too rapidly on the Mountain, temperatures drop and storms come swiftly in. However if we can find a place to shelter and wait out the storm we can find that 'this too shall pass' and that stillness and calm remains, like the Mountains. We may be threatened and buffeted by the emotional and mental storms of life, but like the Mountain, we endure and remain at peace.

This is not to say that we resist change, for as we have already seen, this is necessary on the Quest that is our life. However at our core, as we are here, change is slow and gradual, like the Mountain allows itself the process of erosion. Even Everest is subject to this and grows just a little each year.

The Mountain is home to so many kinds of life and so it is we need to allow those in our lives in to our hearts and minds - we are not by nature creatures of isolation. However we can be reminded that above a certain level the Mountain does not sustain life, it just is. So we can retain a little part of ourselves, our core being, as a place of peace, strength, repose and power to which we can turn whenever we need. This is not to say that it is unreachable by anyone, simply that we know this part of us is there, always has been and always will be and we can rely upon it. This is the gift given to us by this energy.

We also know that the air is thinner the higher we climb the Mountain. The closer we get to our core, the harder we have to work to breathe. So the need is to relax, breathe easily and freely and just accept that peace and stillness is what is required and we will be just fine. In fact, no matter what we are confronted by, however dreadful, this energy tells us it is all just as it should be.

So we climb our metaphorical Mountain to meet ourselves. Any good mountaineer will tell you that the reason to climb a mountain is because it is there. This is much like the Quest we are on by being alive – we do so because we are. It is perhaps fitting here to remind ourselves of the maxim of being good to those we meet on the way up as we may meet them again on the way down. We should include ourselves in this as well.

12 - GLACIER
BACKGROUND

Here the Hanged Man of the Tarot, swinging haplessly and statically from his tree, is transformed into a glacier, equally frozen. A glacier is formed over many years where the accumulation of snow exceeds its melting. It is the weight of this ongoing snowfall that crushes the ice beneath and, slowly and gradually, deforms and flows, to produce the surface features of the glacier.

Glaciers can be found on every continent of the Earth, mostly in mountain ranges but also some oceanic islands of high altitude. Glacier ice represents the largest reservoir of fresh water on Earth, storing about 75% of our supply and supporting one third of the population. Approximately 10% of the land area of Earth is covered with glacial ice, being about 5.8 million square miles in total.

Glaciers can often appear blue in colour, when the ice has become very dense. Years of compression from above force out tiny air pockets between the crystals and the ice then absorbs all other colour in the spectrum, reflecting blue. When a glacier appears only white it is an indication that many air pockets remain in the ice.

Unlike features such as Avalanches, Tornados and Hurricane's, glaciers move slowly. The fastest known glacial surge was the Kutiah Glacier in Pakistan which moved 7.5 miles in 3 months. The Antarctic continent is known to have been at least partially covered by an ice sheet for the past 40 million years.

In the last Ice Age, glaciers covered up to 32% of the land, when cool temperatures enabled advances in the ice flow. Glaciers retreat or advance periodically, depending on the amount of snow that falls. This movement in visible only at the terminus or snout of the glacier and they move in the manner of a conveyor belt. Glaciers are most commonly found above the snow line in mountainous areas. As the temperatures drops with descent, so more snow melts and the glacier releases its store of water.

There are many different features of a glacier, relative to our study here. Ice sheets are enormous continental masses of ice that can expand over 50,000 square kilometres, such as Antarctica and Greenland. Ice caps are defined by being less than the above measurement, such as Iceland in comparison to Greenland. Ice shelves occur when these ice sheets extend over the sea and float on the water, ranging in thickness from a few hundred to over 1000 metres. Smaller than these in turn are ice fields. From these flow ice streams, which move more rapidly than the surrounding ice.

Glaciers themselves can be called by different classifications. Mountain's glaciers develop as their name suggest in these areas, often flowing out of ice fields that span several peaks in a range. Valley Glaciers spill down from these like giant tongues and can flow down beyond the snow line and even reach the sea. Those that flow out from here are hence known as Tidewater Glaciers. When they flow into relatively flat plains, Piedmont Glaciers are formed, which spread out into bulb-like lobes. Hanging Glaciers, also known as ice aprons, cling to steep mountainsides and are wider than they are long. This means their surface can be heavily crevassed and jagged, like teeth.

DESCRIPTION

just as we have seen that the movement of a glacier is slow and at times imperceptible, so their formation is a gradual process. When snow remains in the same area all year round it is transformed into ice. As new layers of snow fall each successive year they bury previous layers, compressing those beneath. This forces the snow to re-crystallise, forming grains that are like those in sugar. Over time these grow larger and the air pockets between them smaller, causing the snow to slowly compact and become denser. After two winters it forms what is called firn, a state between snow and ice, about as half dense as water – it is neither one or the other.

After what can be a hundred years or so, crystals can reach several inches in length. It is the sheer weight of a glacier that enables it to move only very slowly. Glacial ice moves more slowly on its underside than at the top due to the friction created as it slides along the earth's surface.

This is shown to us in the water we see in the foreground, this also appearing completely still, reflecting both another aspect of this card's energy and the glacier above its surface. All part of the energy (and nature of the traditional Hanged Man), the mirror image tells us of the stillness within and how all that we are and encounter in our lives reaches to the very depths and core of our beings and here must be absorbed, responded to appropriately and released, so that we can remain vital and alive, avoiding the potentially poisonous inertia that will surely occur if we freeze in our fear and trepidation.

The largest glacier in the world is acknowledged as the Lambert Glacier in East Antarctica, being approximately 60 miles wide, over 250 miles long and 1.5 miles deep. What we see here is actually only a part of the whole glacier. To view this we lose something of the impact of its size and more importantly sense of impact on its environment. What we can derive from our image here is a sense of slow, deliberate and pains-taking, relentless movement that takes its effect and literally re-shapes all it comes into contact with. Indeed such is the impact of this particular glacier that it is closely monitored for signs of climate change affecting the globe and every one of us.

The ice that feeds this glacier originates in the Antarctic Plateau ice sheet and flows northwards towards the Amery ice Shelf on the north-eastern side of the continent. The Amery ice shelf hangs over Prydz Bay, depositing icebergs and sea ice from chunks that fracture from the glacier. The ice here has three layers, the top being the accumulation of snow in this area, the middle from the Lambert Glacier and the bottom from the freezing sea water beneath.

ENERGY

The Hanged Man of the Tarot, inverted as he is, traditionally represents the state of stillness and even bliss that we can achieve by raising our consciousness. Any good yogi worth their asana will attest to the enlightening aspects of the head-stand posture. This reversal of the mountain pose enables the life-force energy to flow to the head, thereby assisting the enlightenment process.

This process is of course not an instant one, but something that can take a great many years, often a lifetime, just like the formation of a glacier. Indeed we should note here that we can easily define the process and purpose of life as the quest for enlightenment. Here we need to focus on what is above, rather than what is below. Like the glacier that forms from the new snowfall freezing and compressing what lies beneath and already exists, the energy here teaches us that we must always be open to what is new and currently forming in ourselves and lives, rather than clinging to old and out-worn, past experiences, memories, feelings and thoughts.

One of the messages of the Glacier energy is that we must evolve. We have an instinctive need for security, to stay in one place and add layer upon layer to whom and what we

133

are, just as a glacier does. However, as we have seen the glacier squeezes all the air out of itself by piling layer upon layer until it goes blue and crystallises. We cannot live like this; if we cannot breathe we in turn would also go blue! Rather we must continually adapt to the new, the process of ongoing and evolving life.

The Glacier moves, gradually and slowly, and in so doing impacts on all it encounters. It can create features of great beauty such as fjords and whole mountain ranges with dramatic slopes and peaks. So it is that we need to tap into the Glacier energy when this card appears for us and from our awareness of who and what we are and the still acceptance of this, learn to become more aware and observant of the impact of ourselves and our lives on all those we encounter by doing so.

So it is this energy that teaches us to receive what comes from on high, like the new snow on the Glacier each year, whether this be in the form of inspiration, ideas, pure energy or development of awareness. As this is absorbed so it becomes part of our physical reality, like the glacial ice. What is required then is to continue to evolve, by releasing what is no longer needed, just as the glacier melts and releases its vital pure water supply. Then we can be refreshed and drink deeply of what is on offer.

We can also learn from this energy that everything and everyone we touch in our lives is impacted upon in some way, just as the glacier erodes and affects its surrounding landscape. Some features, both of the landscape and us – the one being a reflection of the other – are only touched on a little and perhaps only a small but significant change may be visible. Other aspects of our being and so our actions have much greater, far-reaching impact that can last many years, just as the glacier can carry huge rocks great distances, placing them where they may appear totally out of place.

So the movement of the glacier tells us how we need to be, and how to absorb this energy to greatest effect. The swifter movement (in glacier terms) occurs on the surface whilst our deepest layers do the hard grind of carving out what we resist to create our own peaks and troughs of experience, feeling, thought and awareness. At the centre though, as the glacier is just ice, so we can be still and know that all is as it should be, that we are connected to and part of not only this wondrous and ever-changing landscape around us, but also a greater Universe that we are perhaps now, only just beginning to realise truly exists and lives. Our question now is what we will do with that new consciousness?

13 - DROUGHT

BACKGROUND

The Death card of traditional Tarot is related here to Drought. It is well known that we can survive for approximately three weeks without food but just three days without water, such is our dependency on liquid, our bodies being approximately two-thirds water. A Drought then precedes Death by only a small margin.

The definition of a drought is 'a period of abnormally dry weather sufficiently prolonged for the lack of water to cause serious hydrologic imbalance in the affected area'. This lack of moisture has immediate and profound impact, not only on the Earth and its surrounding area but on the ecosystem and agriculture, preventing any growth but also on any population affected, causing mass migration in an attempt to escape certain death.

There are four different ways that drought can be defined. A meteorological drought is a measure of difference from the normal rainfall in an area, which creates a natural shortage of available water. An Agricultural drought refers to a situation where the amount of moisture in the soil cannot sustain a crop. This normally occurs during hot, dry periods of low rainfall. A Hydrological drought occurs when surface and subsurface water supplies are below normal. This occurs when a deficiency builds up over a period of time, depleting reserves. Lastly Socio-economic drought occurs when demand outstrips supply of available water by the population, rather than any natural phenomena.

Droughts can occur over a prolonged period of time, when weeks without rainfall can turn to months and eventually a drought occurs. However they can also occur swiftly in areas that are traditionally hot and dry, surviving on just a small supply of precipitation. When this is interrupted for any reason, the effects are swift and devastating. It is really the delicate balance between supply and demand that must be maintained for life, of any kind, to survive and flourish.

In what is known as the 'Dust Bowl Days' of the 1930's a drought in the USA affected an area of 50,000,000 acres of land. In 1988 another drought affected at least 35 States of the US when rainfall was up to 85% below normal. This precipitated outbreaks of forest fires with over 4 million acres burnt and half of the Yellowstone National Park charred. The effects of water shortage in Africa are equally well documented resulting in the 'global party' that was Live Aid in attempt to help the millions affected. In the Horn of Africa the drought of 1984 led to famine that killed 750,000 people. Nearly every nation and certainly every continent has endured a major drought, with some, such as India, in constant danger. Since the 1970's the percentage of Earth's surface affected by drought has doubled. Interestingly, given the number of Major Arcana cards in the Tarot, statistics show that a drought occurs in the United States every 22 years.

DESCRIPTION

Most precipitation depends on water vapour carried by winds from an ocean or other water source. If these winds are replaced by winds from a dry region or they are modified by and takes full effect on the ground and growth beneath.

The excessive heat from an abnormally long dry period of time means the unrelenting sunshine causes the Earth's crust to dry out until large cracks appear in this mosaic like pattern. This is further exacerbated since plants cannot live without moisture and their roots cannot play their role on holding the soil together. The soil, like the Bible tells us, our bodies are destined to do, becomes ashes and dust; the embodiment of lifelessness.

First the soil depletes its store of moisture which causes any vegetation it supports to become stressed and then die. The land cannot then support any wildlife resident in the area and these too, must either migrate or more commonly, die. Naturally occurring wildfires are then extremely likely, causing further loss of natural, animal and human life.

During a drought the combined effects of reduced rainfall and increased heat from sunlight create a number of effects on the land, which we can see the end results of here. Decreased levels of rainfall, a reduction in cloud cover, an increase in sunlight and warmer temperatures cause the moisture on the soil to evaporate. The combination of soil aridity and the resultant plant death makes the soil more prone to soil erosion. This causes dust storms and increased sand deposits, which kills further vegetation.

As the soil becomes dry, so do any trees in the area. More intense heat and direct sunlight increase evaporation rates further and without water the trees cannot survive either and die. This creates ideal wildfire conditions. Without tree cover, any shorter shrubs and grasses are exposed and these too dry out and die. This creates the fuels needed for wildfires to spark. The lack of available water swiftly causes death in the animal (and human) population along with a scarcity of food from the death of crops and vegetation.

We need only look at a list of typical effects of drought to see clearly why this card links with the traditional Death card of the Tarot: famine, dehydration, malnutrition, disease, mass migration, wildfires and war. These of course are just the human consequences but here we see the effect on the land itself. We can do well to remind ourselves here that we are part of the land and the living being that is our planet. In short, as bits of the Earth die, so do we.

So it is that in our image here we stare directly at the sun and symbolically stare not only at the source of life but also the architect of death, in drought. This reminds us of our own mortality of course and the almost humorous juxtaposition that 'in the midst of life we are in death'. As we remind ourselves that the Sun represents that goal of our Quest so we can see that we must do what we need to in ourselves and lives to remain alive, not in the physical sense, but living a life of 'deliberate intent', full and conscious so we do not become dry and life or passionless.

ENERGY

Firstly here we can remind ourselves of the likelihood of a drought in the US every 22 years, in keeping with the numerology of the Major Arcana. Added to this, we have seen the four types of drought, which further complements the numerological energy of this card, it being numbered 13 (1+3=4). So it is that we see the inevitability of Death for every human on earth and all that this implies.

However we should also remind ourselves that this is card number 13, not the last one, telling us that this is not the end and indeed, far from it. It is the human body, like the Earth in a drought that dies, but this is not the end. With the return of water to the land life springs forth again, just as the soul outlasts the body and continues to give and support life.

The energy of this card is then telling us that nothing is permanent, or put another way, everything is temporary. The structures and securities that we may have worked hard to achieve and acquire are bound and destined to go. The only true security can then come from within, in our spirit and our acceptance of the inevitability of change and the ending of all physical things. Our work, our home, even our partners and loved ones cannot be a security for us. This energy calls us then to turn within and find what it is within us that can give us a sense of safety and peace inside.

Almost perversely then it is really by letting go of all outer security that we can find what we seek in this sense. It is as if 'to conquer death you only have to die' to quote Jesus in the musical 'Jesus Christ Superstar'. It is as if we need to stare Death in the face, accept and make a friend of it, rather like staring at the sun in our card here.

Death takes away the physical and leaves only the soul, which tells us that when we experience the energy of this card we are reduced to the bare bones and nucleus of what we are experiencing and we are being shown the very core of ourselves. To this we must be true and, as we have said above, learn to accept the inevitability of losing what we perhaps hold most dear and submit to the change that will surely come.

We must realise here too that once we enter the energy of the Death or Drought experience there is no going back. We cannot recreate life as it was. Rather we must embrace the new and seek to create something afresh, newly washed and grown. It is true that there is a place for grief and it is indeed vital to allow the requisite time and space for this so it can truly be released and given to the Earth. Only then can we look ahead fully and completely to what is to come, which is what we choose to create.

I often remind clients in consultations that the Major Arcana card energies are bigger and stronger than we are and that by resisting them we only create pain for ourselves in our struggle. This applies perhaps nowhere more than with this card's energy and so as we can release what we may perhaps hold most dear or fear losing the most, so it is the positive aspects of this energy can begin their work.

It is worth noting too that although we are reduced to our bare bones and even beyond this, that it is these roots in the plants and trees of the Earth that sustain and support life and so it is with us, or needs to be, and this is something else the energy here can illustrate for us.

This comes when we look to what it is that sustains us. When the Earth is dry in a drought it requires water of course to reignite life and return it to health. When we have been through what we can call a Death experience, or a drought in ourselves and lives, in whatever form it may take for us, we need then to look to what it is that gives us life, what sustains our spirit and replenishes the soul, ready for the next phase in the adventure and quest that is our life. What will you give yours?

14 - RAINBOW

BACKGROUND

Following our brush with Death we emerge afresh and renewed and traditionally greeted by the Angel of Temperance. Here, our brave Seeker is granted a vision, that of a rainbow above him and no less than a double rainbow.

This wondrous image has captured the imagination of humanity for thousands of years and always seems to bring a smile in both young and old alike when it appears. It is no surprise then that this traditional card of peace, plenty and balance is brought to us with a multitude of beneficent beliefs and beatitudes.

The Buddhist belief regarding rainbows, that they represent the highest state achievable prior to the attainment of Nirvana or enlightenment, tells us much about the energy of this card. In Buddhism, a rainbow represents the point or place where individual desire and consciousness is extinguished. This card heralds a time of reaching to a higher level of awareness with all that this results in.

As is apparent, a rainbow contains seven colours, akin to the seven levels or degrees of human consciousness that trace our path from ignorance to bliss, or again, enlightenment. This alchemical process is rewarded with the symbolic pot of gold we find at the end of the rainbow, the base self transmuted and raised to purity and finding the Divine, whatever you perceive this to be.

The light spectrum shows how a single ray of white light can be broken into seven colours or rays. This is because the white light contains all the frequencies of each of the colours within it. So it is we see these colours, which are energy, just as our consciousness is. As our consciousness manifests in the physical or material world so it is also split into seven parts, each with its own frequency, colour and characteristics. So our 'Seekers Quest' is here shown to us in the one image of the rainbow, each colour being a different level of our awareness reflecting the Divine.

This is further borne out from the initially Eastern teaching regarding the seven chakras; energy centres that link the physical and energy bodies that the human being consists of. As we learn to develop ourselves at the different levels of consciousness so it is each chakra is 'activated' or opened to a greater degree, allowing more light (and energy) in until we are fully 'en-light-ened'. It is in this way we are a mirror of the Universe and illustrate the principle we see here of 'as above, so below'.

Perhaps this is why the earliest Christians saw the appearance of a rainbow as God's covenant that he would not destroy the world by flooding it. For the Norse peoples the rainbow was Bifrost, a bridge to Asgard, their Otherworld and realm of the gods. They furthered this knowledge that the bridge could only be crossed by those virtuous or good enough, such as warriors or royalty, a theme central to our path to enlightenment.

To the Greeks, the rainbow is Iris, the messenger of the gods dressed in rainbow colours, flying on golden wings on the winds. To the Aborigine's the rainbow is a snake or serpent, the Creator of the 'Dreaming' or the world of energy which has no end. In this way the Rainbow Serpent is the giver of life when it heralds rain.

There is a dual nature of myths concerning the rainbow however, as with all things having an 'equal and opposite' action and reaction. To Hindus the rainbow is Indra, the god of thunder and war who uses the rainbow to shoot arrows of lightning. In many African tribes children are prevented from looking at the rainbow since to do so could risk blindness or oblivion, such is its power. In ancient Japan rainbows were seen as bad omens since they were seen as a serpent and in parts of Amazonian belief rainbows have been seen as malign spirits causing miscarriage and disease.

The rainbow then is part of the wonder of creation, elusive and unpredictable and able to bestow nothing less than immortality and enlightenment but we require great courage and belief to cross the bridge that it is, to that fabled Otherworld.

DESCRIPTION

A rainbow is an optical phenomenon that causes a spectrum of light to appear in the sky when the Sun shines on to droplets of moisture (i.e. rain) in the Earth's atmosphere. In this way, Rainbows always appear in the sky opposite the sun, or put another way, when you look at a rainbow the Sun will be behind you. Light is reflected when it enters a droplet of water giving us the visible colour spectrum in the sky.

The rainbows we are used to seeing are known as 'primary' rainbows, but in our image here we have the additional secondary rainbow, creating the 'double arc' that is more suited to our purposes. It should be noted that in the secondary rainbow, the order of the colours are reversed, confirming visually the principle we saw above that as humans we reflect the Universe in miniature, or 'as above, so below', again. The second rainbow is caused by light reflecting twice inside the water droplet.

A rainbow is sunlight spread out to its colour spectrum. The centre of the 'bow' or arc of the rainbow will always be directly opposite the Sun. The rain will fall in the direction of the rainbow itself. We cannot see a full circle of rainbow

144

colours because the Earth gets in the way! The lower the Sun is to the horizon, the more of the rainbow we see. It is only at sunset that we can see its full half-circle. The higher the Sun is in the sky, the smaller the arc.

As we know a rainbow is displayed in seven colours: red, orange, yellow, green, indigo and violet - the colours linked to the seven main chakras of the human being. There are colours beyond this spectrum that are not visible to our eyes, just as there are said to be further chakras in and beyond our own system. We should also note that sunlight contains all these colours, (as first demonstrated by the great Sir Isaac Newton in 1666) which is why they can appear in the rainbow – in essence a 'lesser' or lower reflection of the Sun, as the symbol of the Divine. The colours themselves are formed by the degree of refraction, between 40 and 42 degrees. In the secondary, double-rainbow the angle is extended to about 50 degrees.

We can see clearly that the sky inside the rainbow is brighter than outside. Basically this is because there is more light inside the arc than outside it, hence it appearing brighter to our eye. This brighter light is a mix of the seven rainbow colours, so it appears white. Following this process logically, this naturally creates a darker region between the rainbows, called Alexander's Dark Band, in honour of the Greek philosopher Alexander Aphrodisias who observed this some 1800 years ago.

The brightness or clarity of the rainbow depends on the size of the rain drops at the time: therefore the larger the droplets, the brighter the colours. With small droplets the colours overlap and appear closer to white. Of course rain when it falls, comes always in a mixture of sizes and shapes. We can also take notice here that because the appearance of a rainbow is dependent on the point of the observer, no rainbow can ever appear the same to anyone else. Beauty is literally, in the eye of the beholder.

We should take note here of the landscape over which our wondrous rainbow appears. This seems to draw us into the image and under the rainbow itself. On the spiritual quest we are often told that whilst we need to have our head in the clouds, we also need to keep our feet on the ground. The land here represents the importance of that grounding and reminds us that it is on this fair Earth that we live, move and have our being. It is here that the wonder of the Universe and of our lives takes root and plays out.

ENERGY

As we have seen, after the Drought comes rain. There is certain inevitability about this, however long it may take. At the soul level which the Major Arcana energies are, our symbolic and spiritual thirst is quenched and we are granted the reward of this vision.

As we drink in the water offered here we are also reminded by its visibility at the same time, of the Sun. In the Tarot the Sun has always been a representation of the Divine and the goal of the quest, or home of the Fool's Journey. Here at card 14, we reach the end of the second septenary of the 21 cards that lie below the Canyon. This second level is the level of the Mind, where we learn and hopefully understand who we are and gain knowledge of our place in the Universe. From here on we enter the realm of the spirit and so we can see the appearance of the Rainbow in our cards as a need to turn more towards the ways of the Spirit and less to the material world.

It can indicate that we have gained self-knowledge and awareness and there is a call here as we absorb that energy to remain grounded and real, as we gaze longingly and lovingly at this wondrous vision in the sky. Perhaps strongest and most immediate of all the qualities this energy brings to us is that principle of 'as above, so below' that we have mentioned above. The rainbow can be seen as the higher reflection of ourselves, each containing those seven colours, chakras and levels of consciousness we explored above.

Not only do we have the rainbow reflecting the single white light that stems from the world of Spirit or the Universe itself, enabling us to absorb it into our being, but we see its reflection in the rare appearance now of the secondary rainbow. Double rainbows are considered symbolic of a time of transformation and here we are given the energy required for that. This can be a time of reaching upward to the world of Spirit and of allowing a little more light into ourselves and lives, on whatever level it may be required when this card appears for you.

Here the energy is that of a blend with the material and the physical, above and below once more. So it is that we are called now to be ourselves - spiritual beings having a human experience. We are Divine and we are Human and it is in the full knowledge and balance of this that we find the peace traditionally associated with this card. The physical cannot exist without the spiritual and vice-versa. The indescribable inner peace this energy can give us now can only be found within, as we blend these two forces together to create that alchemical mix and find our individual pot of gold.

Perhaps we simply need to be outside when a rainbow appears and gaze in awe and wonder at the beauty we can see: the miraculous nature of the Universe and then reflect this back inside ourselves by the realization that we are a part of this creation and we possess that same beauty and wonder.

Along with recognition of our own Divinity the energy here can enable us to calm the fire of any distemper we may possess within our souls. This can lie in the avoidance of extremes, whether of behaviour, emotional response, mental view or opinion or fanatical belief. The balance illustrated by the rainbow of above and below can also be expressed 'as within, so without' and so it is that now we can be guided by this energy to experience this spiritual truth and maxim.

We know that what we project is what we receive; what we give away we possess. When the Rainbow appears for us we need to remind ourselves of the nature of the Universe as a non-judgemental thing that by its scientific or perhaps instinctive nature is duty bound to act like the Genie in the Lamp for each and every one of us – 'your wish is my command'! In other words what we wish for, what drives us, who and what we are within, is given to us in its full measure. The energy of this card can be a full and complete experience of this principle.

More importantly however we know that we always have a choice in how we respond to whom and what we are. We are in control of our own beings and identity. With the energy here we can look within, observe fully, openly and honestly who and what we are and make an informed choice as to what we will now project out to the Universe and so what life and world we will create for ourselves. Be careful what you wish for!

15 - INFERNO

BACKGROUND

For our meeting with the Devil from traditional Tarot we make an analogy with the Inferno. It is well known that a depiction of Hell, where the Devil lives is a place of Fire and eternal torment, so it seems only fitting that we have a look around his house as we attempt to access the energy here and transmute it to our therapeutic, growthful purposes.

To achieve this we focus not on man-made fires, but on the naturally occurring Wildfires that best various parts of our planet at varying intervals. Known also as bushfire and forest fire, the prefix given tells us much of the nature and variety of fires on offer, with grass, hill, peat, desert, vegetation and forest also in the gamut table of blazes that we will call Inferno. What we are focusing on for our purposes here is the uncontrollable and spontaneous nature of such fires, together with the size they can achieve and speed they spread from their source. Other notable features are their seemingly random change of direction and ability to jump apparently insurmountable gaps, such as roads and rivers.

As may be expected, naturally occurring wildfires can be more common in hot, dry climates. To gain some idea of their extent, In the United Sates alone there can be between 60 and 80 thousand wildfires each year, burning between 3 and 10 million acres of land. They have occurred naturally over thousands of years, as fossil records testify. Whilst the damage they can cause is unimaginable we should also note that some species actually depend on the effects of wildfires for growth and reproduction.

There are four major natural causes of wildfire – lightning, volcanic eruption, sparks (from rock fall), and spontaneous combustion, the most common varying throughout the world. We should note here that we are not including those wildfires that result from human cause, which are of course many, varied and equally destructive.

The spread of a wildfire depends on its flammable material and its vertical arrangement. This of course depends on the shape of the land around the fire and these are also given four classifications. Ground fires are fed by subterranean roots and other organic matter which is susceptible to ignition. Ground fires can smoulder for days to months. Crawling or surface fires are fuelled by low-lying vegetation, leaf and timber litter, grass and shrubbery. Ladder fires consume material between vegetation and tree canopies, such as small trees, logs and vines. Lastly, crown, canopy or aerial fires, burn suspended material at the canopy level, such as tall trees, vines and mosses.

Wildfires occur when all the necessary elements for a fire come together in one area. The ignition source is brought into contact with a combustible material that is subjected to sufficient heat coupled with oxygen in the air. If there is enough moisture this can prevent ignition since more heat is first required to evaporate it, meaning of course that droughts can result in more wildfires, especially when coupled with lightning or strong winds.

Of course the daytime hours are more prone to wildfires starting. The burn rate of logs can be up to five times greater during the heat of the day due to lower humidity, increased temperature and higher wind speeds. Sunlight warms the ground during the day which creates air currents that travel uphill. At night the land cools, creating air currents that travel downhill. Wildfires are fanned by these winds and can follow these currents over hills and down valleys.

Wildfires can have an impact upon the weather and environmental conditions we experience too. Smoke plumes from wildfires have been observed at distances exceeding 1,000 miles and can reach heights of 6 to 8 miles, the height of the lower stratosphere. It is here and below that our weather and air pollution takes shape. Wildfires account for up to 14% of our total carbon emissions. Clearly what effects one, affects us all.

DESCRIPTION

Our image here, although lacking the horns and goats feet of the image familiar to those who know the Tarot, can induce a similar sense of awe, fear and recoil. Whilst fire, when in the form of a candle, hearth or camp fire is a very welcome, comforting and protective source of light and warmth, when it is uncontrolled it becomes a fearsome thing against which we have little protection or refuge. When we look at the image here, all we can do to survive is try to get out of the way.

As we observe the height, breadth and power of the flames we are observing what is known as the wildfire front – the point where unburned material meets active flames. As the fire progresses it heats the surrounding air and dries out everything in its path, as if it prepares it for the burning. Any water is vaporized and the wood, in the form of our noble tree, releases flammable gases. Heat transfer from the front warms the air to 800 degrees centigrade, creating faster ignition. This can result in torching, where tree canopies dry and are ignited from below.

The silhouette of our tree here can be analogous to us, helpless before the flames of our own particular Devil and apparently sacrificial at this point. As the tree is, we are dwarfed by the simple size, intensity and power of what is

151

before us. So it is we are apparently helpless before the fire of our destiny. We see the now brittle, charred remnants of trees consumed by the flames, symbolising for us our past, the legacy of what has gone before and how we have dealt with it. Standing still and proud, the tree reaches upward and outward, strong to the last, and echoes our own ego's that must indeed be purged and burned away from us on our Quest. We are not the be all and end all of everything and we must learn humility if we are to progress. This seems a good time to accept this!

We have seen above the fuel required for such a wildfire to burn, and here we can see the grassland that waits to be consumed before the flames. Wildfires are known to have a rapid forward rate of spread when burning through dense and uninterrupted fuel sources. This can be as fast at 6.7 mph (10.8 kph) in forests and 14 mph (22kph) in grasslands, as here.

A further feature of wildfires is their unpredictability, somewhat difficult to show pictorially! Wildfires can display certain characteristics such as flanking, where it advances at a tangent to the front or backing, where it burns in the opposite direction. They can spread by jumping or spotting as winds carry firebrands (hot embers) and other burning materials through the air, allowing the wildfire to cross roads, rivers and other barriers. Amazingly, spotting can occur up to 6 miles (10 kilometres) form a wildfire front.

What is clear as we look at the image here is that this fire will burn and destroy everything in its path and that it will not relent until it runs out of fuel or is starved of air. As we shall see in our next section our response to what may threaten to destroy us, must be similar, as we seek to face and embrace our own Devil, here in the form of our awesome Inferno.

ENERGY

When we examine the nature of the Inferno we can learn much about ourselves and indeed the energy of the card here when it comes to us. We can begin by reminding ourselves that this card is the Devil in traditional Tarot. What can be forgotten is that the Devil was originally an angel and as such, can also exist to teach and guide us, albeit his method being somewhat forceful and confrontational, as our Inferno here tends to be.

We know that the Devil card represents that which we fear and can manifest in such things as obsession and attachment, as the place by which we seek refuge from our fears. We also know that love is the antidote to all that we fear, this being the opposite of that greatest energy of the Universe - love - rather than hate as we might suppose.

So it is that when we are truthful with ourselves, we can see that we can go to the ends of the Earth as we seek to run and hide from confronting and facing our fears, such is the extent and reach of those icy fingers. However, if the Wildfire is the symbolic personification of our fears, we know that there is no escape. Wildfires can occur in any areas, be it forest, desert and so on and so no matter what we do, we are (perhaps), fated on our Quest through life to eventually, somewhere and somehow, face up to our fears and again symbolically, allow ourselves to be consumed by the flames of Hell, depicted here as the Inferno.

Indeed we know that there are many attempts to create natural wildfires as a preventative means of their destructive force occurring. Similarly there are various methods of Wildfire suppression too. Whilst I am, of course, not advocating that we should just let Wildfires burn wherever and whenever they wish, we can make an analogy with the

153

energy of this card here. This is that in terms of the human being, suppression invariably does not work, and especially when it comes to the nature of our energy. If the energy we are experiencing here is primarily that of what we each fear the most, we need to remind ourselves that the nature of energy is to flow and if we seek to suppress it, whether by the use of drugs, alcohol, sex, gambling and many other potential addictions and obsessions, it will win out in the end. The harmful and destructive results of our fears and their consequences cannot be supressed or ignored, they must be allowed identification and admittance so the energy can flow. Only then can we gain dominion, control and ultimately victory over them. In short, if we wish to beat our fears we must fully realise them. Put another way, we must meet the fear, or our Devil, on his own terms – if you wish to defeat your enemy, sing his song!

Here we are reminded of the depiction of Hell in Dante's appropriately named 14th Century epic poem 'The Divine Comedy'. Here Hell, aptly for us, is called the Inferno and shows us nine circles located within the Earth that we each must travel through on our Quest. The Inferno describes the recognition and then rejection of sin, for which we can replace fear.

So we must realise that we each carry our fears with us until we are able to gain freedom and liberation from them. This being the case, like the Wildfire they may break out at any time, given the right conditions. Those conditions are of course of our own making. Such is the nature and arguably intention of the Universe of which we are an intrinsic part, that we are bound or fated to manifest our deepest, darkest fears and phobias. What we must realise is that the Devil is on our side; the Wildfire can purge us of those fears in order to allow the positive effects to begin to grow. In this way we can begin to allow these new shoots that emerge from the burned and scorched landscape of our souls and lives, to reclaim their heritage. As they flourish so do we, this time in the light and total freedom of truth and honesty.

We have seen that only the right conditions can create the spontaneous, natural Wildfire. So it is we need to accept that we create our own Wildfires, internally and externally, in ourselves and lives. We have also seen their rapid spread and size and so we must realise our apparent and seeming inability to have an effect upon them once they have been released. That they jump gaps, both natural and man-made, suggests that no matter what we do, the Inferno we have created must be met with an equal and opposite force for it to be extinguished. This energy can be seen to be truth, honesty and ultimately, love.

The common effect of a Wildfire is demonstrable by its affect upon the global climate and its reach over such large areas. This tells us that, although we may feel it as we experience this energy, we are not alone and there is a connection between us all. So as we contribute to our own quest so it is we shed more light to others on the Quest and we can both give and receive support from and to others. We have seen previously the links between us all and this is a time when that is needed.

Should we choose however, to leave something buried deep within the darkest recesses of ourselves, lives and souls, we know that the Wildfire can smoulder and its power, force and energy may subside but still exists. The heat still festers like inactive cancer within us and may lie dormant for many Moons. Ultimately though, it can and must surface and it is up to us to really decide how this will happen.

The energy of the Inferno then can teach us much about our true selves as we move inexorably onwards on our Quest to the light of wholeness and completion. In this way it is a powerful bringer of light, as the Devil was once called. This energy allows us the empowerment to make a choice as to whether that light will burn or illuminate us.

16 - VOLCANO

BACKGROUND

It is perhaps easy to see the connection between the Tower card of traditional Tarot and our interpretation of the Volcano here. This firstly comes from the image itself, both featuring the fire at the top of their respective towers, the lightning that strikes so forcefully and the depiction of destruction and revelation the images portray.

When we look deeper into the nature of the Volcano however we can see further links. To do this let us look at Volcanos a little closer. We know of them as mountains that erupt, spewing lava and molten fire over the surrounding area. Our Earth itself is really a ball of molten rock with a cooler crust, a bit like a human being – we may strive to appear to be calm and collected on the outside but there is a great deal more going on within!

The Earth's crust consists of plates that float on the ocean of molten rock beneath this mantle. This molten rock or magma has currents. Where it is hotter it rises away from the Earth's core while the cooler magma sinks towards it. This creates the movement of the plates resulting in plate tectonics, being the divergence, collisions and convergence that result between them. Subduction, the forcing of one plate beneath another can then be a common occurrence. The massive force this includes melts the rock of the lower plate, creating magma. The crack or vent here allows magma, debris from the Earth's interior, ash and hot gases to escape, creating the volcanic eruption.

These can often form within oceans, such as the area known as the Mid-Atlantic Ridge. Volcanic eruptions in these areas can create new islands, such as with the Hawaiian Island chain. Other areas, such as the East African Rift and Rio Grande Rift in North America have volcanos formed from the stretching and thinning of tectonic plates, rather than their convergence, often poetically called 'mantle plumes'. Such areas of prime volcanic formation and activity are appropriately called 'Hotspots'.

Volcanos feature a number of different features, such as fissure vents, which are the linear cracks through which lava emerges. Shield volcanos have broad profiles that allow slower moving lava to flow over a great distance, rather than an explosive and dramatic eruption. These create lava domes, formed within the crater of a previous eruption, such as Mount St Helens in Washington, USA. Such volcanos can be prone to bulging, known as a crypto dome, its instability allowing a flow of lava to emerge.

Cinder cones can build up around the vent of a volcano and can create a cone-shaped hill up to 400 meters high from their eruptions. Strato volcanoes are tall, conical mountains formed from the layers of prior ejected material, which is then covered in lave that hardens as it cools, beginning the process all over again. Super volcanoes are seen as the most dangerous volcanos, such is the scale of devastation from their eruptions. The most well-known example here is Yellowstone National Park. Volcanos formed in the ocean are known as submarine volcanos for obvious reasons, whilst sub glacial volcanoes develop beneath icecaps, creating what we call Table Mountains. Volcanos can emit different kinds of lava, depending on their location and the activity causing the eruption. This is classified by the speed of its flow and temperature.

The lifespan of a volcano can vary from months to several million years, making the idea of active, dormant or extinct an anathema to scientists. A volcano can be considered active if it has erupted in the last 10,000 years. Currently the most active volcanos on Earth are Kilauea in Hawaii which has been in continuous eruption for 30 years, Mount Etna and Stromboli in the Mediterranean and Mount Yasur in the South Pacific, which has been on the go for 800 years!

A volcano can be classed as extinct when it no longer has a magma supply or there is simply no written record of its activity. A dormant volcano can be difficult to determine, and can catch us unawares, The famous Vesuvius eruption of AD79 came a time when it is known to have been covered with gardens and vineyards, before it wiped out Pompeii and Herculaneum.

DESCRIPTION

Approximately 90% of all volcanos exist within the Ring of Fire around the edges of the Pacific Ocean, there being thought to be about 1,500 active volcanos on the Earth and many more dormant or extinct. About 50 erupt each year. Our image here is based on an eruption of Mount Rinjani in Indonesia in 1995, which is the perfect example of the volcanic eruption with lightning.

Volcanic lightning can be known as a dirty thunderstorm. Electrical charges are generated when rock fragments, ash and ice particles collide and produce static charges in a volcanic eruption. As the plume of the eruption descends it can produce more charge than it began with, resulting in the lightning, aided and abetted by the large amounts of water it also produces. This is similar to the lightning that can occur in sand dunes, where the positively charged particles run against those negatively charged and sparks, literally, fly. This phenomenon has been compared to the same effect of rubbing a balloon on a woollen jumper – try it and see!

Flows of volcanic lava can reach temperatures of 1,250 degrees Celsius (2,000 Fahrenheit) which simply burn everything they come across. Boulders of lava can rain down from the volcano on the surrounding area and mud flows from rapidly melting snow can strip valleys bare, including all that is in them. Volcanic eruptions can be accompanied by Earthquakes, hot springs, mud pots and geysers, creating a multitude of threats. In recent years volcanic eruptions in Iceland grounded the aircraft of Europe and beyond, since volcanic ash particles can be melted and stick to the turbine blades of jet engines.

We can also remind ourselves again of the spiritual maxim 'as above, so below' which can also be termed 'as within, so without'. As we look at the image on this card this is brought to mind when we observe the upward motion of the volcanic plume, coupled with the descent of the lightning. This maxim reminds us that we are spiritual beings having a human experience and that everything is a reflection of our truth. In other words, as we release that which we are within to the higher energy of the spiritual realms, so we are rewarded with the flash of insight, revelation and understanding that comes with what we can call enlightenment, which rarely comes quietly.

We can also see the tree to the side of the volcano in the foreground. This reminds us of the tree from our previous image and tells us that we must be stripped bare, taken to our core here, and release and offer up all that we know and that which we do not know but must acknowledge lies within, if we are to avoid the destruction and symbolic famine that result from its forceful expulsion.

To the ancient Greeks volcanos could only be explained as the actions of the gods which we can see as the inevitable consequences of leaving alone or trying to ignore that which we prefer not to look at. The German astronomer Johannes Kepler believed volcanos to be ducts for the Earth's tears. Tears are often seen as healing things, the sting of their salt compensated for by the sweet release of emotional pressure and burden we may have carried for a long time. The analogy with our image here is easy to make.

ENERGY

We saw how the nature of the Inferno can contain the danger of leaving anything buried to smoulder, believing it to be extinguished, only for it to re-ignite sometime later. Just as with our deeper selves, with which we are concerned at this stage of the Quest, so all that we contain within must be brought into the light. The Inferno seeks to literally burn away that which limits restrains and restricts us but cannot plumb the depths of our core selves. Here lie our past, sometimes shameful memories, regrets and unresolved mistakes and issues which lie smouldering, apparently extinct but in reality only dormant. Given the right conditions then, this Volcano within our beings will eventually erupt, shoving to the surface that which we may have convinced ourselves was done. On the spiritual Quest, which is in reality just normal, everyday life, all must be exposed and come to the light and this is the message, purpose and ultimately healing of the energy of this card.

The word Volcano is derived from the name of Volcano, a volcanic island in the Aeolian Islands of Italy, which name in turn originated from Vulcan, the Roman god of fire and sadly not connected with Star Trek! However, we can dip into those ongoing missions to make a further analogy here. Vulcans are the masters of logic and seek to develop themselves as a race and individually by its use and application. However, every seven years all Vulcans must endure the 'pon-farr', which results in explosions of violence and loss of control, or an eruption, unless they mate. If they do not, they die. Notably, attempts were made to suppress or control these inner urges in several episodes, each time not successfully. In the end, as we have noted above, what is above, must come out.

We have seen that volcanos erupt because of collisions or merging of its plates beneath the surface. This clearly tells us that as human beings our own tectonic plates, such as deeply held resentments, long-festering anger, rejection, frustration, denial and so on, can become amplified as we pile on more and more layers and something must give. I have often said that the Major Arcana energies are bigger and stronger than we are and if we don't do something about them, they will do it for us. In this case, if we do not pay due attention to our symbolic tectonic plates, through such things as therapy, counselling, energy work (of the many kinds now available) and simple, plain and brutal honesty, then the nature of this energy will do what it must.

This means an eruption of some kind. How we experience our own particular volcano depends on each person but be aware that 'what goes us, must come down'. This says that we will experience first-hand and direct the result and effect of who and what we truly are. This can either have catastrophic and deeply painful effect or we can release our volcano willingly and experience some pain yes, but with the knowledge or even a tiny glimmer of hope, that healing is on its way. Be assured however, that we all have a volcano and all must erupt; that is what they do and are bound to by their very nature.

We saw also that some tectonic plates can be stretched and thinned, a little like the practice of 'papering over the cracks'. However it is this very action that results in the eruption where we are weakest and stretched thinnest that the truth, that brutal honesty again, will emerge. We may apply our metaphorical wallpaper for years and try different patterns, glue and styles but in the end we must strip back to the bare walls and properly prepare the material we find there, in order to finally create something beautiful. To illustrate this for yourself, try holding on to a handful of sand and squeezing to ensure you don't spill it and see what happens!

We also know that lava can begin to flow from vents or cracks in the volcanos surface, perhaps caused by that stretching or surface repairs we try to make for ourselves. Bulges can also appear in the volcanic mountain as what is within seeks release and expression. This intensity builds and in effect tears open the surface in order to seek the light, just as our inherent nature and energy is to find its way back home again, to the Upper world, Spirit Realm, Heaven, Universe or whatever term you choose to use. We are bound and instinctively motivated to rise and refine that which we are and in order to find our way home, to become enlightened, whole and experience true peace, we have to allow all that we are and may wish to avoid or cannot admit, to come to our surface.

We should also note here that volcanos can lay dormant for many a long year but following their eruption begins the formation of new layers. This can tell us that although we may have understandably massive fear and trepidation as to what may happen if we reveal our true selves, something solid and secure will result and so we are granted the gift of hope that is always there, beneath whatever it is our own tectonic plates are formed from. We can begin this process by asking ourselves what we need to do to find the light beneath the volcano.

17 - FIRMAMENT

BACKGROUND

Following the literally earth-shattering and personal upheaval of the Volcano, we find ourselves blessed now with the emergence of the light of The Star to guide us on our way. So traditional Tarot has it and here we expand our vision from within to view and observe the Firmament the 'vault of the sky' as the word means, deriving from the 'firm structure' of its Latin origins. Specifically, the term is taken to refer to the imaginary sphere on which the celestial bodies appear to be projected.

This view followed naturally from the discovery of the Earth as a globe in the 4th century BC. Many ancient civilisations, including Greek, Egyptian, Chinese, Indian and Native American supported this. Indeed the creation myths of the ancient Mesopotamian, Sumerian and Indo-European cultures saw the sky as a solid dome arching over the Earth. The Bible tells us in Genesis that God created this firmament to separate the 'waters above' the Earth from those below – rain and oceans. The firmament was 'heaven'. The firmament was also viewed as a 'tower' with many windows which opened and closed at intervals through which the light shone, as the Stars, which fits nicely with the progression to this card from the last.

Later, mediaeval scholars adopted the idea of the Greek philosophers Aristotle and Ptolemy, which determined that these celestial bodies revolved around an orbit with the Earth at the centre. Interestingly, given the magical and esoteric significance of the energy and workings of the number Seven, it was viewed that there were seven inner orbs beneath the orb of the Firmament, each preserved in the naming of the days of our week. It was the observation of comets in the 16th Century that challenged the idea of the Firmament as a fixed, solid thing. After Galileo's telescopic observations confirmed this, this idea was abandoned.

The progress that science has since given us tells us a great deal about the Firmament and its inhabitants, the energy of which concerns us here. Each Star is an enormous glowing ball of gas that can live for millions of years. Basically, the bigger the Star the shorter its life span. A Star is born when a cloud of hydrogen gas collapses. It then becomes hot enough to burn nuclear fuel and after billions of years the Star expands and the core contracts, which eventually explodes and turns into a dim and cool object, such as a black dwarf or black hole, depending on its initial mass.

The energy produced by stars is as a product of its nuclear fusion. This radiates into space and manifests as a stellar wind. This flows from its outer layers as protons and alpha and beta particles, showing us that even here the male/female, dark/light principle of 'complementary opposites' exists and takes form.

Most stars occur in groups of (at least) two. These are locked in elliptical orbit around their centre of mass, which is called a binary star system. These are held together by gravitational forces. Larger groups are called clusters, which can be up to 1000 stars, which include the Pleiades and Hyades. Huge collections of stars are called Galaxies, in which we live, our Solar System being located within the Milky Way Galaxy, which we see on this card. It is likely that the majority of stars in the Milky Way are red dwarves, meaning that like us, they are single from birth.

DESCRIPTION

Observation techniques have evolved drastically since this

process was first known to have begun, about 1500 BC. Now we have telescopes that operate from space itself, sending us amazing and profound images of deep space. In our image here we view the spiral image of our home in the Universe, the Milky Way. It is here that we have been able to catalogue the stars in our Firmament. Constellations are first known to have been categorised during the Babylonian period, around 600 BC, which were aligned to their myths. It was this that gave rise to the science of Astrology.

A typical galaxy, such as the Milky Way that we see here in all its majesty and splendour, contains hundreds of billions of stars and there are more than 100 billion galaxies in the known Universe. Most stars are between 1 and 10 billion years old. Stars are essentially giant nuclear reactors, which makes them hot and bright in the Firmament. Our closest and therefore brightest star is of course the Sun, which we'll visit shortly. Next comes Proxima Centauri, 4.3 light years from the Sun, which is itself just over 90 million miles away.

The scintillation of stars, their twinkling, is caused by the thick layers of turbulent air in our atmosphere. As the light of the star travels through the cosmos is it bent many times by the layers of our atmosphere and in many directions, causing the source of the light to appear to twinkle. When two or more atomic nuclei fuse together at a star's core they produce a heavier element. By the time this energy reaches the outer layers of the star it has reached the spectrum of visible light, which is what we see. The colour of the stars that we see is dependent on its temperature at this outer edge. There is also electromagnetic radiation that stars emit that is beyond our sight but is no less significant as a flow of energy. The luminosity of a star is determined by its radius and temperature. This can fluctuate, giving us star spots; areas of darker colour on their surface, as they appear to us.

There is something of a reminder of the Tornado in the cards image, all those aeons ago when we began our Quest in that the aspect of the Firmament we view appears to touch the Earth yet also reach the heavens, telling us something of what we can achieve with the energy of this card.

Set against the blackness of the silhouetted landscape, the brightness of the centre of the Milky Way depicts the densest star clusters and also strongest energy force emanating from them. This appears radiant and beautiful, almost enticing us onwards and upwards on our Quest, set to explore now the outer reaches of our known Galaxy and ever onwards 'straight on till sunrise' (where we find 'Never Land' according to JM Barrie). The last vestige of the setting Sun is visible in the corner, enabling us to see the glory above and reminding us that we are another day nearer our home and goal.

The stars are at once comforting and familiar to our view, guiding lights above and around us through which we can orient and steer ourselves along our Quest. Yet they are also distant and unknown, a vast expanse away of unexplored and unknown territory that seems to beg us to stretch out, both physically and in our imagination and go boldly or otherwise where we have not gone before (there had to be a Star Trek reference in this card somewhere!). So it is we are called to lift our vision, become 'starry-eyed' and rise up, fuelled by the promise of the light above as it guides us forever onwards.

ENERGY

The Firmament appears in all its glory to us as we emerge from the dark recesses of the Volcano's eruption. Here its energy stretches out from across the Universe to call us to connect with a greater awareness, an expanded vision of both ourselves and the reality which we inhabit. From a 'cosmic' standpoint as well as an individual one, we can see that we can attach to the energy from the Firmament. We are called on our Quest now to expand our awareness, our sense of knowing, to attach ourselves to our destiny and step up to the plate by living it.

The energy of this card can guide us on how we do this. It may appear as a tall order but remember that at this stage of our Quest we have weathered, survived and ultimately triumphed over Tornado's, Hurricanes, Earthquakes and much more. Rather like the experience of life itself we must battle against the myriad forces of adversity, shown in these cards but experienced variously as depression, rage, bitterness, poverty and despair that would seek to malign and destroy us and throw us off the path of the fulfilment of our destiny and Quest.

To look at how we do this, we can turn to a great source of wisdom, demonstrated also in the practical reality that he lived: the words of Mohandas K Ghandi. He told us that when we despair we should remind ourselves that the tyrants of the world can appear invincible but in the end the way of love and truth will always triumph. The energy of this card asks us to identify our own tyrants within and replace them with love and truth.

Such is the repository of wisdom that Ghandi offered and left with us that we can turn again to him to learn how we do this. The Firmament offers us a chance to align and live with our highest capability and destiny. This comes down to what we believe and what we believe directly creates the reality we experience, not just on a level of overall life direction but daily, in each hour, each minute, even each second. Ghandi quite correctly told us that our beliefs become our thoughts; our thoughts become our words; our words become our actions; our actions become our habits; our habits become our values and our values become our destiny.

It is notable that Ghandi gives us seven stages by which we create our own reality. The original image on the Star card of the Tarot shows us seven main stars, relating to the seven chakras of our intrinsic energy system. It is through their development (aided and abetted by our own developing awareness) that we can connect with the Firmament here. This allows us to move to a place of metaphoric low light pollution and our vision is cleared, as the dust settles form the volcanic eruption we have just experienced.

So here the energy we experience and receive can connect us to our beliefs. By looking at our core beliefs, the programming we may have received both from previous lifetimes as well as our upbringing and conditioning from this lifetime, parentally and socially, we can expand our awareness to move beyond any limited or apparently 'negative' patterns. By taking an honest and clear look at what we really believe, from our true heart and mind, we can determine those we know we need to change and work on this.

It takes only three weeks on average to acquire a new habit to our thinking. We can re-programme our minds to believe what we choose and this energy can align us with our highest beliefs; like the stars above and around us we can reach seemingly impossible and distant goals by realising that we create our own reality. Put another way, aim for the Moon and you'll land somewhere amongst the Stars!

We saw above that the majority of the stars in our Firmament are, like us, born alone. Yet, like stars that exist in pairs, we are pulled by an invisible force, or energy, that compels us to find a mate. This is not just to populate the species but to find our connection and wholeness, to experience a stronger flow of the strongest energy in the Universe, that of love. Yet we can only find this when we believe it is possible.

Now we have broken free of the individual prison that prevented the eruption of our Volcano. Now we are exposed, naked and free beneath the Stars and here we can realise and learn that we are indeed all connected to and part of a greater whole. This whole is that of each other, all humanity on Earth, without exception, as well as the wonderful planet we share our daily existence with and then the wider Universe we came from and will return to.

Part of the energy of this card is an opportunity then to realise our reality. This is not the downtrodden, individual plaything of destiny but a part of a wider creation and reality that we determine for ourselves. Here we are exhorted to 'be the change we want to see' (a paraphrase from the beloved Ghandi) and in so doing this energy can lift us beyond any limitation we care to imagine.

The twinkling of the Firmament can remind us that it is not an easy thing we can accomplish here and that we need to continually strive to rise above the mire of everyday platitudes to living and miserable, pious 'existence'. The light and therefore energy we see and receive from the great Firmament can fluctuate but even though it may fade and flicker at times, it will not be extinguished. Our challenge and opportunity here then is to lift ourselves beyond individual limitation and rise to collective possibility. We have seen that when a Star reaches the end of its lifespan it is effectively absorbed back into the Universe, as its energy collapses. So it is that we die and our energy becomes part of the collective Universe once again, from whence it came. In the brief time allotted to us we can achieve great things. In this way we can become our own Star, in every sense that this can be applied. Which Star will you be?

18 - MOON

BACKGROUND

Allowing ourselves to be guided to the dizzying heights of the Firmament brings us to the Moon. Here the energy we need to explore and assimilate is a strange one, just as the Moon has fascinated, bemused and befuddled us for centuries.

The Moon is the Earth's only natural satellite and is the fifth largest of our Solar System, being the largest planetary satellite relative to the size of the planet. It is about 27% the diameter of the Earth and It is the brightest object in our sky next to the Sun of course, despite its surface being dark. Its gravitational influence produces the tides of our oceans and seas and the lengthening and shortening of our days, by about three minutes to each. It lies about 384,000 kilometres from the Earth and has a diameter of 3,475 kilometres.

It is thought the Moon was formed about 4.5 billion years ago, not long after the Earth. The most widely accepted theory is that it was formed from the debris left over after a giant impact between the Earth and another body which was about the size of Mars, called Theia. The collision blasted material into orbit around the Earth and we had our Moon.

The Moon has a distinct mantle, crust and core. Its inner core is solid iron and the outer core fluid, liquid iron. This is surrounded by a molten layer, formed by the crystallisation of the magma ocean that originally covered its surface.

The Moon makes a complete orbit around the Earth about once every 27.3 days, called its sidereal period. Due to the fact that our Earth is orbiting the Sun at the same time, it takes 29.5 days for the 'phase' of the Moon to be complete around us, which is called its synodic period. The effect of its gravitational pull on the Earth causes our planet's crust to bulge upwards, creating the tides. Although you don't notice it, when the Moon is overhead, you move upwards by a few metres!

The Moon's orbit is actually taking it away from the Earth, by a distance of about 4 centimetres per year. However it will settle down to a steady orbit, after 50 billion years, when it will then take 47 years to complete its phase. That is if course, if the Sun doesn't consume the Earth about then, as it is theorized will happen!

DESCRIPTION

Due to its synchronous orbit with the Earth, the Moon always shows us its same face. It is estimated that about 14,000 square kilometres of the Moon's surface is in permanent shadow, the fabled 'dark side of the Moon'. The light of the Moon that we see is of course, reflected sunlight.

Although the Sun in reality is much bigger than the Moon, they appear relatively the same size in our sky. This is because the Sun is about 400 times larger than the Moon but is about 400 times further away.

The Moons' appearance is somewhat pock-marked, featuring dark volcanic matter between its impact craters and the brighter highland areas. The largest crater on the Moon is the South-Pole Aitken Basin, about 13 kilometres deep and 2,240 kilometres wide. The darker areas we see on our image of the Moon here are the lunar plains known as 'Maria' (from the Latin for 'seas'). They are so-called due to early astronomers' belief that they were filled with water. They are in fact solidified lava pools. These Maria are nearly all found on the Moon's near side, covering 31% of its surface, but just 2% on the far 'dark' side. This is due to the thicker crust on the far side.

The lighter coloured areas we can see are called terrae or highlands, simply because they are higher than the Maria. The craters on the Moon we can see were formed from collisions with asteroids and comets. On the near side of the Moon alone it is estimated there are about 300,000 craters wider than 1 kilometre.

The Full Moon phase occurs when the Moon is completely illuminated as seen from the Earth. This happens when the Moon is on the opposite side of the Earth from the Sun. This means the near side of the Moon is fully lit by the Sun and appears round to us, as we see on our card here.

What we are actually seeing here is a mixture of Maria (seas) and crater areas. These all have their own names, such as the well-known Sea of Tranquillity, and Sea of Waves, Vapours, Serenity, Clouds, Nectar, Islands, Cleverness, Moisture, Showers, Cold, Fecundity, Crises, Serpent and lastly, Ocean of Storms. Some of the crater names that we can see on the card are Copernicus, Grimaldi, Kepler and Plato. These names may conjure up quite an amazing place but also tell us something of the nature and effect the Moon has upon us, as we shall see.

ENERGY

The effect and the energy the Moon has upon us has been well researched and documented, although still open to much debate. Although they are a subtle influence, operating deep within us, they are no less powerful because of it.

The traditional image of the Moon card gives us some clues as to its energy and influence. There is a theory that we are more prone to mating and love-making at the time of the Full Moon. The traditional Tarot image has a crab emerging from the waters, taken to symbolize the depths of the Mind, the sub-conscious. The crab deposits its eggs in the high water tides that occur at the Full moon. The dog and wolf that sit opposite the path coming from this show the tame and wild sides that our mind contains, rather like the two spheres of the human brain, being the logical and intuitive, rational and irrational sides alike.

Indeed this irrationality is dominated by the energy we experience under the influence of this card. Termed 'lunacy' from the lunar body that is the Moon, those with mental instability are known to experience more profound symptoms at the Full Moon, just as we are prone to bleed more at this time. Whether this energy is experienced in what can be termed a positive or negative effect can be dependent on whether we have tamed something of that unknown wild side of our minds.

So here we are challenged to face what we remain fearful of. This energy can bring to light that which remains in darkness to us. We are challenged to give answers to what our deepest fears and fantasies are and expose them to the light of reality. This may be our darker impulses but if we can make a friend of that we emerge fuller and more complete, like the roundness of the Moon at its Full phase, as we see on the card here.

The effect of the Moon is felt both on a physical and mental level. Due to its impact upon the waters of the Earth, the effect of its energy on us, since we are at least two-thirds water and other fluid, is striking. What we ingest at this time is absorbed to a much greater degree, be this the purification of water, health inducing vitamins and minerals or the altering effect of alcohol or drugs.

Fear is the opposite of love, rather than hate as we might suppose. Indeed some unfortunate people suffer from a fear of the Moon and its influence, called Selenophobia. Exposure to the moon for these people can induce panic attacks, sweating and trembling, these symptoms being stronger at the Full Moon. Perhaps the remedy here is the knowledge that 'there is nothing to fear but fear itself'. This tells us much about the energy we receive from this card and of course, the Moon itself.

This energy is ultimately one of illumination. However to find that light we must turn within, to our own individual darkness. We need to realise now that nothing can remain in darkness if we are to find wholeness and completion, as we surely must if we are to complete our Quest. Our Quest is of course our life and now we must utilise the courage we have acquired along the way, the faith we have experienced and the knowledge that nothing is permanent, only energy. This is confirmed by the transient nature of the Moon and its persistent energy that will eventually draw forth from within us that which we seek to keep hidden, for whatever reason.

However, it is clear that however we seek to impose ourselves upon it to maintain order and control, the Universe and the process of life itself is not a logical, structured thing. Like the waxing and waning of the Moon, all things have their tides and their seasons, including ourselves and our own phases. Sometimes we are up, at others down. Happiness is not something that we attain and retain; it is more a state of understanding. That understanding is what the energy here can give us, if we are ready to accept that we are more than we may have supposed.

This could be termed to be that elusive 'sixth sense' or intuition, the gift from the energy of the Moon. This is the blend and balance that emerges naturally from the tame and wild sides of the brain, the positive/negative poles that exist in all things. It is when they are successfully blended and so balanced that our fears can limit and restrict us no longer. Many people struggle with this inner knowing, allowing the mind to give them confusion, unable to decipher reality from illusion, just as moonlight can play tricks on our eyes.

This is the part of us that 'knows because we know' and is a natural part of the human condition. The Moon and the energy of this card offer us a path now to that blessed state of awareness, understanding and inner peace, if we can but put the fear aside of releasing outer control for apparent inner chaos, subtlety and irrationality. It is then that we are strong enough to feel the full force of the Sun, which we now see.

19 - SUN

BACKGROUND

Having dragged our darkness out into the light, willingly or otherwise, we are now exposed to the full force and glare of that light, this being the Sun.

Our Sun was formed about 4.6 billion years ago from the collapse of a region in a large molecular cloud which is thought to have given birth to many other stars. The majority of matter in the molecular cloud gathered in the centre, the rest forming our known Solar System. The Sun is approximately halfway through the most stable part of its life and will remain unchanged for several billion years more. The Sun is actually white in colour but from Earth appears yellow because of the atmospheric scattering of blue light. Its surface temperature is about 5505 degrees Centigrade and it generates its energy by nuclear fusion of hydrogen into helium. The coolest layer of the Sun is about 500 kilometres above the photosphere (where its visible light radiates to) and allows for the existence of carbon monoxide and water molecules.

As the star closest to Earth it is the brightest object in our sky and is brighter than 85% of the stars in our Milky Way. The hot corona, the plasma surrounding the Sun that we see during its eclipse, continually expands, creating solar winds which are a stream of charged particles. These solar winds extend throughout the Solar System.

The Sun orbits the centre of the Milky Way, taking about 225 million years to complete this. The light that we see from the Sun is about 8 minutes old, it taking this long to reach us. The energy from this supports almost all life on Earth, by the process of photosynthesis, the name given to the conversion process of light into chemical energy.

Perhaps due to our utter dependence on it for life, the Sun has of course been an object of veneration across the Earth. The Egyptians saw the sun as Ra, being carried across the sky in a ship accompanied by other gods. The Greeks saw him as Helios, carried by a chariot of fiery horses. To the Incas the Sun was Inti and to the Aztecs Tonatiuh. To the Romans the sun became 'solar invictus' - the 'unconquered sun'.

Babylonian astronomers observed the Sun's motion in the first millennium BC and there are ancient monuments across the globe fixed to the position of the Sun as it travels through the year, such as Stonehenge, New grange in Ireland, the pyramids of Egypt and those in Guatemala, Mexico and Peru, the Serpent Mound in Ohio, amongst many others. The position, workings and effect of the Sun has been studied since Chinese astronomers in 206 BC, then by Ptolemy in 100 AD, Copernicus in the 16th Century and then with the telescope by Galileo in the 17th Century. Isaac Newton and William Herschel contributed their observations, then Joseph Lockyer in the late 1800's, and then Albert Einstein's great Theory of Relativity allowed us to calculate the sun's energy output.

DESCRIPTION

The Sun is of course at the centre of our Solar System and is almost perfectly spherical in shape. It lies close to the inner rim of the Milky Way's Orion Arm. It consists of hot plasma interwoven with magnetic fields. Its diameter is about 1.4 million kilometres, being about 109 times the size of the Earth. Its mass accounts for 99.86 of the total mass of the Solar System. Three quarters of this is hydrogen, the remainder being mostly helium. The Sun rotates faster at its equator than at its poles since it is not solid and due to the temperature differences between the two.

The Sun does not have a definite boundary as rocky planets do. The last visible layer of the Sun that we can see here is called the photosphere. Anything beyond this is too thin or cool to radiate enough light to be visible to the naked eye. The photosphere can be up to hundreds of kilometres thick. The Sun's core is considered to be about 25% of its total radius and this part of the Sun appears brighter than the outer edges, due to the increased heat here. The areas beyond the photosphere are known as the solar atmosphere, rather like our own energy body or aura, consisting of five layers, rather than our own seven. Sunlight at the top of our atmosphere is composed of about 50% infrared light, 40% visible light and 10% ultraviolet light. This atmosphere filters out over 70% of ultraviolet light.

When observing the Sun (which we must not do with the naked eye of course), the most obvious features are sunspots, which are darker areas on the surface, due to their lower temperature. These can be tens of thousands of kilometres across and have intense magnetic activity that reduces the energy flow from the interior to the surface. The number of visible sunspots varies over an 11 'solar cycle' and usually appears as pairs with opposite magnetic polarity. The solar cycle has a direct influence on our climate due to the magnetic. At a basic level the fewer solar activity within its cycle, the cooler temperatures we experience.

Here we see the Sun at the height of its power, the differing colours we see created by the differences in temperature as described above. As the Sun set and rises we can observe other colours from within its spectrum, due to the wavelengths being bent or scattered, showing us light that is violet and blue but seen as green. As we gaze at this image it is easy to feel the heat from this direct encounter from our nearest Star.

ENERGY

One of the easiest ways to quantify and explain the energy that we receive from this card is to observe and experience the effect when the Sun comes out on a cloudy day. It is as if everyone beneath it and indeed the Earth herself breathes a collective sigh of relief. There is a palpable rise in energy, along with a rise in temperature of course. There is a greater height above us as the clouds clear and we can feel an irresistible urge to stretch out and expand our bodies.

If we relate to this at an energetic level we can also generate and experience an expansion of our energy. Firstly, there is more of it seemingly available to us, since we receive a greater flow and concentration of that life-force which we have termed energy. This comes in a physical form of course from the warmth we feel on our skin but energetically this reaches all levels of our being, the physical, emotional, mental and spiritual levels, as defined by the suits of the Minor Arcana and here the soul level of the Major Arcana.

The energy of the Sun creates an opportunity for growth, expansion and achievement, of whatever it is we are choosing to focus on in ourselves and lives at the time this card appears for us. In times before electricity dominated, we were much more dependent on this natural light to guide the level of our activity. Energetically we find that the appearance of this card heralds a time of activity and a need for us to act, a time to 'do' rather than simply 'be'. As we veer towards the completion of the Seekers Quest this is not a time to rest on our laurels but strive to fulfil our potential that we have a firm grasp of now. Now is a time when nothing is beyond our capability and we are fuelled and empowered in whatever way we need. This comes from within, from the accumulation of what we have absorbed on our Quest thus far. Now it is time to put this into practice.

We know that the higher temperatures of the Sun are closer to its centre and just as we work towards the centre and goal of our Quest so it is that the energy here can indicate a need for an increased intensity. This is not a time of test but of opportunity. We can find that we have within us now a deeper source and well of what we need. It is a time when we can dig deep and find, just as surely as the Sun will rise each day, just what we as an individual need.

We do need to ensure that we do not 'burn out' but the Sun will not; not for billions of years at least, when all will evolve to a different level. Spending too long in the full glare of the Sun only burns us of course but this can be a time when we may need to sweat a little with the effort, but nothing in life comes from no effort or work. Now it is a time to focus on the achievement of our goals and do what is necessary to bring them home.

That we know the effect, reach and energy of the Sun reaches throughout our solar system, through its solar winds, is indicative that we will feel the energy of this card at all levels of our being. Whilst the 'sunspots' of intense activity described above can occur, so do we need to allow their energy to permeate every level and aspect of who and what we are. We know that the Sun has a primal effect on our global climate and so it is with our energy here.

It is noteworthy that the Sun follows an 11 year cycle, this being of course half the number of cards in the Major Arcana. At card 11, the Mountain we find ourselves at the roof of the world. Having surmounted the seemingly insurmountable now we can journey on with a clear view of the goal of our Quest, personified as the Sun. We can also note how Sunspots have magnetic poles in the duality of their existence. We have seen how these twin 'complementary opposite' energies exist through our Universe and hence throughout our Major Arcana, in different forms. Here then we have an opportunity to perhaps unite the polarity of those energies and find a wholeness within ourselves hitherto unknown and hidden. It is this that the light of the Sun illuminates for us.

One of the traditional interpretations given to this card in the Tarot is that it brings an assuredly positive outcome and happiness. In our therapeutic and energetic terminology here, we can see this as a cycle of contentment from the achievement we are capable of now. We will shortly see the effect of this from a higher standpoint in our next card, but for now it is enough to bask in that energy, absorb all we need and release both inwardly to our being and outwardly to our life.

20 - METEOR

BACKGROUND

The result of the absorption of this divine sunlight is that we are given the capability of rising – rising to a level beyond our everyday, mundane consciousness to a level where we can perceive something deeper, more profound and closer to our soul. Traditionally this is depicted as Judgement but for our therapeutic purposes becomes a Meteor.

This is a natural object, the word deriving from the Latin, Old French and Greek origins meaning to lift up, to rise, or high in the air, as in the state of our awareness and level of our soul at this stage on the Quest. A meteor itself is also called a shooting star and refers to the bright trail or streak seen in the sky when a meteorite (a lump of rock falling through space) is heated to incandescence by friction with the Earth's atmosphere. The majority are fragments of comets or asteroids but can also be debris from collided objects throughout space. They are called Fireballs when they are observed to be brighter than any of the planets.

Meteorites were traditionally divided into three categories. Stony, being those comprised of silicate minerals, Iron, being comprised of metallic iron-nickel and Sony-Iron, which contain both. Now they are classified by their structure, chemical composition and mineralogy. Each year about 15 tonnes of meteoroids and different forms of space dust enter the atmosphere of the Earth. Meteorites can move at speeds of up to 42 kilometres per second. By way of comparison, the Earth moves at 29.6 kilometres per second. It is the heat of their entry and force of impact upon the Earth's atmosphere that transforms their structure and chemistry.

Meteors have been known since ancient times but were not recognised as astronomical phenomena until early in the 19th Century, being seen until then as atmospheric occurrences. A spectacular meteor storm in 1833 in the USA allowed observers to see they originated from a single point that moved with the stars. Other notable meteors have been the Peekskill Meteorite in New York 1992, Bine in Indonesia in 2009 and at Chelyabinsk Oblast in Russia in 2013. Meteorites that survive to impact on the Earth, usually of iron, can leave behind a crater, the most famous of these being the Barringer Meteor Crater in Arizona which occurred about 50,000 years ago and is 1.2 kilometres wide and 550 feet deep. Some meteors can explode above the Earth's surface, as happened over Siberia in 1908, destroying hundreds of square miles of forest.

In ancient times meteors were the subject of superstition and were linked to the gods. Meteorites were seen as gifts from angels or the gods displaying their anger, sometimes called 'thunderstones'. Knives have been recovered from tombs of Egyptian Pharaohs and Mesopotamian, Aztec, Mayan and Incan graves made from iron from meteorites, long before the Iron Age. Some Inuit tribes saw meteors as the faeces of stars or fiery urine from the cosmos. Meteorites have been venerated as sacred objects by different cultures and ancient civilisations across the world, such as Greenland, Tibet, India, Mongolia and Australia.

The temple of Apollo at Delphi is said to contain a sacred stone believed to have been thrown to Earth by Kronos, the Supreme Being, to mark the omphalos, 'the navel of the world'. In ancient Rome there was also the 'needle of Cybele', the goddess of fertility, and this meteorite being worshipped for over 500 years. In the Bible Jacob laid his head on a meteorite and begat his dream of the ladder that was the 'stairway to heaven'.

It was thought that the stones held supernatural powers and meteors have always sparked our imagination, still being seen as omens in some European areas and invoking 'shock and awe' as well as fear. The folklore to 'wish upon a star' to make your dreams come true is well documented, even in fabled Disneyland!

DESCRIPTION

Meteorites themselves can be as small as a speck of dust or up to 100 metres diameter, although the majority are pebble-sized. In collections across the world there have been over 1000 observed 'falls' of meteorites and about 40,000 'finds' of meteorites that were not seen as meteors. When we see many meteors only seconds apart we refer to this as a meteor shower, the trails and sparks usually coming from the same source.

The spectrum of light that we can see trailing a meteorite can depend on its trajectory and density. They become visible between 75 and 120 kilometres above the Earth and typically disintegrate at altitudes of 50-95 kilometres. Of course we can see more meteors at night as the darkness allows us to see more, but of course they do occur in our daytime too, actually being about half of all.

The trails that we see behind the meteorite is a trail of gases that heats up when it enters the atmosphere of the Earth and melted or vaporized particles from the rock or stone. Most meteors glow for only about one second, so we see a rare and wondrous thing in our image here. The visible light produced by a meteor may take on various hues, depending on the chemical composition of the meteoroid and the speed of its movement through the atmosphere. As layers of the meteoroid are rubbed away and become ionized the colour of the light we see can change according to the layering of its minerals. These include red from potassium, orange and yellow from iron, green and blue from copper and purple from potassium.

Again we see a silhouetted tree, something of a mainstay in the cards, symbolising ourselves as we stand in awe at the phenomenon and energy we experience and absorb at each card in turn. Imagining this, we gaze from our lofty position amongst the hill tops, lit to beautiful effect by the light of the firmament above us, at the wonder manifesting there. It is easy to see the various Meteors as shooting directly toward us as we look at the image and we are at once dwarfed and made humble by this display. We realise we are but a tiny speck in the vastness just of our own little corner of the Galaxy, yet alone the total Universe. Yet we are still as vital as every other living being.

It is worth noting here too that alongside the twin effects of molecular ionization and dust vaporization, meteors also produce noise, known as a 'sound of passage', which is of course impossible to show on our card! We hear this sound many seconds after seeing the meteor. The sound can feature 'crackling', 'swishing' and a 'hissing' sound. Although unproven, one theory says that the meteor produces radio waves, the energy they release as the trail dissipates occurring at audio frequency, hence the noise we can hear.

Due to their known orbit some meteors can be predicted to occur. The most visible of these are the Persids, which peak on August 12th each year. The image we see here is that of the most spectacular meteor shower, called the Leonids. These occur about every 33 years in their most dramatic way (the next being due 2032). The much anticipated event of 1999 was sadly not so spectacular. The Sioux and other plains Native American nations maintained records of the Leonid meteor storms, that they called 'winter counts', being pictographic records on animal skins. These clearly show the dramatic impact of the 1833 Leonid showers.

ENERGY

We have seen that the appearance of a meteor has always been held in what we can call a powerful regard. Our response to the energy we receive from this card should be no less powerful or significant. It is up to us how we perceive and choose to respond to the signs and omens we can observe in our lives.

The appearance of the Meteor in your cards is a call to arms in many ways. This call is to look at yourself and determine who is the architect of your life – is it you or is it some bigger, greater or apparently more powerful force then you, be this your employer, money itself, your Government, family, partner and so on. We are called to rise above the limitations of prescribed living or accepted society and live instead by our own code, or to quote one of my favourite songs' there's only one way of life and that's your own'. (The Levellers).

The fleeting but wondrous sign from above we see in the Meteor asks us to respond to the purpose and meaning of our life. Are we living to work or working to live, are we living or just existing? In short we can experience this energy as a 'wake-up call', a rattle from the heavens that we can both see and hear reverberating through our soul to our very bones. It can be so easy to muddle through our lives sometimes perhaps rising above the minutiae of mundane days but forever slipping back into the morass. The energy on offer here gives you the opportunity to once and for all live fully to 'live and live well' to quote Ralph Waldo Emerson.

How we do that is a matter for each individual. At this stage of the Seekers Quest we do not operate from the ego and indeed we cannot be motivated by self-aggrandisement if we

187

are to successfully respond to this cards energy. Preceding cards should have burnt the ego from our soul so now we can find higher purpose and meaning in the quality of who we are and how we are. This may well require us to dig deep, deeper than we ever have before and force ourselves to complete our potential.

Meteor then really offers us the chance to realise self-mastery. This is not in an abstract sense of a feeling of being 'spiritual' but in a practical, daily way. Similar to the Buddhist approach of mindfulness and the Toltec shamanic approach of First Attention, we need to apply the higher energy of this card to everything we are doing, with more alertness, concentration and focus. This may seem like hard work but once the habit is acquired we step into a flow of life that removes this.

Here we can see that the energy of this card is then a need to not merely go with the flow; this smacks of mediocrity and we are far above and beyond this now. We must create our own flow then hold it, stick to it and give every ounce of everything that we have become and are to not let go. This applies from the moment we wake to the second we sleep and at all points between, and even in our dream state, which we can also learn to direct. In order to accede to the energy here and live a life of full intent and purpose, as surely must befit its true meaning and purpose, we must exercise this direct and totally practical method of self-mastery.

To do this we must also take a moral look at the structure of ourselves and lives. Along with the glory of intentioned living that this energy brings must also come responsibility. This is a responsibility for ourselves, both inwardly and outwardly, in terms of our thoughts and feelings as well as our actions. We know that what we do is but a reflection of what we are within. Here we must accept the full reality of this and if we do not like it, step into the power we are given and change it.

It is only when ourselves and lives again inwardly and outwardly are fully in keeping with what it is intended for us to do that we can step into fulfilment and completion of our Quest. What it is that we are intended to do is simply what we decide. When we have striven and risen above everyday existence and created our own flow, the nature of existence is such that we align ourselves with a higher purpose than cannot but manifest in what is right for us to do. This is shown for us in the coloured light trial from our meteor, being the colours of the chakra system that is in more reality than our physical being - our true existence.

Far from being an omen of disaster, disapproval or disempowerment, the Meteor offers us the chance to 'live as if you will die tomorrow' (Ghandi) and experience the profound truth that 'life is either a daring adventure or nothing at all' (Helen Keller). Now we can operate the machinery of our own mortality, realise that there is ever really only one moment, that of the present and experience it to the maximum. It is only when we can live this way that we can ever hope to find the fulfilment of our goal, find our way home and complete our Quest, as we are now required to do and is the destiny of all of us.

21 - EARTH

BACKGROUND

The purpose of our Quest has been to find our goal, to find our way back home once we took the plunge over the Canyon and into life. Our metaphorical climb back up to reach the source of light again has brought us here. Just as in traditional Tarot the Fool completes his journey and finds himself again, so it is we realise that we were always home, already there but without knowing we were. Traditional Tarot gives us the World here, we present the Earth, in all her glory and magnificence, as our home and of which we are a part. It is in this way that we can know and experience the wholeness, enlightenment and completion of our Quest.

Our Earth is of course the third planet from the Sun and fifth largest in this Solar System. The planet is approximately 4.5 billion years old and life first appeared on her in the first billion years. The formation of the ozone layer and the Earth's magnetic field allowed previously ocean restricted life to move to land. About 70% of the planet's surface is covered by water, the rest covered by lands with lakes and the polar ice caps. Inside the planet there is a solid iron core, a liquid outer core and a thick layer of mantle. The Earth interacts through gravity with the Sun and Moon, as we have seen. We should note here that from the surface, the Sun and Moon appear approximately the same size. Since the Earth rotates about 365 times on its orbit around the Sun, this gives us the days in a year. The Earth's future is closely tied to the Sun – as it becomes brighter and hotter life as we know it cannot exist, but we have a while to go yet – over 2 billion years.

We know that the rigid outer layer of the planet contains tectonic plates that move in relation to one another at their boundaries. It is noteworthy that there are seven major tectonic plates covering the globe. The surface of the planet is continually changing and evolving due to these tectonics and the process of erosion. Beyond the planet, the Earth's atmosphere has no definite boundary, gradually becoming thinner and fading into outer space. The majority of the atmosphere is within the first 11 kilometres of the surface.

Scientifically speaking life as we know it on Earth is thought to have evolved through the process of photosynthesis, allowing the harvesting of the Sun's energy. With oxygen these allowed cells to develop from which various life forms came. There have been five mass extinctions in our evolution, the last being 66 million years ago when an asteroid may have caused the extinction of the dinosaurs. Smaller mammals survived and these evolved into ape-like creatures from where we apparently came. Other theories of course exist, such as Adam and Eve and extra-terrestrial origins.

Belief in the planet as a deity, usually as Mother Earth or some kind of female goddess, has existed fittingly, across the globe. The Aztecs call her Tonantzin (our mother), the Incas Pachamama (mother earth), the Greeks Gaia, the Chinese Hou Tu, the Hindus Bhuma Devi (goddess of Earth). To the Egyptians the Earth is the male Geb, the sky being female as Nut. To many she is simply Mother Earth, the personification of the planet and exists alongside her male counterpart, as Goddess and God, representative of the twin poles that we have seen persist in many differing ways in all life and perpetually through our quest and the Major Arcana. It is thought that prior to the conquering of much of the Middle East, Europe and Asia by barbarian warlords and their worship of war gods that a single, peaceful acknowledgement and veneration of a Mother Goddess existed across the majority of humanity.

DESCRIPTION

The shape of the Earth is actually an oblate spheroid, meaning it is flattened along the axis from pole to pole with a bulge around the equator. At the Equator the Earth is 43 kilometres larger than the pole to pole diameter. The image of the Earth is sometimes referred to as 'The Blue Planet' in reference to the majority of its surface being covered by water, as we have seen. This was verified in awe inspiring beauty when we began to receive images of our planet taken from satellites in space which continue to be improved in detail as our technology evolves.

The image we see here was taken on the Apollo 17 mission in 1972 and is often referred to as 'The Blue Marble'. This was taken en route to the Moon and we see the Earth from a distance of about 29,000 kilometres. set amidst the myriad stars in which we exist. We can see the southern polar ice cap, the Antarctic, along with the land mass continents of India and the Arabian Peninsula. We can also gain a clearer idea of the coverage of the planet's surface by water, in its different forms, along with our dependence on this, falling as rain from the clouds we see and the melting of ice. Fresh water forms just 2.5% of the total water on the planet.

It has been well documented that those who have visited space and the Moon have been changed by the experience. Those who journeyed to discover the Moon have written about how they really discovered the Earth, in its fragility and beauty and how the differences of race and nation seemed so inconsequential and ridiculous. It became clear to these souls that we are really all one and connected and living on the same living planet together. Its smallness becomes apparent and its majesty, along with the fact that it is alive. It is to that which we aspire on our Quest. It has been described as a 'tear drop of green' (Ron McNair, NASA astronaut on board the

Space Shuttle) and affording us a 'glimpse of divinity' (Edgar Mitchel, Apollo 14 astronaut).

It is not just the beauty and wondrousness of the Earth that struck those who viewed us from space, but what they saw around us that changed their perception of life and its purpose. That the Earth appeared so small and perfect was hugely significant along with the fact that it and we exist in the vastness of the blackness of space. The Earth has been seen to emit colour around it, notably the same chakra colours of our own energy system from red at the horizon, through orange, yellow then blues turning to black amidst the stars. Above all it is the oneness of our existence and our togetherness that those from space speak of as the overriding transformative effect of their view of the Earth and that we can learn from here.

ENERGY

We began our Quest looking out at the vista of the land before us from our high vantage point at the edge of the Canyon. We have traversed through that landscape now, both inwardly and outwardly, the one reflecting the other. We have learnt and discovered much, experienced pleasure, pain, torment and wonder, each in equal measure and again seen the reflection and cohesion between these states. Now we can view all things from a higher perspective and one that is now complete and true.

Traditional Tarot teaches us that the Fool begins his journey not knowing anything and at its conclusion knows that he knows nothing. In this way he becomes the Wisest Fool. He achieves this by a process of questioning everything he encounters. In Tarot Therapy we can apply this analogy to ourselves, coming to the realisation that what we now know, we knew all along, but just did not realise it. Our Quest has been a process of bringing this to our consciousness.

What it is that we have come to know may of course be different for each of us and only we can know what this is. Part of the process of life and its purpose, for each of us, is to move beyond our fears, limitations, faults and mistakes. We can only do this by facing each and every one as we go, admitting to them and so finding a liberation and freedom from whatever it is that is restricting us at any one time. It is only by this process of becoming honest and self-aware that we can find ourselves as we truly are and love ourselves for it. Indeed we can easily say that love of self, just as we are, is the object and goal of our quest.

Once we have truly come to love ourselves we are free. This is what the energy of this card can grant us, if we can truly say that we do love all that we have been, are and will be. This requires of course that we accept that we are not perfect; we are after all, still human and not yet re-united with the spiritual realm of existence when we leave human frailty behind. It is in self-love that we are able to move beyond and above limited thinking, fearful feeling and incorrect action. Rather than a motivation of fear we are motivated by love. When this becomes the case we can be truly untroubled by the trials and tribulations life may seek to throw at us.

Along with this comes a change in our view of who we are, along with our perspective of why we are alive at this time and the purpose and product of that life. It is here that the energy of this card can also kick in at a somewhat higher, or perhaps deeper level. It is here that we recognise the connection, link and bond between all humanity and further to the Earth herself and then the wider Universe. When we realise that there is actually no separation, either physically, emotionally, mentally and spiritually, we can cease to act only for ourselves and instead be freely motivated within and respond without, for the good of all, the health of our fellow humans and the planet and Universe to which we identify.

Of course these things remain empty words until we know their truth for ourselves. The energy from this Earth card does however contain reminders and pointers as we realise that we are now and always have been, home. It is said that there are seven main 'chakras', energy centres or points of power spread across the planet. This is again an outer reflection of that same energy system within every human being and highlights for us the connection not only between all of us but also to our home, the Earth.

When the Earth appears in your cards it can be an indication that what we are engaged in can teach us nothing more and we should come to accept that what we need, we have already. This of course has always been the case and it is only, ultimately, our fear that has prevented us seeing this from the start.

At various stages we have experienced Tornadoes, Hurricanes, Earthquakes, Volcanoes and more and still we have survived. When we look back we can see that at the root of all these things has been love, the single greatest and strongest energy in the Universe. This energy brings to us the love of self that perpetuates our existence and naturally is expressed in the person that we are and what we do. It is in this that we find the fulfilment and enlightenment with which this card is usually associated. Once this is realised, our whole life and world changes, just as it did with those astronauts on seeing our little pea of a planet from space. Transformation and enlightenment is not only possible, it is already yours and the energy here is the simple, subtle yet powerful and revelatory realisation, awareness and knowledge of this.

THE MINOR ARCANA

As we have previously seen, the structure of the Tarot reflects the structure of the human being. The Major Arcana symbolises the soul, the whole or collective human being, as the sum that is greater than its parts, in true holistic vision. Now, in the Minor Arcana, we turn to the parts of that collective.

These are broken down into four levels, shown most directly in the four Elements of classic medieval thought, but that are traceable back much further to ancient times. For our Tarot Therapy purposes, in applying the energy of the cards directly to ourselves and our lives at this causal level, we take these Elements as the constituent parts of the human being. This is easily shown thus:

SUIT	HUMAN ASPECT
EARTH	PHYSICAL
WATER	EMOTIONAL
AIR	MENTAL
FIRE	SPIRITUAL

So it is we have our four Tarot Therapy suits for the Minor Arcana. Rather than being symbolised by Pentacles, Cups, Swords and Wands respectively, we apply the elements on which these are based directly.

We start, literally, from the ground up, beginning with the formation of the physical life, just as we each do in our mother's womb. We then learn to assimilate our feelings and emotions, in the element of Water. Next comes our mental understanding and thought processes and finally their outworking in our aspirations, motivations, dreams and wishes, encapsulated in the Fire element within us, the driving force that gives us our 'get up and go'.

In energetic terms this can also be traced the other way, as a depiction of how we receive and respond to the energy we receive from the Universe. In this we can see a demonstration of the old spiritual law 'as above, so below', so central to much esoteric thought, understanding and working.

In this respect, we receive an inspiration and motivation – an inner impulse that we instinctively respond to – this is classified as the Fire element. As we integrate this into our self, we work it out in our heads; we 'get our head around it' (whatever 'it' may be for each of us), we come to an understanding and logical processing of our subject – this is the Air element. Next comes how we feel about it, what emotions does it provide us with and what we will do about it? This is the Water element. Finally we act on it, or not as the case may be. The actions we take in this way, define our being and purpose of life. This is the Earth element.

What is important to realise here is that for the human being to be healthy and whole and living a life in accordance with their highest aspirations, fulfilling their true and intended purpose in life, we must respond to the energy we receive at each level in turn. If we do not, then energy cannot do what it does naturally, which is to flow and move.

We cannot prevent the nature of energy and if we do not respond to our motivation, through laziness or whatever reason, then the energy present at that level become stuck. If we ignore or do not accept what we are capable of, then the energy has to flow somewhere else. This it does by becoming heavier in its vibration, its particles become denser and so it descends to the level of our minds. This can result in our feeling a conflict mentally. It is as if we do not 'get it' and understand what is troubling us, then this motivation lodges in our heads and starts to drive us mad. In reality this is the 'Universe', or the natural order of things, giving us an opportunity to work it out and align ourselves once more with our highest purpose and motivation.

Again, if we do not accept the messages in our heads or resist the way we are thinking in some way, then that energy will again be unable to flow in its natural method. Our heads become muddled and we cannot see our way forward. Neither can the energy. The quantum particles it consist of become a little denser and as consequence it descends further down in the human being. So it is engages with our feelings and emotions. It is then that we either respond to our emotional impulses and learn to 'follow our heart' or we become frustrated and block what we really want to do, instead following that logic we have learned to obey, rather than the intuitive knowledge of what is right for us as we should have done before we got into this mess!

Lastly in this descending journey if we do not follow what is our true heats desire and do what we want, then the energy will seek further release and expression. By now the energy particles become so dense as to manifest physically. We will receive impulses within our physical beings giving us the chance and opportunity to what we are supposed to be doing. If we have successfully and naturally absorbed the energy in its descending evolutionary path then this will not be a problem. If however we have allowed ourselves to be diverted from our intended and true purpose in life, then the energy will manifest physically in some way, in some last, desperate attempt to get us back on track.

This means that we become ill and the nature of that illness or – dis-ease' as it is holistically seen, will tell us in quite plain language what is wrong, where and why we are not functioning as we should. In this the quantum nature of the

Universe is always supportive of us and does all it can to help us fulfil our souls path and evolution. Rather than resenting the illness and physical maladies that we may experience, we need in this view to see them instead as opportunities to put right wherever it is we have lost our way and gone wrong. When we are able to correct the energy imbalance, the rest ultimately takes care of itself.

One of the functions then of Tarot Therapy and specifically here, the Minor Arcana, is that the cards can point us towards interruptions and imbalances in our energies. The lay of the cards can show us not just the level at which the imbalance lies but more specifically its nature and response required from us to put it right.

This of course is because we see and use the cards as energies themselves and if we take them in the manner described here, we can use them to our advantage, as an essential guide to the fulfilment of ourselves at any and all levels, and ultimately of our souls path and evolution.

Now that we have seen the workings of the natural energy of all human beings, as it is shown in the natural world we inhabit and are intrinsically linked to at this same energetic level, it follows that the images and information contained in the cards reflects that model. So it is that that we begin our journey through these inner and outer worlds is a simultaneous one, and begins with the realm of Earth.

COMPOUND CARDS

We come now to the traditional Court Cards of the Tarot, here called Compound Cards. As we shall see, the energy of these cards is determined by the combination of the two Elements of which it consists. In Chemistry, a compound is a substance consisting of two or more different kinds of elements. For example the Element Water as many know is known in chemistry as H20, i.e. two parts Hydrogen, one part oxygen.

Traditionally speaking the Court Cards are seen as representing the involvement or presence of people involved in the client's life or subject of reading in some form or another. The type, appearance, age and some character aspects are defined by which court card appears in the reading. In Tarot Therapy of course, this changes. As we take the cards directly from what we have come to know as their energy, we see them still in their directly elemental form and expression.

We know already that each of the four suits of Earth, Water, Air and Fire relate to the Physical, Emotional, Mental and Spiritual levels and aspects of the human being. Here we extend that a little further and see that each Compound card is really a combination of two elemental forces, or energies. In this way, each Compound card also is based on, relates to and expresses an element. There can be different ways of aligning these as a survey of Tarot decks and books will show you. In terms of the Tarot Therapy approach, the following are chosen:

TRADITIONAL TAROT	TAROT THERAPY
PAGE	EARTH
KNIGHT	FIRE
QUEEN	WATER
KING	AIR

It is then a simple step to combining the elemental ascriptions above with that of the suit. So, the Page of Pentacles of traditional Tarot becomes Earth of Earth, the Knight of Swords becomes Fire of Air, the Queen of Wands becomes Water of Fire and the King of Cups becomes Air of Water.

Each card will be described individually as we work through them, but for now we can look at how these elemental combinations essentially work. Here we must remember that cards are simply a depiction of energy. In the Compound Cards that depiction is as a combined force of two energies, each with a different emphasis, operation and effect.

Firstly, the suit or Element to which the card belongs is its foundation, its basic nature on which it relies and is supported. This could be seen as our basis of operation, our essential being and instinctive reaction – akin in some respects to the Sun Sign in astrology – our basic identity and general awareness of self. So, the Earth Compound cards will be those which are slower to act, and more methodical, grounded and realistic by way of example. The Water cards apply to those through their heart, those of deep, impassioned feelings fraught sometimes with sensitivity and caring. The Air cards will be the intellectuals of the bunch, those that must pre-plan and understand all before them, then be able to analyse it afterwards. Lastly the Fire cards will be those quick to act, eager to progress, impatient and potentially explosive.

Of course this does not necessarily mean that someone of this type is bound to appear when these cards appear in your reading. In Tarot Therapy it tells us that there is energy active within us that may cause or require us to be any of these aspects – i.e. cautious and slow-moving for Earth, feel our way with Water, think ahead with Air and go for it with Fire!

If we then look at how this basic approach, level and manner of being is or needs to be expressed, we see this through which individual card it is – whether the traditional Page,

Knight, Queen or King, but again Earth, Fire, Water or Air respectively.

So the suit to which the card belongs is its foundation, the outer nature if you will and its inner expression and manifestation the other element. So the Page of Pentacles becomes Earth of Earth. This energy is then one that we receive slowly and gradually and brings to us stability and security. Once we have received this as our foundation (inner), so we can then proceed with equal caution and patience (outer).

Continuing the examples from the above paragraph, the Knight of Swords becomes Fire of Air. Here we establish ideas, understanding, logic and plans (inner). This is then acted upon as soon as we are clear and we give our all, without doubt or pause. We are highly motivated and act with fervour (outer).

Our Queen of Wands becomes Water of Fire. Here the motivations within are strong and we change or quit for no-one, being fervent and full of vigour (inner). This is responded to with an emotional passion, met with an equally strong force, with a care that will hurt no-one without denying or diluting our beliefs (outer)

Lastly, the King of Cups becomes Air of Water. This is someone that cares deeply and is possessed of sensitivity and understanding of self and thence others (inner). This is related in eloquent and often poetic terms and explained and expressed logically (outer).

I have illustrated the nature of the Compound Cards in Tarot Therapy as these twin energies and shown a basic sample of how they would be seen in people, in order to help you adjust from the way in which they are used in Tarot Therapy. This does not mean however that they are limited to this in Tarot Therapy. What we must now do is to expand our understanding of the energy of the Compound cards to realise that they, as with all cards, are energies and energy simply is.

Your job as Tarot Therapist is really to describe the nature of that energy and, using the cards that also appear in the reading, determine how it might be experienced in the client and their life. This may, or may not be through a person, whether themselves or another. It is about understanding the nature of the Elements and their workings, both within us as human beings and the natural world. As mentioned above, we are part of the world and so it is hoped that study and use of the Minor Arcana cards here will establish and aid this understanding.

EARTH ELEMENT

The Earth element relates to the physical realm, the everyday aspect of our existence. This regards what we do with our bodies; how we live as the outworking of our souls' intent – or not as the case may be.

When we give a Tarot Therapy reading, the cards from Earth tell us about the expression of our energy at this level. They will show us the relevance of our actions as they relate to our path in life. The Earth supports us all, just as our individual bodies are the vehicle for our soul.

In these cards we trace the path from the beginnings of a physical life, as a Seed, and follow its evolutionary journey to completion and Hibernation. We take as our model for this what is known as the BBCH scale, which is the phenological (the scientific study of biological life) study of plant and animal life. This are used in a number of scientific and agricultural disciplines and is a decimal system, meaning it is divided and classified in ten stages. These of course equate to each one of the ten numbered cards of the Earth suit in the Tarot Therapy deck.

The Earth cards tell us the condition and use of our physical energy. These may have their expression and manifestation in our work and what we do each day. This can include all tangible phenomena we encounter in our lives, including health, money, possessions and all levels of materiality. This is quite normal in traditional Tarot but we should stress again here that the Tarot Therapy approach focusses on the energy behind or within these things. This is causal to that everyday reality and so by working with this energy we can learn to create and manifest the reality we want, as that which helps us grow and be the best we can be.

As we follow the system of energy descending as described in the introduction to the Minor Arcana, we can see the Earth cards as depictions of the energy as it outworks through our bodies and finds its expression and manifestation in what we do, all day every day. This is the lowest, densest formulation of divine energy, as it all is. The energy we speak of may be showing itself to us in our lives as, for example, a need to be cautious with one's spending, but this is still a manifestation of an energy that is sacred, or divine.

In the approach of Tarot Therapy we see all life is sacred and since the energy is alive, it could be said to be life itself, it is also therefore sacred. So do not mistake this 'lowest' form of energy as base or below any other form of energy – it is still an aspect of the divine, or sacred and as such should be treated with the same regard as the energy depicted in any other card, be it The Fool, The Sun or any other Minor Arcana card.

So these cards can then be seen as determining the extent to which are fulfilling our mission on Earth at this time, or perhaps better put, whether we are being the best we can be, fulfilling our potential, destiny and what could be seen as the sacred plan for us. For us this simply means that we have to work hard at it, once we know what 'it' is and these cards show us how we can do that.

EARTH

1 - SEED

BACKGROUND

We begin our Earthly journey with a Seed. It is from the Seed that most growth comes, whether literally or symbolically, in the natural and human kingdoms. The Seed contains the potential for physical growth but requires an external force to act upon it in order for this manifestation to happen. Of and by itself, it is just a seed.

That external force is Germination. The most common example of this is the sprouting of the seedling that comes from within the Seed, as we shall see. In a more general sense however, germination can imply the process by which anything expands into something greater than which it is.

All fully developed seeds contain an embryo, from which the seedling sprouts. Some plants produce a number of seeds, called 'empty seeds' that lack embryos and never sprout. Most seeds also go through a period of dormancy when there is no active growth. This occurs when there is no external environment favourable to produce that growth.

Successful germination depends on both internal and external factors. The most important of these are temperature, water and oxygen. We can easily equate these with the remaining three elements of our quarter, being Fire, Water and Air respectively. There can be much more to it than this of course and different plants require these things in different degrees and conditions but this is the basic essence of germination.

The Water that needs to be received for germination must be relative to the dry weight of the seed – to moisture rather than soak them. This is called 'imbition', as in 'to imbibe'. This leads to the swelling, then breaking of the seed coat. Oxygen is required for metabolism. This comes from within the soil, requiring the seed to be placed at the right depth. Lastly, the correct range of temperature needs to be maintained for germination, which can vary depending on the type of seed. Typically this is above freezing but not over hot – a pleasant atmosphere really. It should also be noted that it is as this stage where there is most vulnerability to injury, stress and disease. From above, many seeds also require light, again not a high intensity and not continual, like day and night.

Many seeds enter a period of dormancy until the above combination of forces is present. Then the seed coat breaks and the seedling is produced, which takes us to the next card of this suit.

DESCRIPTION

The Seeds we see here are that of the Sunflower. Of course there are a huge number and variety of seeds to choose from, but I have chosen Sunflower for two reasons. Firstly, many people are familiar with a sunflower seed and we can eat them, in various forms. Secondly, the symbolism - that it will one day grow into a beautiful Sunflower, in turn producing hundreds more seeds - fits well with the symbolism of the Sun itself. In the Major Arcana, the Sun becomes a symbol of the goal of the Seeker's Quest, the whole, complete self and soul and the home to which we all belong and will one day return.

The image is set within a green outline, (as are all the Earth cards) to symbolise the Earth, the element that is this suit. There is also a brown hue within this green, to remind us that it is of the Earth herself, as that which we are all dependent on and that gives rise to the physical aspect of all life shared with and part of her.

ENERGY

This is the foundation of life, the essence from which all life springs forth. This is symbolised here as the Seed. All action begins with a step and this is the first one. Each of the number One cards for the suits are the essence and pure energy of their Element. Here we have the seed, as that which from all physicality emerges.

We note that the seed is not the life itself, but is the potential for it. This tells us when we see this card that we have this potential within us at that time. However, we must then create the right conditions to respond to this potential. Just as the right balance of environmental conditions is required for the Seed to sprout, so we must add emotion, and ambition to bring our potential to life.

These must be in balance and proportionate to each other. It is when these four combined factors blend that we can turn the potential to action. The energy of this card tells us that with this correct structure, anything is possible and we are capable of anything. All we must do is achieve that favourable balance of forces within us.

That there is a period of dormancy with some Seeds tells us that we may need to pause before we act and that what may be required in the now (when this card appears in a reading) is to look to see our feelings about our project or plan, what we think about this and what our motivation is. Once these are clear then the need is to make a beginning, however small. Nothing happens without effort so unless we make some physical, active action, then then energy of potential and possibility here will remain dormant.

As we see with the Seed, these things must be applied within, at the emotional, mental and spiritual levels within us, then acted on without, in order for us to achieve the highest and best we can possible be. This energy brings us to the point of beginning.

2 - ROOT
BACKGROUND

The part of a plant that emerges first from the Seed is the embryonic root, known as the primary or radicle root. This allows the seedling to become anchored into the ground and to begin absorbing water. As it does this, a shoot emerges from the seed, but for now we are focussed on the root. We should also note here that some roots can be aerial, or above ground. In this way we can further define a root as the non-leaf, non-nodes bearings part of a plant's body.

Roots have four main functions – absorption of water and inorganic nutrients, anchoring and supporting the plant in to the ground, storage of nutrients, vegetative reproduction. The roots become elongated, pushing the tip further into the ground. Gradually these cells continue to divide and mature into root tissues. During the germination of the seed, it is a process called gravitropism that causes the root to grow downwards and the shoot to grow upward – each according to their instinctive nature.

It is known that some roots sense their physical environment in which to grow, including light sensitivity and any physical barriers. Because of this, roots will grow in the direction where the required combination of air, nutrients and water exist to enable its growth and progress.

Root growth is classed into two main areas – primary growth being the length or elongation of the roots and secondary growth which encompasses its width or diameter. Each root has tissues that can be classified in the order they are found within the root. Each root has three layers; the Epidermis, its outermost layer and protective covering; the Cortex, the storage area for food and water and the Endodermis, the inner boundary of the Cortex that prevents water moving into it.

The innermost area of the root contains vascular tissue which fittingly here is comprised of two cells – xylem and phloem cells. Xylem cells dissolve minerals and water into the stem and Phloem cells carry food from photosynthesis into the root. A root is composed of several regions of development. These blend from one into the next from bottom to top.

DESCRIPTION

We continue with the growth of the Sunflower seed in our image here. What we see is a depiction of the primary root of a sunflower seed. Here it is seen in its natural habitat, i.e. the Earth, of course. What we can notice as we look at the image is the thin protuberance of the root in contrast to the oval shape of the Seed. There is something of a reminder in this of the male and female respectively.

We can also note the twists and turns of the root as it grows, adapting and responding to obstacles it may encounter in its path and as its response to seeking the sources of food, water and light that it needs.

ENERGY

With the One of Earth we saw the need for responding to the potential energy symbolised by the Seed. Here we see something of the result of our investment into that energy. So from the Seed we have the root – the one item becomes two, not by division but by the natural outworking and response to the energy and life-force it possesses. What is clear is that in order for something that is lasting and of worth to grow, we must first put down roots. This gives us something to draw upon as well as establishing our project or whatever it is we are engaged in, into the real world.

We have seen that some plants can establish roots that begin above ground. So it is we are visible by our actions and these must be rooted in reality, based on truth and solidity if they are to last and become established and grow. We have seen that function of our roots is to provide anchoring and support, so here we can learn that we must give time and effort to looking at and acting upon the basic level of what we wish to manifest and achieve. Roots also provide storage for food and nutrients so as we progress with a project we must ensure we have the necessary tools for the job, both within and without ourselves. This can be in terms of ability, function and whatever is required to sustain this and ourselves, long term. This produces a natural, knock-on effect, in the plant of more tissues and roots, and in us of the consequences of our actions. The natural tendency of energy being to flow as we have seen means that what we invest now in these early stages is of vital importance in determining what we will produce and experience as a result.

It is this flow and natural evolution that brings about the forward movement of what we do and are. Roots extend further down into the ground and so as we take care to supply ourselves with what and all that is required so we become more secure in it and strengthened by it. The essential thing here is that we become and remain grounded, by whatever means is necessary to achieve this. This can take the form of becoming fully in the world and taking a conscious, active role within it, in whatever way we choose. It may be that we need to ground our own energy and continue to do this, on a daily basis, by means of a grounding meditation or suchlike.

We have seen the three layers of the root – the outer, the inner and the storage in-between. For us this tells us that the energy is needed to be protected at its innermost level, in other words our core reason for being. This is fed by what we store – what we have within us – what we are made of, in different levels and ways. It is this that produces the natural growth, with the elongation and further establishment of the root system – in other words the support network which we must now provide.

When these factors are created and nurtured, we find that we are responding to the energy we receive with this card in such a way that more energy flows and is produced. In plant terms this means that the energy is caused to flow upwards, as a result of the downward flow of the root, and a shoot is produced, this being the third stage and so the next card.

3 - SHOOT

BACKGROUND

Once the primary root is well-embedded in the ground and receiving all it requires the natural produce is the shoot. Shoot refers essentially to any new plant growth and they include stems (an essential part of the shoot, not the shoot itself), along with flowering buds and leaves. In our process of growth the one Seed became two with a root and is now three with a Shoot. Of importance to our process here is that the shoot is that which grows upwards, unlike the downward movement of the root.

Within the Shoot there is the stem. The stem provides an axis for buds, fruits and leaves, called nodes. These shoots are vulnerable to prey and can become a source of food for small animals and suchlike. There are many things that want the goodies within! These shoots are vulnerable when they have not developed what is called their secondary cell wall, meaning they are easier to chew and digest. It is only when a shoot completes its cell wall that is has a hard and tough structure and so inedible to others, in the main. The nodes are the nodule, bulging parts of the shoot from which other shoots emerge.

One of the four main functions of the shoot, or stem, is the production of new living tissue, the others being support for flowers, leaves and fruits; transport of fluids and storage of nutrients. In other words it does all that is required for future growth.

DESCRIPTION

Here we see three newly formed shoots emerging above ground from the sunflower seed. Such is its strength and power to be created and grow that we can see it has forced the Seed itself up, which it now utilises to some degree, in this early and vulnerable stage of its young life, as a protective shield.

There is something beautiful and perfect as we look at the emergence of any new life and it is indeed a thing of wonder. It is perhaps in that vulnerability that we marvel as we notice too, the lushness and freshness of its green colouring. We can also see the beginnings of a leaf formation on the shoot furthest from us, as it seeks to shed the shell that was the seed.

ENERGY

We know from numerology that the energy of the number Three is essentially a creative, productive one. The energy here is the natural outworking of the two forces combining to produce a third, as so many things in nature do – humans included of course. Here the absorption of nutrients in the root causes the shoot to emerge from the Seed and appear above ground. This creative energy is what we are offered in terms of the energy we receive from this card.

The essential question to pose ourselves now is what will we do with that energy? We are being given and indeed have generated for ourselves a force of creativity, an energy that will cause us to act. We need to ensure now that our actions go towards producing what we intend and to the very best of our ability. This can also create an upsurge in confidence and expertise in what we do, which should also be utilised and put to the good.

We saw above the importance of the role of the stem, reminding ourselves that the stem is within the shoot, is a part of it, not the whole of it. The nodes tell us that there can be critical times and situations we may encounter now as we work with the energy we have produced. As we respond to the energy of this card there can be a need to examine what

214

we are doing to determine if there are important things we have either over-looked, put-off or avoided, or are fearful of doing and strike out and do them! This can be a time not for fear but of joyful response. We could in many senses, look at this card as a time of quality-control. Symbolically speaking from our analysis of the Shoot, if the stems are not right at these critical points, then the quality, durability and splendour of what is finally produced – the buds, leaf and fruit - will not be as good or as useful.

We can also learn from the vulnerability of the shoot to being eaten by predators. It is when we begin to put ourselves 'out there' in the world, with whatever we are doing that we can become vulnerable. This may be to criticism but more so at this Earth level, to others stealing our produce and taking away what is good for themselves. We can learn then of the need for protection and safety, amidst the produce that is going on now.

In spiritual growth I am always teaching that we must first become grounded, like our Root, then connected above, to our highest potential and purpose. What matters then is that we are protected, secure in ourselves and strong. There are always those opposing forces in life, which may manifest in those around us who may seek to extract for themselves what we are doing, so ensure you have whatever necessary protection is required to prevent this now. This energy can enable you to have this.

Future growth being the predominant function of the shoot and indeed a symbol of it here, we need to realise that with the energy of this card we are at a stage where what we do in the present creates our future reality, and ask ourselves what we want to manifest.

215

4 - LEAF

BACKGROUND

We are now at a more recognisable stage that most people would see with any plant or natural growth, when the leaves appear and it can be seen as 'established'. This is the 4th card in our suit and it is noticeable that stem elongation has stopped by the fourth week of production of the plant.

Leaves originate from the apex of the shoot. Cells divide and mark the very beginning of a leaf. These cells enlarge and form a structure known as the leaf buttress. The leaf which then grows is specialised for the process of photosynthesis. Many leaves are thin and flat, maximising the surface area exposed to light, which promotes better function when it comes to the photosynthesis process.

Externally, leaves are commonly arranged on a plant so as to expose themselves to the light as efficiently as possible, avoiding shading each other. Plants will however adapt to their conditions, since survival comes first. Internally, leaves are also organised for maximum exposure for photosynthesis. For some, this means that they need to regulate the amount of light they absorb due to excessive heat or for protection against being eaten, available nutrients, humidity, cold, drought and so on. Leaves will often produce a formation known as a rosette to help with protection, leaving the leaves to come away easily but leaving the root intact.

The shape and structure of leaves will vary considerably from plant to plant of course to provide for maximum adaptation to all the above factors. Considerable changes can occur as the leaf and the overall plant matures. Storage of food and water is an important function of the leaf, again making them a vital source of in the diet of other species, both animal and human.

Leaves are therefore a heavy investment on the part of the host plant. Many come equipped with a necessary armoury, both for protection and long-term survival, such as thorns. Once their job is done, typically in the autumn, the leaf is shed, taking its nutrients to the ground beneath, to further the production of this and future plants.

DESCRIPTION

Here we stay with the sunflower and we see the emergence from the previous Shoot, into fully formed leaves. In our image here we can see four leaves, in keeping with the number for this card and its energy.

We can see that two of these leaves are fully-formed and complete, while a further two are newly-formed. This fits with the process of numerology, giving us something of the energetic structure of the energy here. The balance of forces that forms with the Two, when multiplied by itself produces further growth and leads to a more stable existence. As we have seen the production and formation of leaves equips the plants with the necessary forces it needs for sustenance and survival, in short the outer establishment of itself and its life.

ENERGY

In the journey of our everyday existence and manifestation which this suit covers and guides us through, we have reached the stage of manifestation of that which we are striving for and to achieve.

The appearance of the Leaf in our cards tells us that we need to strike out into the world with our project and our endeavours. If we have followed the necessary growth pattern through, we will have established strong roots, well-embedded within us and our lives, then nurtured the Shoot that we produced through to formation of our leaf now. This being the case, we have seen that the leaf forms so as to

217

obtain and provide the maximum efficiency for its intended purpose. This tells us that we have achieved the necessary means within us to succeed and thrive.

Leaves play a lead role in the storage and supply of food and drink for the plant. This is indicative of our need now to draw on the reserves we have within and without us to focus on the supply of what we need. We strengthen from within and maintain those resources until we need to call on them. The energy here is one of establishment and consolidation. It is shielding our defences and strengthening our boundaries and barriers so we are able to create stored within that will led us through what is to come.

We have seen both the internal and external function that leaves have and here the energy is the same for us – we are required to create and consolidate within ourselves the steadfastness and resilience we need to take our product, our endeavours and aims out into the world, in order for the fulfilment of our lives and selves. We can take the energy coming to us with this card to ensure a firm foundation and basis for our present and then future existence.

That leaves adapt to their structure and surroundings tells us that we may need to do the same. If we drink fully of this energy this will not be a problem. If we have strong foundations established now we can twist and turn as circumstances require and still be strong enough to produce the best result.

Of course we need to ensure that all this strengthening does not result in a fear of moving forward. Consolidate yes, but supply from within so it leads outward. If we are not sure to keep the energy moving now we can become stuck and without realising it a prisoner of our own making. This can manifest in boredom and a lack of challenge upon which to thrive.

If we continue to seek to strive for filling in behind us as we go we are building upon what we have achieved so far with determination, protection and power that will, literally as we move to the next card, flower.

5 - BUD
BACKGROUND

We come now to the stage in the growth of plants life, which we are following with the Sunflower, but that can be applied across all vegetative species, when the first flower (or fruit) buds appear. Whilst we give this card the title of Bud, since it is more readily understood, the correct phenological term goes under the much better word Inflorescence.

An Inflorescence is then a group or cluster of flowers that are arranged on a main branch or stem. Specifically it refers to the part of the seed plant or shoot where the flowers are formed, the title of our card Bud here being a reference to the budding of flowers. The stem that holds the inflorescence is called the peduncle, with the stalk of each single flower called the pedicel.

We should note here that a feature of the process of inflorescence is that it varies from plant species to species, there being no general consensus that defines it. The main groups are distinguished by their branching, and the intersections these make. A further point of note is that inflorescence is characterised by the different arrangement of the flower buds, the order in which they bloom and how the flower clusters are arranged.

The foliage is often different from the vegetative part of the plant, differences being something of a theme at this stage of growth in the natural world. Leaves associated with this part of the plant are called a Bract. Bracts serve a variety of purposes, including protection of the budding flowers and attraction of pollination. Where there are unequal growth rates in the plant, it can be common for the plants organs to grow out of their expected position, which is process called Metatopy.

DESCRIPTION

Here we see the sunflower caught at the moment of its budding. The full beauty and splendour of its flower is not yet seen but we can see something of the colour in the bud which is as yet curled up, awaiting the moment to unleash its display to the world.

At this stage, as we have seen above, anything is possible. The Sunflower here is about to embark on its biggest process of change. The previous four leaves now are beneath the growth that has occurred since and the flower in bud has been produced above them. The flower has literally, branched out. In the centre of the bud we can see a circular pattern and we can determine that the outer flowering when it happens will move out in all directions.

ENERGY

The energy that comes with this card can best be summed up in one word – change. The process of the bud about to burst into flower is one of exponential change. Previously with the four we received energy of consolidation and foundation and now we release the energy that was received and stored.

This can be a process that brigs with some fear, since change can be uncomfortable and somewhat unpredictable, since at this stage we do not know the result of these changes. They are however, inevitable and contain the promise, like the flower, of producing something wonderful and beautiful.

We have seen that the budding process, if we call it that for ease, varies from species to species. This tells us that we need now to 'branch out', more on our or at least by embracing our individuality. We need to go and make our own way in the world and embrace and be proud of what we have achieved so far. In putting ourselves 'out there' we do now know what may happen, but for now we need to display our product and self to the world.

There can be a need with this energy to accept that branching out is required if we are to reach our fullest potential. This may manifest in some unseen events. We have seen that part of the function of the flower clusters is to attract pollinators – those that can contribute and bring something that helps us to thrive. This may means that our energy now needs to be more open. This may mean taking a risk in what we our doing a little, but opening ourselves to the help and guidance of others. Sometimes it can be hard to accept that we need help, we cannot go it totally alone and this can be risky. If we are brave enough however, with the energy here we can produce something startling and beyond all expectation – this can be both within ourselves as well as outwardly in what we do in the world, this being the level the Earth suit governs.

6 - FLOWER
BACKGROUND

Flowering plants, known as Angiosperms, account for 90% of all known plant species, with more being added to the list annually. Each family of plant species has its own characteristics and all important food source plants are flowering. Flowering plants are distinguishable from other plants species by various developmental and anatomical features. Obviously they produce flowers, these being a series of closely spaced leaves designed to facilitate pollination – sepals and petals. They also bear the plants organs of sexual reproduction – stamens pistils.

Many scientists agree that the function of the flower was also to attract insects, birds and animals to carry the resultant seeds and fruits in order to propagate the species. This is also seen as the reason for the bright and beautiful colours of flowers. Pollinators are attracted to individual plants by colour, scent and nectar. What is clear is that the primary and overall function of the flower is sexual reproduction and pursuance of life.

Flowers vary hugely in their form and appearance, to provide the most reliable characteristics for establishing relationships and reproduction. Most flowers produce both male and female cells, these being microspores and macros spores respectively. The former are borne in the stamen, the latter in the carpel. It is these that the petals serve to protect, the outer leaves in turn protecting the bud and flower.

It should also be noted in our brief study here that flowering plants are fund in almost every habitat from forest, grasslands, sea margins and desert. Angiosperms encompass a huge variety of life forms, including trees, herbs, aquatics and bulbs. About a quarter of all known plant species come from three families alone – orchids, legumes and sunflowers, our choice here for just one of many reasons.

DESCRIPTION

Here we see our chosen species, the Sunflower, as it emerges into its glory. We have seen above the function and role of the flower of plants species, but here we can bask and glow in the promise of its majesty and splendour.

We can see something of the Sun in its appearance, in its circular formation as well as its colouring. This reminds us of the Sun card again, acting as it does for so long in the Major Arcana as the goal of the Quest of life upon which we are all engaged.

We can see that progression above the leaves we have already encountered on our Earth journey, manifesting here as the flower. We can notice the protective surrounding of the yellow petals, these acting as a bright beacon to attract those that would come to it. The many seeds to be produced from all this can then be safely carried in the central pod we can see at the heart of the sunflower, rather like the centre of our own selves and the centre of our quest at this Earth level too.

ENERGY

We have seen that the plant expresses its productivity through its sexual reproduction, encompassed in its flower. This tells us that the major energy we receive with this card is one of a need for self-expression – to act on what we are producing within us. Of course whether this manifests in a sexual encounter or expression may be of our own choosing and making, so long as it is appropriate and not abusive in any way.

We have seen that the necessary layers of protection and safety must first be in place for the flower to appear. This shows us that in order for us to express ourselves fully and freely, to the greatest effect and in the best possible manner, we must first feel safe. We may need to look at our boundaries now and assess whether we our actions create the necessary sense of safety and solidity from the structure of ourselves and lives.

We may also have a need now to look at our exactly what we are manifesting in our lives – what are we doing in the outer, everyday world? Does this reflect us at our best and do we gain satisfaction from it? The flower is a plants most beautiful expression and display so this energy asks us whether we too reflect these things. This can also cause us to look at ourselves and ask whether we see our own beauty and allow this to show on the outside. This may be in a physical way but also in terms of what we do with our time in the day.

That flowering plants are found in almost every habitat on Earth tells us that we may need to look at where we find ourselves at this point in our lives. This does not necessarily mean geographically but in terms of an assessment of what we have achieved so far and what we wish to do or where we wish to go, next. This cards energy calls us to look at what we have achieved and where we wish to put our efforts to take us to where we wish to go next and what we wish to do, to further fulfil ourselves on our outer path in the everyday world.

7 - POLLEN
BACKGROUND

Pollen production is a critical part of the reproduction process of a plant. Pollen is produced in the male, stamen of the plant and is a powder of grains that produces the sperm seeds of plants. The pollen is then spread by the wind, via water or by insects or birds, dependent on the type of pollen produced by a specific plant. Pollen distributed by insects is typically sticky and produces a scent so as to be attractive to insects. Approximately 90% of all plants rely on these external forces for their successful pollination.

Pollen grains have a hard coat that protects the sperm cells during their movement from the male to the female part of the plant. Pollen grains can come in a wide variety of shapes and sizes, dependent on the individual plant. They are comprised of two types of cells, vegetative and generative. Within the generative cells there are two nuclei, one of which produces the pollen tube.

When pollen grains land on the stigma of a flower, it germinates. A pollen tube is produced through the tissues of the flower until it reaches the ovary. The nucleus within the pollen grain, its male part, passes along the pollen tube and joins with the nucleus of the female ovule. This process is fertilisation. Pollen tubes respond to a combination of chemical, electrical and mechanical stimulus for their growth, which comes in a pulsating pattern rather than steady growth and they grow only at their very tip. The pollen tube is basically a passageway for the sperm cells to do their job of pollination.

Plants can be either self-pollinating or cross pollinating. Self-pollination is when the pollen attached to the necessary part of the same plant for fertilisation to occur, which is known to produce weaker plants. Cross-pollination is when pollen is transferred by one of the above factors to a different plant of the same species, thereby continuing its genetic line and ensuring successful survival and progress.

DESCRIPTION

Here we see a close-up of sunflower pollen tubes emerging within the fully opened flower. The open pores of this central section of the sunflower attract bees for their pollen, thereby spreading and sustaining life. The remainder of the image is of course comprised of the sunflower leaves.

We should remember here that the sunflower is simply our chosen plant species but that there are a great many plants in the flowering plant kingdom that all produce pollen tubes and that these vary a great deal in size, shape and formation. It is the process of pollination that is relevant for our card here and this image encapsulates that in this beautiful and almost symmetrical way.

ENERGY

At this stage in the life-cycle of plants we witness the process of how the plant reaches out to ensure its' continued, developing existence. It has reached a stage in its life where its impulse is to go forth and multiply! Similarly, the energy we receive when this card appears in our reading is one that prompts and even compels us to move forward, to strike beyond our known, established and safe boundaries. It is a case now of living rather than existing.

In order to do this we must strive to be better and more than we have been. The energy here calls us to look to the future and determine not only how we will flourish and develop who we are and what we are doing, but how we will achieve this. It is this that the pollination process guides us to do within ourselves and our own lives.

It may well be that at this stage we must seek the help, guidance or abilities of another, just as many plants require that external agent of wind, water or insect to extend its' self and life. Our own abilities may have got us this far and we may have a solid, established degree of independence that will get us through our lives but for a further fulfilment we may now need to seek to join with another, not necessarily on a physical level, but at the level of the practical in our lives, this being the realm of the Earth suit. Of course this can be extended to the physical in a sexual way as well.

The process of self and cross pollination in plants tells us that if we choose to continue to 'go it alone' in life and not join and merge with other and their abilities may result in a weaker state of self and achievement in the world. By seeking out those who are compatible with us however, we can produce a result that is 'greater than the sum of its parts' as the holistic paradigm has it.

This cards energy tells us that we have all the necessary abilities and skills required for who we wish to be in the world and what we wish to do and achieve within it. Now is the time to develop these things to their next stage. We must move forward if we are not only to survive but flourish, as we are most certainly called to do now. Contained within us, like our symbolic pollen, is what is required to get there – it is protected by our past shell of achievements, but it is up to us now to reach beyond these limitations and become more than this.

8 - FRUIT
BACKGROUND

The fruit of a plant is formed by the enlargement of its flower parts, hence it following on from our previous cards of Flowers and Pollen. The Fruit is frequently a seed-dispersal tool that attracts animals (and humans) to eat or otherwise disturb it, thereby scattering the seeds it contains. Many seeds will of course not survive but the practice and method is successful enough to endure.

It is the female parts of the flower that develop into the fruit. After fertilisation from the Pollen, the ovules within the plant become seeds and the ovary wall then forms the rest of the fruit. The different types of fruit, fleshy, dry and hard are created dependent on the three layers of the ovary wall. As the ovules develop into seeds, the ovary begins to ripen and the ovary wall (called the pericarp) then become either fleshy, as with berries, or hard as with nuts.

The simplest fruits are those that form from a single flower with one or more carpels (its female parts). Plants with multiple fruits can form from many different flowers, so there is a wide variety of fruits from an equally wide variety of flowers. Fruits are classed in this way as simple, aggregate, multiple or accessory, indicating their origin. Fruits are classed as consisting of three parts, the skin, middle and inner. In many species, these three layers fuse together as the fruit ripens and cannot be distinguished. Some fruits release their seeds immediately while others rely on the process of ripening and decay to do so.

When we think of the term fruit, we immediately think of apples, oranges, strawberries, peaches and so on. These are the fleshy, seed-associated part of the plant that can be eaten in their raw state, whether tasting sweet or sour. However, botanically and equally important to our way of working here is that the fruit of the plant can be many others things, such as bean pods, corn kernels, wheat grains and even spores from fungus. This reminds us that the primary function of the fruit is to disperse its seeds.

Often external factors are required for the successful dispersion of the seeds. These can again be wind, water or animals, again emphasising the interdependence and exchange of all life in the natural world. Some of these take the amazing from of tiny parachutes (as with dandelions) to ensure sufficient dispersal and maximum opportunity for propagation, or the 'helicopter blades' of trees such as the maple and elm.

DESCRIPTION

We have seen previously that the sunflower is one of those flowering plants that are classed as inflorescent, meaning that they are formed from a cluster of flowers, the flowering head of which we see in close-up detail here.

This being the case, the fruit of the sunflower is the many packets at the centre of the head, rather than the seed itself. These are known as florets in the case of the sunflower, which we see here from the shading of bright yellow at the outside to the green in the centre.

We should also note that the formation of these seed packets is in a spiral formation, and are really quite beautiful, almost forming a mosaic pattern. It is known from studies now that there are so many spiral formations in the natural world, not least of course our own DNA, the building blocks of life. The links between us and the natural world we inhabit are actually far more intrinsic, inter-dependent and primal than we perhaps allow for.

ENERGY

When we examine the energy of this card we can begin with the perhaps predictable but accurate surmise that here we see and experience the fruits of our labours. Whilst we can perhaps sit back just a little and admire the results and what we have produced we should also remind ourselves now that the primary function of the fruit is not only survival, but also continued existence and propagation. In this way we can receive an energy now that propels us to move onwards and look at how we need to keep developing, multiplying, moving onwards and upward with what we do. It is not enough to simply rest on our laurels and think that we have achieved everything we can and will do now. This is the Eight, still not the end of the process.

This energy can then indicate a time when we are still or need to be strongly motivated to develop, to hone our skills and expertise, even to fine-tune that which we do. It offers us a chance to shine, above and beyond the norm and to excel at who we are and what we do. It is a time of going deeper and starting to move towards perfection.

We have seen that fruits are classed as either simple, aggregate, multiple or accessory. This tells us that we need to look now at our state of being in the world and consider whether we have achieved what we set out to by ourselves, and what the involvement with others has been. It is said we come into and go out of this world alone, but really we are dependent on at least two others for our being, mother and father of course and in many ways on the interaction and input of others as we grow. The energy of this card then calls us to look at our state of independence and interdependence and to use these things, not just for our own, selfish growth, but the good of the whole, just as the plant disperses its seed via its fruit for its continued and developing existence and its reliance in a great many cases on external factors and other beings.

This is a time for looking at the detail of who we are and what we do, the seed within, as well as the effect this has upon the whole. This could be expressed another way on the environmental maxim we can learn so much from – 'think locally, act globally'. This energy can bring to us the direct realisation that who and what we are within manifests and has effect without, both locally and globally.

Lastly here, we have seen that many plants evolve wondrous methods of dispersing their seeds, in the parachutes and helicopter attachments mentioned above. This tells us that we need to adapt to the ever changing environment of our lives, again both physically within our being and externally with what we choose to do. It is only by this continual development and evolution that we will succeed and achieve and be the best we possibly can.

9 - HARVEST
BACKGROUND

We have seen that the fruit of a plant grows so as to disperse the seeds it has worked so hard to produce. We have also seen how the plant is to a large degree dependent on external environmental and animals factors for those seeds to be dispersed, a process we can now call harvest and examine a little here. In order to avoid simple waste, nature abhorring a vacuum, the plant must do all it can to attract those that will want its seed and carry them further afield for distribution. In other words, harvest is essential for life; it is the culmination and high-point of its life-cycle, rather than the flower as one might think. This may look and smell beautiful but alone is not enough for continued survival and existence.

First we must observe and be aware that fruit will only ripen while it is still attached to its parent plant. Injury can cause an early ripening and consequently missing out on the pure ripeness possible. Similar to the humans, plants owe their fruit ripening to a surge of hormones. The hormone within plants is called ethylene, which causes the cells walls, previously used for protection and solidity of form, to soften. The pectin, the glue that holds the plants' cells together is also dissolved by ethylene. This results in a mingling of compounds that creates the fruits juices and soften it.

The flavour increases inside the ripening fruit. The trick is to harvest when the fruit is as its peak, which we catch here with the Nine of Earth, that high point between pollination and rot. Again similar to humans, fruits consist of 65 to 95 percent water. It is when these fluid reserves are exhausted that decay begins. Therefore the ripeness of the fruit is affected by its environment, especially high temperatures and humidity, as well as injury, such as bruising or skin breaks.

Fruit is also subject to a respiration process, which cannot be stopped without damage to the produce. Respiration depends on a good air supply and if this is not received in the correct quantity and quality, ageing occurs and the fruit quickly decays. The process of water loss also continues after harvest, requiring most conditions for best maintenance.

DESCRIPTION

Following our chosen Sunflower species, we find it is very helpful when it comes to telling us when it is the correct time to harvest its abundant seeds. The plant hangs its head and the now underside turns yellow then brown and the petals fall off, making it easy to determine ripeness in this particular plant.

The Sunflower is the epitome of the spirit of giving from the abundance it produces. Birds perch on the stalks to help themselves to the seeds, along with fowl, squirrel and many others that collect and gather that seeds that are then dropped to the ground.

We can clearly see from the image here, the principle of harvest. Stretching from where we observe into the far distance is a field of sunflowers, all either ready for harvest or having given of their seed in the quest for continuance of survival and life.

ENERGY

Sunflowers can be seen as the epitome of the abundance that can be found in nature and particularly here, plants that bear fruit. As such they symbolise for us that abundance and the height of produce in the energy of this card. As we have seen the result of this energy is the maximum amount of outer produce that we have been able to manifest from all the effort and toil previously invested.

234

We have seen that it is a matter of correct timing as to when to harvest for maximum effect. When this card appears, it is usual that this time is now. We have seen that to delay is to miss the peak and the energy of this card brings with it the possibility of the best and peak of our own achievement and the energy required to go with this.

This energy brings with it physical energy and manifestation at its best and at our own peak. We may have been bruised and perhaps even a little battered along the way, but if we act now, then the effects of those injuries can be minimised and we can reap the rewards of our own harvest. This cards energy then tells us that we need to act and act swiftly. The energy of the card gives us what we need.

The giving nature of the sunflower especially, but of all fruits, tells us that this is a time to release and out our there what we have been working on and achieving. It may be that this has previously been for us and this is as it should be. Now however, as we have reached our peak, it is time for release and sharing. We have seen previously the interdependent nature of plants for their survival and growth and here there is no exception to this. This tells us that in our own lives we now need to stretch out and share who and what we are with others, for their won growth and aggrandisement. If we choose instead to keep everything for ourselves, we can be subject to unnecessary decay and loss.

This cards energy can bring us to the experience of full ripeness, the fulfilment of our previous actions and the manifestation of what we desire and what is good and correct for us to do. The nature of energy being always to move and flow, it is vital that we keep doing this too, offering, sharing and giving of ourselves, perhaps to a greater good now. This is a time of celebration of all that we have done and the realisation, followed by the action, that it is not all about ourselves, but those around us too.

10 - COMPOST
BACKGROUND

One thing that is abundantly clear from the natural world on an annual basis, is the process of birth, life and decay. It therefore follows that in the last card for our Earth suit we look at that process of decay, known variously as dormancy or hibernation and classified here as Compost.

This dormancy as we choose to call it here (we have explored the dormant principle as it applies to the Volcano before), is really a period of arrested growth in a plant. This being the case, it is primarily a process of survival and it this which we must be clear about here. Part of the year may be unsuitable for growth of a plant and so they adopt a strategy of hibernation in order to survive.

This period is often dictated by an internal biological clock that tells them instinctively when to slow down their activity and to prepare their soft tissues for a period of, for example, freezing temperatures, water shortage, shortened light periods and reduction of rainfall. Whatever the environmental cause, what we need to see here is that this is a temporary period of inactivity and a means of conserving energy.

What is interesting is that many plants will enter a period known as predictive dormancy, this being when the organism enters the dormant phase before the onset of freezing temperatures, water shortage etc. It is literally as if the plant senses and knows what to do and when, something known as senescence, which we can apply to ourselves here and learn much from. Equally consequential dormancy begins after the adverse environmental conditions have begun, which occur more often in unpredictable climates.

Another feature of dormancy in plants is that from the outside, the plant can appear dead, but on the inside it is still very much alive. If cut into, there will always be at least a small amount of living, green tissue. External to this a hard coat to the seed is created for protection of these living tissues and to preserve its energy reserves. In this way, during the period of dormancy, however long this may last in each individual species, it creates a storehouse of energy for when it is next required.

Plants can also shed their mantle of soft leaves and stems to leave the bare, hard wood, rather like a suit of armour. This copes with the cold and dry conditions as may be experienced without affecting the sleeping seeds within, ready to sprout forth come spring. Plants generally have buds always at the ready, those highest on the plant sending chemical signals to those beneath not to grow unless needed to take over in the event of their death.

Lastly we can also note that some plant species have no visible means of survival above ground, but retreat below the soil to preserve and continue their life. Just because we cannot see it, does not mean it is not there! In particular this applies to herbaceous plants.

DESCRIPTION

The image here is that of naturally occurring Compost, from fallen leaves and twigs, like nature's home-made carpet each Autumn. Any gardener knows the value of Compost in begetting and feeding the new life that awaits within, or beneath. Compost is simply the organic matter that decomposes, ready to be recycled to feed new crops or plants that will grow next season.

Although of no use in itself Compost has a great use for the land. It is rich in nutrients, as well as acting as a fertilizer and pesticide. So it is that when we view the image here we are reminded that although everything may appear to be dormant or in decay, we are still amidst new life and its potential.

ENERGY

First and perhaps most obviously in our brief study here is the basic necessity of the process of decay and that this is not a death. When we consider the energy of decay we may see this with gloomy eyes and despondency but here this energy is in fact quite the opposite, when we care to look within. When we do this we see that we must submit and go with the process of release and decay in order to maintain that which we hold most dear and sacred – life itself.

Of course all material lives must eventually die but this is not the case here. This is instead a time for hibernation or dormancy, exemplified in our Compost. We saw that this is an instinctive thing, often beginning before it is required, for maximum effect. This cards' energy then tells us to tune into our inner instincts and know when to leave well alone, when not to act sometimes being as important as when to act.

Dormancy then is an inner as well as an outer process. The outer process of decay tells the world that we are now finished as were, we are no longer that person doing that thing. On the inner side what is not always immediately obvious though is that we have learnt from and absorbed the best of what we have done and achieved, as evidenced by the living tissue preserves in the plant. This tells us that we must take what we have learned from our activities and achievements and apply this to our future seeds, potential and activity.

Now may not be the time for outer activity but for a turn within. We recall here that for the plant dormancy is a period

239

when they store energy within. We are guided to do this now as well and in doing so we ensure not just our survival but the preservation, continuation and future development of what we have done. In this sense, this is a time of the past creating the future but we must rest and recuperate if this is to be the best it can possibly be.

The plant is taken or stripped to its core, releasing all it does not require or that serves no purpose now. It presents a face to the world that is cold and hard and the energy here can give us this outer edge and face that can help us be tough when we need to be, the wold can be a cold, desolate and lonely place at times after all. On the inside however we remain soft and vital and it is here that life is preserves and thrives.

Of course this is only what is visible to others and as we have seen plants exist below ground too. This shows us that we may need to keep hidden and private some aspects of ourselves. This is not in the sense of keeping things secret when they should not be, but of the wisdom of keeping your own counsel and applying our natural, instinctive knowing of when to wait, rest and retain until we are ready once more to spring forward with renewed vigour and activity. This will not happen if we not go dormant once in a while. The energy of this card teaches us the value of composting our own actions.

EARTH OF EARTH - BEDROCK
BACKGROUND

Following the previous description of the Tarot Therapy approach to the traditional Court cards, we begin our brief examination of these here with what was once the Page of Pentacles. Pentacles being Earth and the Pages equivalent to the same, we are dealing here with an energy that is expressed through this card as Earth of Earth.

Of course this gives us a simple equation with which to work – Earth of Earth simply means more Earth, expressed for our purposes here as rocks. The solid casing of the Earth's crust, known as the Mantle constitutes about 70% of the Earth's mass. If we dig deep enough into the surface of the Earth, we will always hit rock. Beneath the largely loose layers of soil, sand and crumbled rocks we find bedrock, which is a solid form of rock.

The rocks we see around us consist of 2 or more minerals. There are over 3000 minerals in existence, one of their features being that they are the same throughout, so all rocks come from a single source in this respect. Like the majority of living things in the natural world, Rocks are also continually being formed, eroded and then formed again. This is known as the Rock cycle and as we shall see with our Water element, follows a similar process, but over a much great period of time.

Rocks are actually classified in three ways – Igneous, Sedimentary and Metamorphic. Igneous rocks are formed from fire or some other heat source. This is usually magma from volcanoes, that when solidified again become granite. Sedimentary rocks are formed from pieces of sand and small rock that are then very slowly formed into layers of new rock.

Metamorphic rocks are those that have changed from igneous or sedimentary due to movement of the Earth's crust.

To return to the solid Bedrock mentioned above, this is consolidated rock, meaning that it is solid and tightly bound, and so most suitable for our Earth on Earth combination here. Bedrock underlies sand and other sediments beneath water and above the surface can be unconsolidated rock, meaning there are loose particles visible. Bedrock can extend for hundreds of metres below the surface of the Earth. Some bedrock is known to be over 4 billion years old.

Despite the great depths it can reach, bedrock can also be visible on some mountain ranges, rocky coastlines and on plateaus. Known as outcrops, these are exposed through natural processes such as erosion and uplift of the Earth's tectonic plates.

DESCRIPTION

The image presented here is shows us clearly the form and structure of bedrock and its role in providing a solid foundation for the life that grows above it. It can be seen how the pressure from the uppermost layers pushes down on the layers of rock below, creating the founding layer or bedrock visible here, at the darker white area. The bedrock will, as we have seen, extend much further down beneath what is visible here.

We can also observe how the upper layers of the bedrock are interspersed with the deepest areas of soil that have penetrated down. Here the rock appears spaced apart rather than in one solid form. This gradually gives way to the layer of soil that forms the surface of our little cross-section.

Above this we can see a shaft of light from the sky, in the top right-hand of the card. In the upper most corner here we can see a tree, a reminder of the growth and produce that can come, in this case over many years in keeping with the slow moving evolution of rock and the Earth, from the solid, apparently immovable bedrock upon which our surface is based.

ENERGY

We have seen that approximately 70% of the Earth's mass is formed or rock. This mass of solidity tells us much about the nature and energy brought to us with this card. It is solid, strong, slow-moving but evolving, of its own accord and at its own pace.

We have also seen how the bedrock can penetrate very deeply within the planet. This tells us that the energy here both goes to and comes from way down deep within our soul, and can be felt in the core of our bones and bodies. The energy here tells us to take our time, do everything at only our own pace and allow everything the time and pace it needs to bed down as firmly as possible to become as strong as possible.

This energy is not just about putting down roots however; this has been done with prior Earth cards. Rather it is about ensuring we establish a structure that will last for as long as possible, no matter how much effort, time, blood, sweat and tears this may take. The end result is more important than all these things for without this done there will be no future growth.

It is what lies deeply buried within us, like the sedimentary rock of our Bedrock here that sustains best and longest. That which is beneath is where the most strength is held. For us now, this can mean we may need to adopt an attitude of being immovable and digging deep within to attest to this.

This energy can also cause us to look within to ask ourselves have we buried something so deep that we can no longer know of its existence. It may be that we need to remove and reveal some of what we have chosen to ignore or perhaps even pretend does not exist within us and allow it to become clear and acknowledged. This is when that supportive energy turns in on itself, a little like the metamorphic rock that forms from tectonic shifts deep within the Earth, and cause an instability within us. We may need to ask ourselves what is our rock in life based on, on what are we basing our actions, modus operandi, and way of life?

Overall all then, the energy here is one of consolidation, since we are here able to apply a direct analogy with the consolidated rock that forms the safest, surest and strongest layer within both our Earth and ourselves that we need to depend on. Will this sustain you for the rest of your life and allow for future growth of all your plans and actions?

EARTH OF FIRE - CHARCOAL

BACKGROUND

Here we subvert the traditional Knight of Pentacles to Fire of Earth. For our purposes here, this produces Charcoal. A dictionary definition of Charcoal is 'a carbonaceous material obtained by heating wood or other organic matter in the absence of air'.

As we know, a fire must have a source of fuel for it to burn. This is our Earth energy here, be this wood or some other fuel. Once a fire has been established and burning for a time, most of the gases and smoke particles (smoke is produced when there is not enough oxygen to burn all the fuel) have been released. All that is left now is pure charcoal, which is almost pure carbon, with some minerals.

The hot charcoal burns with a red glow, but no flames since charcoal will only produce carbon dioxide, which cannot be burned any further. The quicker a fire burns to charcoal, the greater heat and less smoke is produced. So charcoal is really formed once the oxygen (air) is removed and the water vanished to vapour, so we can see here the removal of two of our four elements and the result of the combination of the remaining two.

The process of making charcoal deliberately is known to date back at least 30,000 years, to make some of the earliest cave paintings. Charcoal has been utilised in different ways by humanity since then. Its' use as a fuel was crucial in the development of metallurgy and its qualities as an artistic medium are still employed. Charcoal is of great importance today in the purification of water and air. Its' most common use is as a fuel and for cooking, but is also used in the manufacture of objects from crayons to filters.

DESCRIPTION

245

We can see clearly from our image how Charcoal is the combination of Fire with Earth. The combination of the beautiful colours of the Fire from the deep red close to the charcoal edges to the almost luminescent areas of orange and yellow lie in blended contrast to the black and grey of the charcoal itself.

It is noticeable from our image too that the Fire is underneath the charcoal, or that it is within it. This ties in with the way in which we have previously seen (In the introduction to the Compound Cards) that the inner energy of the card is the first Element of its title, and its outer energy the Elemental suit to which it belongs.

ENERGY

The energy of this card takes time to become established within us, like the fire that must burn for a time to produce charcoal. This occurs only once the other elements have been removed, as we saw. It is when we get down to hat is our basic fuel, our motivation, that this energy can take expression within us.

The energy this card brings to us is one that we need time to absorb and may counsel us to slow down and absorb our initial impulses to see what will last and what we have already established. It is only when we have stripped away all that is superfluous and unnecessary that we can truly see who and what we are.

Removal of excess may be required from us now, so that we become more rarefied in ourselves and who we are. From this we can become more intense, like the great heat that is produced from the charcoal following the removal of air and water.

Charcoal being of great versatility, we can found ourselves becoming very adaptable and willing, over a period of time, to apply our talents and abilities in diverse ways. This energy can be a very good one for when we want to try out new things.

It can indicate a time when we may be a little slow on the uptake and find things hard to absorb or understand but once this is achieved, the fierce devotion to principle and action is unshakeable. The energy here can push and prompt us to see things as they really are and to establish a foundation of practice ad action that will last, and then apply ourselves in a focussed and passionate way.

In short, it is about becoming and being who we truly are in a more direct way and thence with greater vision and intensity – turning up the heat from within, effectively.

EARTH OF WATER – QUICKSAND
BACKGROUND

Here the Queen of Pentacles becomes our Water of Earth – inwardly she is watery, outwardly earthy. For us this results in Quicksand, which is simply solid ground that has become liquefied by water. The 'quick' part of its title refers only to the swiftness the sand can move in its semi-liquid state.

Quicksand is actually just another type of soil, usually sand or a grainy soil, being a mixture of sand and water. Under the right conditions it can occur anywhere. It is formed when an area of loose sand becomes saturated with water and the sand becomes agitated. The water becomes trapped and cannot flow away. This creates a liquefied soil that cannot support weight. There are two ways in which this process can occur.

The first is from flowing underground water, such as an underground spring. The force of the upward water flow is in opposition to gravity and this causes the sand granules to be more buoyant. The second way is from Earthquakes. The force of the ground movement increases the pressure of shallow groundwater which liquefies the sand and soil deposits.

The liquefaction is increased by vibration, increasing its 'quickness'. What is first solid then becomes soft and then 'quick'. It is the vibration that reduces the friction between the sand particles and results in it behaving like a liquid, from the loss of its strength.

It is notable that although quicksand can occur anywhere given the right conditions, the most common places are those of natural interaction between water and earth – riverbanks, beaches, lake shorelines, and marshes and near underground springs.

A simple exampleto illustrate our point here is to think how the sand changes when we walk out to sea a little. From the beach the sand supports you with no problem but as you encounter wet sand your feet sink down a little as you walk.

It is when it becomes too watery that the sand cannot support you, although just a moderate amount of water allows the sand to clump together – the kind of sand that allows us to build castles and so on.

Lastly for our purposes here, we should note that should the human body become trapped in quicksand, it is basically necessary only to relax and allow ourselves to be carried to the surface. Panic results in separation of the sand and so we sink further. Relax however and we float. It is slow movement here that will succeed, not mad thrashing about.

DESCRIPTION

Many of us when we think of or picture something called Quicksand imagine something from a bad movie where some unfortunate person sinks in something resembling slurry until the hero of the hour appears to drag them out by some ingenious means.

However as we have seen above, any area of wet sand is in effect Quicksand, by definition. Our combination here of Water of Earth finds its natural home and habitat at the beach and so it is we settle for our image on an expanse of wet sand, specifically from a beach in Cornwall, in this case.

The sand creates a quite beautiful expanse in many ways and is fuelled by the interplay of light from the Sun. The movement and saturation of water has resulted in the sculpted flats and ridges that we see, the subtle interplay of water and sand offering its semi-solid support to those who would seek to travel its surface.

ENERGY

We have seen that the nature of Earth when it becomes effectively 'waterlogged' is that it becomes porous. In our example, which is that of sand, we get the beautiful expanse and feeling of the wet, or quick sand between our toes and over our feet and we slowly submerge a little.

This illustrates the energy of this card neatly for us. What is solid and stable within us, that of our outer lives, our actions and everyday materiality we depend upon, is subject to our emotions and feelings. These may create a necessary softness but as with all things in life, we need to maintain a balance lest we become threatened with sinking and ultimately disappearing beneath the tides and flow of our emotion.

This card's energy has a real strength with it that can appear from the outside tough. It is rather like the principle of tough love in action here. The down to Earth quality of this energy is then blended with the softness of empathy, feeling and understanding within that creates the ability to do what is absolutely necessary whatever the conditions and more than this to do this with an understanding, openness of heart and ultimately, love.

Of course should the Earthy energy over balance that inner love then this energy can bring a toughness that is too harsh, but this does in turn allow us to 'get on' and carry out necessary actions when things may be tough. It's rather like a maxim in my gym – 'tough times don't last, people do'. This energy brings the understanding that the toughest of all people know how to live in the face of adversity, ridicule, anger or bitterness.

This does not mean becoming so 'wet' that we allow ourselves to be manipulated. We have seen that the more vibration there is, the more the sand absorbs any weight upon it. This tells us that we need to remain still and calm when things are tough or we are challenged. Yielding to whatever we may be feeling completely is not a balanced response or answer. Just as when we fall in love it is in part a sickness that we must allow to pass before we will know whether the love will last. The beauty of the energy here is that the possibility of this is high when we get that balance right.

As with so many things in life, if we do not panic but remain still and calm we can let ourselves float, just as is the correct response when we find ourselves sinking in sand. This is not that passive acquiescence that comes from total inertia or passivity, but a lightness of being and action that loves what we do and do what we love. The action in floating here is not a passive one, it is our considered response and doing what we know to be right. We must go with the flow yes, but we must first create that flow, something which is unique and individual to each of us.

EARTH OF AIR – DUST STORM
BACKGROUND

Now the King of Pentacles becomes a Dust Storm, as Air of Earth. A dust storm arises when a strong wind blows loose sand and dirt from a dry surface, showing us this blend. The wind blows these particles from one place to another, in a process called saltation. Perhaps predictably, dust storms are most common in dry and arid regions. When occurring in a desert, such as the Sahara, they become known as sandstorms.

It is often the combination of colder air as gusts blowing over heated earth that causes a dust storm to occur. This often follows a prolonged dry period which leaves loose particles to be gathered by the wind. The leading edge of a dust storm commonly consists of a wall of thick dust.

The fine, loose and surface particles are caused to 'Saltate' or leap after the wind causes them to first vibrate. As they repeatedly strike the ground they loosen and break off smaller particles of dust which then begin to travel in suspension. As the wind speed increases so the particles are transported. The vertical limits the particles can be raised is largely determined by the stability of the atmosphere above the ground, as well as the weight of the particles. Dust has been known to be lifted up to 20,000 feet above the ground.

It is now known that a static electric field is created by the friction of the particles. The negative charges of the particles relative to the earth can double the number of particles raised – this is the same effect on your hair when you rub a balloon on it. Visibility is often obscured almost completely during a dust storm. This can also be especially so in a desert sandstorm, when in addition to fine sand particles, larger ones are also blown over long distances. Dust storms are often known by the Arabic name 'haboob' which means 'strong wind' but are also termed 'black blizzards'.

Up to 20 million tonnes of dust are transported from the Bodele Depression, a dry lake bed in the Sahara, to the Amazon basin each year. This supplies the rainforest with essential minerals and nutrients to maintain its fertility and keep it thriving. Dust storms can range from a small burst lasting just a few minutes to a storm that can blow for 50 days at speeds close to a hurricane.

A wind blowing at just 9 miles per hour can be enough to raise dust particles if the conditions are right. The smallest particles become airborne while the larger ones are blown across the ground, which is known as creeping. Once a wind increased these larger particles begin to bounce and the field created gets things going to provide the storm.

DESCRIPTION

Here we see a dust storm in full flight. We can see the dry condition of the earth in the foreground and have some idea of the looseness of sand and soil created by this condition. It is easy to see the source of what we see above in these conditions.

It is also possible to see the thickness of the front of the dust storm from its denser appearance at this stage – in other terms the clouds of dust look heavier and thicker than elsewhere due to the larger number of particles of sand and soil they contain. They are also darker in appearance.

We can also gain some perspective of the height and overall scale of the dust storm when we observe the size of the dust cloud. From what may not appear to be all that high on the left of the image we see that the dust cloud spiral up and out beyond our view to the right to a level we can only then imagine. Imposing and threatening as it is, we can also gain a sense of wonder and marvel at the awesomeness of the natural world, as indeed we can with every card in the deck.

ENERGY

We have seen that the conditions need to be right for a dust storm to happen. This requires dryness of earth and strength of wind. This tells us that we receive this combination as energy when this card appears for us. This may be in the form of dissatisfaction or lack of passion and feeling with hat we are doing in life, but that we are, or may need to, think about it first before we do anything.

The combination of earth outwardly and air inwardly leads to thinking, taking an objective view of what we see around us and then making careful and well-thought plans on how to respond. The energy here may suggest too that we need to analyse our actions and then allow the storm to blow through them to stir things up. This energy often comes in when there is a need for some immediate effect over what has become too stale and dry in our life.

The effects of such an occurrence may be unknown but we need to remind ourselves here of the life-affirming effect the Sahara dust storms have on the Amazon. We have seen massively from our studies so far that nature never sits still. The Earth aspect of this energy may seek to do so and we have usually created a stable foundation on which we have built our kingdom when we experience this card. However foundations can weaken and crumble if we do not keep them strong and give them attention. However, long with that stability can creep laziness and a lack of attention.

It is now that this cards' energy tells us to think carefully and see objectively and coolly what is needed and required to be done in order the (re)create that fertility that we once enjoyed. We saw that it is by colder winds blowing that the storm arises so we need to think clearly, honestly and unemotionally as we build and begin to act on our plans.

We know too that visibility is reduced or removed during the 'black blizzard' of the dust storm. This tells us that we need to look within as we make our plans and consider our future and where we go next and what we need to do. The logic must be tempered without outer visibility. In other words, we cannot see the effects our thinking will have on our and perhaps others future until we begin to operate and act on them.

We need then to be sure about the way our mind is working and we are not coloured by emotion or fantasy. If we get our thinking correct and work to ensure we are building on what we know and is established then we can move confidently towards and unknown but more exciting and fulfilling future.

WATER ELEMENT

The Water element relates to the emotional realm and the feeling aspect of our existence. These cards demonstrate the energies of our feelings and emotions and how we can choose to respond to and deal with what arises for us at this level.

Largely an inner thing, our feelings of course have a profound and direct impact on our actions. Put another way, we invariably do what we really want to do. However the wisdom of this can be open to question and it is here that we can gain and learn from the knowledge of the energy of the cards of this suit.

Our emotional energy can be seen as betwixt and between our mental understanding and our actions. As we receive energy from the Universe, so we assess what it is at a mental level, in our minds and respond to this in our hearts – it gives us feelings and this determines our actions. So often our feelings and emotions can arise due to past experiences and unresolved issues. The great use of the cards from this Water suit can be in helping to understand why we feel the way we do and what we need to do about it.

The cards of this suit follow the process in nature of the coming into being of Water and the process it follows through its life cycle, known as the Water Cycle or Hydrologic Cycle. This process follows the way in which we receive Water in the natural world, through its development while here in different forms and the uses we can make of it, through to its 'disappearance' into vapour at the end. These cards depict the journey water takes as it circulates from the land to sky and back again. The process of the Water Cycle is classified in different ways and describes the process of how we receive water as rain, through its 'runoff' into and across the land, its absorption into it and subsequent emergence, thence evaporation. It is the manifestation of this process in the natural world that forms the basis for the Water cards.

We are of course, completely dependent on fresh water in order to live. We have already seen the interactive nature of the Elements and so how we are dependent on each and all of them and we very soon become critically aware of our need for Water. The mass of Water on the Earth at any one time remains fairly constant over time but as the water moves from one 'reservoir', be it a sea, ocean or whatever, to another, the amount can be variable. We can also see something of the interaction of Water with the other Elements when we see that water takes energy from its surroundings and cools the environment when it evaporates. Equally, when it condenses it releases energy and warms the environment. When water evaporates it is purified which then replenishes the land with freshwater. Its flow transports minerals across the Earth and it helps to reshape geological features, through erosion.

These Water cards then show us that rather than being subservient to our emotions and the tides of our feelings, we can instead implement choices as to how to respond to what we are feeling. In this way we gain dominion over our feelings, not by crushing or repressing them but instead but the full—bloodied, whole-hearted openness that allows us to feel everything fully and completely, knowing this is part of our functioning as whole spiritual beings on the human path.

WATER

1 - DROP
BACKGROUND

I have always taught that the Aces of each suit of the Tarot are the essence of their particular Element – in this case the essence of Water being a single drop. In addition to this, as the pure essence of their element, the first card of each suit requires a response in order for it to evolve and continue existing. In this case a single drop of water will soon evaporate but if it added to other drops, as we shall see, great oceans can form.

For emphasis of this principle we can look at the way water is formed. It is not simply a matter of a combination of hydrogen and oxygen molecules – energy must be brought into the mixture too, in order for the atoms to mix and fit together. This energy takes the form of an electrical spark, which when it passes through a mixture of gases, creates a hydrogen product. This combines with oxygen, and water is produced.

As many know, chemically water is H20 – two hydrogen atoms and one oxygen atom – these are bound together by shared electrons. The resultant water molecule is V shaped – or perhaps more accurately boomerang shaped - one side carrying a negative charge (the oxygen atom) and the other a positive charge (hydrogen). It is this which makes water conductor energy, rather like a magnet. This means that water attracts other water molecules to itself - this is why we can see crystalline structures when it is frozen.

Water molecules tend to form long, fragile chains as they attract each other, making them too heavy to fly around at low temperatures. This is why water is a liquid. It is the bend in its molecules that cause it to be liquid rather than a gas. The formation of water is also dependent on the external temperature when the hydrogen and oxygen is combined. If the temperature is too hot then the liquid vaporises to form steam and if the temperature is too low, then it creates a solid, such as ice.

The Earth is approximately two-thirds covered in water, about the same ratio that we humans are water also. It is not known specifically how water came to be here and formed the oceans etc. Generally speaking it is thought that as the various gases cooled and were held in an atmosphere of sufficient pressure for water to form, although it is quite possible that water also arose from within the Earth itself, formed via vapour from volcanic eruption, then falling as rain.

We know that only 2.5 % of the Earth's water is fresh and so useable by us. Of that 98.85 is ice and groundwater. Our dependency on fresh water is total and complete. Like energy the nature of Water is to flow and move. It follows the Water cycle describe above in an ongoing and continual process, telling us much about the energy we receive from all the cards of this suit, as we shall see.

DESCRIPTION

Our image here shows a single drop of water. It is actually very hard to depict one naturally occurring drop of water by itself, as per the cards title, since as we have seen, they naturally attract more. So it is that in our image we see this taking place. As one drop, or to actually use its correct term, a droplet, is released into a body of water, it creates the beautiful rippling effect we see here.

We can see the image of the single drop as if it is held in suspension above the body of water beneath it. It is easy to imagine and see as we look at the image how it will shortly fall into and merge with the water body below, adding its own unique pattern to the ripple effect we can see.

So it is that we can see how water is analogous to our emotions and feelings in so many ways, as we shall see on our journey through these cards.

ENERGY

As we have seen this cards' energy is all about the essence of the element, in this case Water. It is the formation of Water with which we are concerned here and as we have also sense, this requires energy to be present. The energy in human form we relate to and receive with this card is that of our emotion and feeling.

The question which this card brings to its recipient is 'how do you feel'? Its' energy requires us firstly and simply to connect with our feeling in that moment. First we have to be aware of and notice this, before we can then follow a response through to action. Much of the spiritual path and quest is to become more fully conscious of our whole selves as human being. Through the process of Tarot Therapy we do this by engagement with and awareness of the four constituent and elemental parts of our human being and here it is that of feeling.

By becoming conscious of our feeling we can begin to learn control of them. This is not by suppression and in fact, by the opposite. The energy of this card is about learning to respond rather than react to our feelings. It is really only by allowing ourselves to feel our emotion fully and engage with it that we can hope to learn how to integrate this part of our being into the whole.

So we can learn recognise through the energy of this card that this a vital aspect of our completeness and wholeness and that we are dependent on this for our very existence. We cannot deny our emotion, nor suppress or ignore it. Like water, its' nature is to move and flow and here we need to begin to learn how to do that in an appropriate and healthy way. This starts here, through this energy, by learning to consider how we feel and embrace and accept those feelings as valid, whatever they may be.

Emotion, if left to its' own devices, can flow unchecked and cause us to behave outrageously and out of control. Here we can work with the energy offered to us by seeking a more considered, appropriate response brought about by the conscious understanding and acceptance of whatever we are feeling in each moment. It is in the complete embrace of the fullness of our feeling that we integrate the energy here and bring about the understanding we speak of.

This of course is no easy thing as many of us will immediately realise, given the depth of feeling we are capable of and the power of those emotions upon us, just as with the nature of water, our dependence on it and its' possible behaviour and expression on Earth. For now, it is enough to marvel at its' beauty and the purity of our feelings and drink deeply of them.

2 - RAIN
BACKGROUND

As every resident of the British Isles knows, rain is never far away. In these lands, it is quite logical for one drop of water to be followed by rain, as it is with our cards here! Oddly enough, when we think of rain we tend to think of it being cold, especially in Great Britain! However, droplets of water from which rain comes actually form from warm air. As this warm air rises, it cools. Water vapour always exists in the air and together with the droplets formed from the cooling air, clouds are formed. When there are enough water droplets, the clouds join together and the water droplets collide, forming bigger drops. These are, like everything else on Earth, subject to gravity and fall, as rain.

The source of all this water is the formations on the Earth, principally oceans, but of course lakes and rivers too. Heat from the Sun evaporates the water, which remains in the atmosphere until it condenses, forming clouds and then rain. Rainfall occurs when the water vapour has cooled enough to become liquid again. So it is in the formation of rain, from its source, through its fall and back to source that we can see the whole water cycle in one connected movement.

Rain is of course the prime source for many ecosystems of the Earth. The direst continent on the planet is Antarctica. The average rainfall over the landmasses of Earth is 7.15mm, but if take this over the whole planet it leaps to 990mm – water it would seem, attracts more water. Of course in the raid, dry regions of the planet rainfall is welcomed as a blessing when the 'rainy season' begins, but elsewhere it can bring the constant threat of flood and all that this engenders.

Rain is typically classified in one of four groups, due to its severity. These are light, moderate, heavy and violent. A peculiar phenomenon can be sometimes witnessed in the hot, deserts of Earth, known as phantom rain. A band of rain can be seen to be falling from the clouds above, but it never reaches the ground due to the hot conditions, the water simply evaporating before it does so.

The type and manner of rainfall is subject to various causes. Stratiform rainfall is caused by a broad sheet of precipitation with a smaller intensity, as opposed to dynamic precipitation which is showery in nature and its intensity. These variations are due to the condition and change in the movements of warm and cold air.

Rainfall is measured in units of length per unit time, usually millimetres per hour. This is the depth of rainfall that would occur on a flat, horizontal and impermeable surface over one hour. Much as we may not like to be underneath it, we cannot avoid not just the importance of rain but our utter dependence upon it, no matter where on the globe we are situated.

DESCRIPTION

Here we have an image of rain! There is not a great deal of description needed, since this image speaks for itself. We can see above the rainfall the clouds formed by the rising air as described above and the rather torrential rainfall that results in this case.

We can gain a sense of the power and intensity, as well as something of the beauty, of the rain as it makes its way downwards, back to the Earth from whence it came. The darker areas juxtapose nicely with the lighter clouds, reminding us that even here, in the midst of a downpour, the balance inherent in all nature, persists.

ENERGY

We saw with the One of Water how it is vital that we are connected to our emotions; that we must carry an awareness of this aspect and level of our being at all times. Water is symbolically and in many ways, literally, linked to the emotions, because they both share an instinct – to flow.

We see with this card the complete round of the Water cycle, in the formation of rain from the oceans and so on of the Earth and their subsequent rise in vapour and fall as rain. From this we can align our need for expression of our emotions and what we are feeling at any given moment. The energy of this card tells you to express your feelings and to share them with another. It is often through this exchange with other people that the most beautiful things can be experienced.

Of course not all emotions are pleasant and what we would wish for. However just as rain can be a refreshing light shower it can also be a deluge leading to flood. So it can be with our emotions. We need to ensure that we are refreshed and enlivened by our feelings rather than letting them well up and burst out like the walls of a dam breaking. The energy here tells us to allow our feelings expression in an appropriate and healthy way, for our growthful development.

Although we tend to think of rain as unwelcome we must also remind ourselves of our reliance upon it. Just as we need fresh water to survive, so do we need to acknowledge and give and receive this emotional flow with others. It can be an all too common refrain to say 'you made me feel' this or that emotion. In fact, no-one can 'make' us feel anything, our feelings are our own. When we express what we are feeling, without judgement or expectation, so we free ourselves of the danger of pollution from resentment, rejection and so on.

The energy with this card can cause us to see the need for the sharing of our emotional being with another, not just with the beauty of love (although can certainly manifest with this energy) but the delight in everyday exchanges. This cards energy tells us to be open in our hearts so that the wonder, joy and freedom of emotional sharing can be experienced to the full. This results in a freedom and celebration of life at the emotional level.

Rain occurs quite naturally, all by itself, with no interference or influence from us. The energy here reminds us of the natural flow of our emotions and the watery aspects of our being. This can be in the form of tears, which can of course bring their own healing. Tears can be joyful as well as sad and here the energy tells us to celebrate and even indulge in the full gamut of our feelings and the relief and connection that comes with sharing them.

3 - SPRING
BACKGROUND

We have already seen of our dependence on a fresh water supply for our survival and when we look at our history and where we have chosen to settle, the closeness of a supply of groundwater has always been a vital factor. In the case of a spring or seep, pressurised groundwater emerges from beneath the earth in a steady flow, or stream, thereby offering ongoing sustenance.

Springs however, can be ephemeral or perennial, or temporary or permanent. Whatever it may be, the underground source of a spring is known as an aquifer. This consists of an underground area of porous rock or matter into which water has flown. The water table is the top level of an aquifer, which is subject to change due to rainfall and geological movement. When the water table reaches a sufficient level surface water will flow and emerge from the soil.

For a spring to be formed the aquifer must be 'confined', meaning it is limited by a layer of non-porous material. When the confined aquifer is at a lower level than the water table it cannot rise and becomes pressurised. When the pressure is intense enough this forces the water upwards, defying gravity and a spring emerges through whatever outlet is possible.

Springs can emerge either directly onto the grounds surface or into the beds of rivers or directly into the ocean below sea level. Springs can vary in volume from being barely detectable to 30,000 litres per second. Temperatures can range from being barely above freezing to boiling point. With advent of technology to bottle it, we nowadays tend to associate fresh, spring water with quality and purity.

The majority of water in a spring is meteoric in nature, meaning it originally feel as rain or snow to the Earth. Spring water can also be ancient sea water, usually diluted with meteoric water. The exact nature of the spring, including its age, temperature and volume is dependent on the topography of its surrounding area. Where there are larger faults and fractures larger springs can result.

Often in areas of recent volcanic activity, hot springs can be formed when water falls between cracks in the earth onto the hot rock below. The deeper the rock the warmer they usually are. The water moves slowly to a great depth, warming as it goes. If it ten reaches a large area of less resistance it can rise more quickly then it descended, giving it no time to cool and so emerges as a hot or thermal spring.

DESCRIPTION

When we think of a spring we may be tempted to picture a bubbling brook scenario, with water bursting forth from lush greenery before flowing prettily away in a crystal clear water spring. Whilst there are many such sources for this image, spring can emerge in a wide variety of settings.

Here we can see the manner in which a Spring will always seek to break free, and the water to follow its natural course. The image clearly shows us how the water will always flow to the lowest level, taking it ever forwards on its course to the Sea. The light reflects beautifully in the water creating an almost mystical appearance to its cascade.

ENERGY

In the previous card we saw the need for emotional expression and sharing with others at this level, coupled with what we can both give and receive from this experience. There are echoes of this in the energy we receive from this

267

card in the nature of the spring. Since this is water coming forth from beneath the ground we can make a relationship with our need to express emotionally what we keep within.

We can take this analogy a little further here however, when we look at the depth from which the water of a spring can come. Allayed with our emotions, this cards energy can teach us that we may need to first sit with our feelings, absorb them allow them to ferment a little, so that we can become clear as to what we are feeling, why and what we need to do in response. It is then, symbolically when the temperature is right, that our emotions can come upwards and outwards and be expressed to the best possible effect. In short then, the energy of this card is about the appropriate and positive expression of emotion to help us create the best possible outcome, both for ourselves and others affected by them.

A further aspect of the energy here can be that we need to connect with the depth of our feeling. If we remind ourselves of the spiritual maxim of 'as within, so without', we can see that if we allow ourselves to feel our feelings fully, to absorb completely the full weight of our emotions then it follows there may be an equally powerful expression of them. This is in keeping with the varying amounts of flow of water than springs can produce. Aligning ourselves with our true feelings then becomes a goal and a need from this energy.

We know that the source of the water for the majority of springs in the Earth came first from rain and snow. This tells us that we need to look at what feelings we have received from external sources – in other words the energy here prompts us to observe our feelings and decide how we best need to respond to them so that we create a positive and fruitful outcome. This is in keeping with the numerical energy of the three, the number of creativity and production.

So the energy we receive now can enable us to create powerfully positive feelings and the creative expression of our emotional response.

4 - POND
BACKGROUND

From the creative expression of Water in the form of a spring we flow into the next stage of the water cycle, seen here as a pond. The definition of a pond is 'a body of water, smaller than a lake, as by damming a stream'. The word itself stems from the Old English pynding, meaning to impound. Ponds can arise naturally in flood plains as part of a river system or in isolated depressions. There are a few animals, such as beavers and alligators that can make ponds.

There is no universally recognised and agreed definition of a pond, as oppose say to a lake. A characteristic a natural (as opposed to man-made) pond, is that its depth is no greater 1.8 metres and that it features standing water. The temperature of the water in a pond is about the same from top to bottom and changes with the air temperature.

Natural ponds can be filled from an underground spring or by rainwater, where they can be termed 'dewponds'. Ponds can be formed in natural areas of depression following the spring flooding of a river as it retreats, as well as retreating glacier in the same way. Melting snow can also create a pond, albeit a temporary one. These can be known as 'Vernal Ponds' meaning they occur in the spring season.

For a pond to be 'successful' in terms of life-support, it needs to have native plants growing in it. This is for the provision of food, oxygen and shelter for wildlife. Pond plants tend to grow in 'zones'. These include meadowsweet, growing in the bankside, yellow iris growing in the marsh zone (near the edge), duckweed in the aquatic zone – in the pond itself and starwort, which grows entirely submerged.

Ponds can be teeming with all manner of life, not just plants. There can upwards of 1,000 animal species living in plants, although not all in the same one! Most pond animals cannot travel from one pond to another so they become like a complete eco-system of themselves. The water in a pond must remain clean if it is to provide a healthy environment for all the life it contains and supports. The type of life in a pond can be determined by a number of factors, including the depth of the water, available sunlight and shade, determining the oxygen available, plus the effect of grazing animals and the waters salinity. Water-lilies can be a staple of pond life, as can frogs, turtles and herons, with geese and muskrats for grazing.

Historically, ponds were an essential part of life, with nearly every village and farm having one, the water being used for both human and animal purposes. With the advance of technology and the provision of tap water, many ponds disappeared from neglect.

DESCRIPTION

The image here is of a natural occurring pond. This is a temporary pond, forming in the spring flood but dried up in the summer heat, reminding us of the temporary nature of our feelings.

The sense of stillness and stability in its presence and nature is apparent when we view its image. The grass growing beside it in an almost protective manner and the stillness of the water allows for the reflection of what is within to emerge, just as we see reflections of colour and forms in the water. The different zone of life as referred to above are visible in the grass for grazing around its edges, the marsh areas of plants and the many unseen creatures within and beneath the water.

ENERGY

We can see immediately the restrictive and limiting influence as opposed to the free-flowing nature of the spring. This is consistent with the energy of the number four, allotted to this card. The water of a pond is also usually defined as being still, further indicating its nature here. The numerical energy of four can indicate stagnation, standing still, along with imposing limitation and the safety and security this brings. These emotional conditions can be those which the appearance of this card can give rise to.

This is in keeping with the 'impounding' origin of the pond itself. This can mean that when we experience this energy we may need to look at our emotional self and consider whether we are polluting ourselves by a lack of expression or inability to allow our emotions to flow. As we have seen with the pond, it is dependent on different things to avoid stagnation and pollution and this is the case with our feelings and emotions – we need oxygen to breathe – if we do not our emotions can cause us to suffocate beneath them.

Ponds needs areas of shelter too and so it may be that this cards energy heralds a time of needing to consolidate our feelings, taking an assessment before we do then see the need to release them. The balance required here for the successful outworking of the energy is to stabilise our feelings and emotions so we can them know what and when the appropriate expression is.

As the water of a pond is a similar temperature throughout this can indicate a time of emotional consistency, with few or little 'ups and down's – a time and energy of emotional calm from this point of view. Of course this may be the need indicated by this card, especially if it follows a time of upset, loss etc.

The need for varying forms of life within a pond can show us the need to look at the source or origin of our feelings.

External factors loom large here of course but the need with this energy can be to see how we are choosing to respond, rather than out thinking that it 'makes us' feel a certain way., We can need to see here that our emotions and feelings are of our own choice and making. If we then look to their source we can establish a control over our emotional make –up and condition and so contribute to the successful nurturing of our well-being at this level.

In closing it may be worth mentioning that a majority of ponds – symbolic here in summary of our emotional stability – simply disappeared from neglect, a reminder we cannot ever ignore our feelings, lest we become emotionally barren.

5 - STREAM
BACKGROUND

For this card we are focussing on a stream as a body of water with a current confined within a bed and banks, as a stream has been defined. A stream can be classified under many different names, often regional in use, such as a brook, creek, rivulet and runnel, amongst others.

Streams play an important role in the water cycle, with which we are concerned in this suit of the deck. Streams fulfil a role in the recharge of groundwater, as well as providing a habitat for fish and wildlife migration. Streams are seen as a link, maintaining biodiversity in a region and its immediate habitat.

Streams are typically formed from the runoff from rain or snow. Whilst most of this water evaporates back into the atmosphere, some flows into the ground (infiltration) and becomes groundwater. This follows its natural course dependent on various factors such as wind, humidity, vegetation and rock type. This 'runoff' starts as a thin film of water called sheet wash and combined with a network of other tiny flows (rills). As these combine and focus into a channel, a stream is formed.

For a stream to qualify as such it must be wither perennial or recurring. Parts of some streams can begin underground before there emergence above the surface. A critical factor in the character of a stream is its gradient, determined by its base level of erosion, this being the point at which the stream enters the sea, or a lake or pond. Streams are also 'ranked' as first, second or third order streams. A first order stream has no other channels flowing into it and become a second order stream when this happens. When two second order streams combine, they create a third order.

Streams are also seen as having a particular profile. This starts with a steep gradient, no flood plain and few meanders, evolving into a low gradient and wide flood plain and extensive meanders. At their beginning streams are known as young, later mature or old as the above changes occur. Streams also carry a load, the sediment it displaces, dependent on its velocity.

Streams form a network of waterways across the land, flowing into other bodies of water to create rivers, then seas and so, which is shown in the progression of cards through this suit. This also echoes the human circulatory system and the manner in which air is circulated when we breathe.

DESCRIPTION

The stream we see here is located in the Cairngorm National Park in the Highlands of Scotland, close to the hamlet of the Skye of Curr. It is easy to see the current, flowing steadily and creating the small areas of white water on its surface as it bubbles its way forwards. The bank is distinguishable, albeit shallow, on the right hand side of the image and further downstream as it moved into the sunlight.

Of course there are thousands of such streams possible to choose from for the image here. This one is chosen due to its 'typical' nature that we imagine when we think of a how a stream 'should' look, so as to maximise the potency of the symbol here in our minds.

In the poetic way in which the stream begins in the shade and flows into sunlight, we are reminded of the beginning of many streams underground (and therefore impossible to show in an image!) and that the energy of our emotions moves naturally towards the light.

ENERGY

From the background information given above it is clear to see that a stream typifies the process of change that the water cycle undergoes at this stage. This is keeping with the numerical energy here, five being essentially energy of change. This is primarily evident in the current that a stream must possess to be such. This carries the water onwards and so reminds us that our feelings and emotions will not stay the same forever; like energy itself it must flow, move and so change.

The energy here then, counsels us to identify the need for that flow within our feelings. We can be assured that when we our feelings do change, outer events will evolve too and this card brings the promise of this.

We should note too that the many streams begin underground before breaking through to the surface. This tells us that we may need at this time to allow what we have been keeping in emotionally to find expression, to enable us to move forwards. Although we know that streams can carry sediment, reminding us that in the short-term we may not be free of what weighs us down emotionally, we are making progress towards a better, purer feeling.

The numerical energy of five is often one that is influenced by external factors. This is in alignment with the influence upon a streams course, depth and more, from factors such as wind, humidity and so on. This tells us that when this card appears for us we may need to see what emotional impact we are subject to from others around us as well as our environment. This is not to say we have to agree with or submit to these feelings, only that an awareness of them and their impact upon us may be required.

Contact with others feelings is also encouraged with this energy. We are shown this when we look to the networking nature of streams in the manner in which they link to other bodies of water in the landscape. We may therefore need to guard against isolation and cutting ourselves off from others at an emotional level. It may be necessary to allow what has previously been kept underground or within ourselves to emerge into the sunlight. It may be that we can surprise ourselves with the reception we may be granted when we do so. Often emotional fear can prevent expression but the energy here shows us that all must eventually find its way into the light.

6 - RIVER
BACKGROUND

Rivers exist as a combination of many tributary streams and as such are bigger movements of water on the Earth than a stream. We saw previously how streams are classified in 'order', from first to second and so on. Following this same classification structure a stream effectively becomes a river when it reaches sixth order and upwards, to twelfth order, the class of the Amazon, the worlds' largest river.

Medium and larger rivers are usually less steep than smaller ones and flow slower. They tend to have larger volumes of water within them as well as collecting debris from the smaller tributaries than run into them. Most rivers are formed from the many tributaries flowing in to them, in the higher altitudes and elevations of mountain and hills.

As the river progresses they can create a valley between the mountains and hills, which typically with have steep v-shaped sides where the river has carved its course. Running water in this way can change the earth's surface more than earthquakes or volcanoes, over a greater period of time. As the river flows, it collects pieces of frock and carries them with it, breaking them into smaller pieces as it goes, and eventually creating sediment.

Once a river has left the higher altitudes it slows down as it enters the flat plains. When this happens the sediment can sink to the bottom of the water and be deposited there. As the water continues to flow over them these rocks and pebbles are worn smooth. This, while process from source to sea can take thousands of years to form.

It is when the river travels through the flat areas of land that it 'meanders' creating the 'S' shapes we can see in many. When a river floods, it can then spread out over many miles of the surrounding area. During a flood, tiny pieces of sediment are deposited, further sculpting and smoothing the valley, such as the mighty Mississippi in the USA.

Eventually a river will flow into a greater body of water, such as a lake, sea or ocean as the water cycle continues. The transition between these areas is known as a delta, where the single river diverges into many channel and the fresh water can mix with the salt water ahead and completes its journey.

A river then does not just flow into the sea. Along the way it carves rocks, moves boulders, deposits sediment and creates valleys, all the while pursuing its goal of creating a smooth and wide plain to enable it to flow smoothly on to reach the end of its course.

DESCRIPTION

The image here is of the Iskut River, as its flows south into the Kinaskan Lake. This is in a Provincial Park in north-western British Columbia in Canada. The Iskut is the second largest tributary of the Stikine River and the area in which it originates in known by the First Nation people as The Sacred Headwaters.

This image has been chosen as it illustrates perfectly for us the features described above. We can see the seemingly haphazard meandering the river takes in the foreground, along with a potential flood plain surrounding its course. The steep sides of the lake above it show the manner in which the river has carved out its present feature in its inimitable, relentless manner. We can also note the contrast between the straight and meandering course the river follows in the two halves of the card.

ENERGY

Following the order of the Water cycle we know that we must reach a level of 'sixth order' or more for a river to become such. So it is that with the energy of the number applied to this card that we know that what we can receive from this card is a feeling of openness and sharing. When we receive this card in our readings we may need to look at a need to express our feelings openly and to share who we are with others, as well as receive their feelings with an open heart.

The results of this open expression can also therefore be felt through the energy of this card. This can mean that our feelings can flow outwards, just like the river can flood over the area of the plains surrounding it and which is has previously established. We may need therefore to look at what ground we have emotionally prepared previously to lead up to this point.

This may also mean that there will be many twists and turns in our emotional feelings at the time this card appears or is placed in your reading. The natural meandering of the river shows us that an emotional course is rarely true and straight so we may need to be open to our emotions taking unexpected changes of direction now.

We also know and can see from the image that the river has established itself over a period of many years, carving its presence into the valley through the rock. From this we can learn that our emotions can be relentless and human nature is such that ultimately we will follow our hearts and do what we want to do, rather than what our heads may direct us towards. We may need now to look into our hearts and accept what we find there and look at the possible future direction we may carve out for ourselves by following its lead.

We are also reminded of this when we look at that nature of a river to eventually flow into a larger body of water, which we can also see in the image. The nature of emotions is to connect with others and very rarely can we truly 'go it alone' or create such a state of emotional independence as to not need the company and interaction of others. We may wish to look at the company we choose to keep now and if this allows for us to be who we truly are, along with what impact our emotional interaction has both from and to others.

Our emotions may appear to be flowing along smoothly on the surface as this river may seem to do, but we should also remind ourselves of the activity beneath, with the sediment carried and deposited further downstream. This tells us to look at the emotional impact upon us of anything may seek to keep hidden from view and buried beneath the surface. We know deep in our hearts we are not free of such feelings and eventually they will surface, somewhere down the line. It is now that we must ask ourselves if we and others may be better off if we let these feelings rise to the surface and find expression.

7 - LAKE
BACKGROUND

A lake can be defined as a large body of water that is relatively still, surrounded by land aside from a river or other outlet which serves to feed or drain the water. By this definition they are deeper and larger than ponds, although there is no widespread acceptance of the difference between the two. Natural lakes are generally found in mountainous areas, rift zones and areas with ongoing glaciation.

All lakes are temporary over geologic time scales, as they will slowly fill in with sediments or spill out of the basin containing them. Some lakes, such as Lake Eyre, are a dry basin, only filling with water under the appropriate seasonal conditions. Lakes can have a wave action at a shoreline or where win turbulence comes into play.

The majority of lakes lie in the Northern Hemisphere of the Earth and consist of fresh water. Most lakes have at least one natural outflow, such as a river or stream, which serves to maintain its average water level by the drainage of excess water. Lakes with no natural outlet, known as endorheic, lose water purely from evaporation and underground seepage.

A lake can be formed by a recently occurring tectonic lift, creating a depression that can accumulate water to form a lake. Glaciers, as they advance and retreat can also scrape a depression in the land which water can then fill, such as the Great Lakes of North America. Lakes can also be formed from the consequences of a landslide.

There can be many different types of lakes including: Salk Lakes, where there is no natural outlet; Oxbow lakes which form as crescent-shapes in valleys from a river and its meandering course; Crater lakes from volcanic craters and sub-glacial lakes where the water sits below a layer of thick ice such as Lake Vostok in Antarctica, plus many more.

Lakes typically have numerous features and these include a drainage basin or catchment area where the surface water and from rainfall will flow to at its lowest elevation; the inflow and outflow – the source of water to and from the lake; its nutrient content showing the contents of the water; plus pollutants and sedimentation. All these combine to produce the overall character of the lake itself.

A lake's volume can be changed by the difference between its inflow and outflow. This can depend on a number of factors including precipitation, runoff, groundwater channels and evaporation. Lakes have a distinct feature in that they form layers called thermoclines, where the layers vary drastically in temperature. The deeper layers are oxygen starved and it is only when the surface temperature meets the temperature at depth that the water can mix.

At the bottom of a lake, the lake bed, can be found silt, sand and organic material such as decaying plant and animal matter. This matter all contributes to the flora and fauna found in the environs of the lake. Natural lakes are such that they can be seen as a microcosm of their surrounding environment.

DESCRIPTION

The image used here is of the beautiful Lake Tahoe, in the Sierra Nevada on the border between California and Nevada in the USA. This is the largest alpine lake in North America and the second deepest, after Crater Lake and is approximately 2 billion years old. It is featured here due to its being known for the clarity of its water and its surrounding panorama of mountains. The lake has just one outlet, the Truckee River.

ENERGY

From the flowing nature of the previous River card we come to an energy that by definition is still. The last couple of cards' energies have emphasised the need for expression of feeling and emotion, but here that shifts t a need for contemplation and looking within. Traditionally associated with fantasy and the illusion of emotion, here the Lake invites us to symbolically (or perhaps literally) to dive within and see what lies beneath.

The depth of lakes is one feature here that calls us with the appearance of this card to look deeply within our own emotional selves to see what may lie buried within and how this may affect us. We have seen how lakes typically have at least one outlet so we may need to look at how our deepest emotions are finding their way out of us and indeed, if this is happening.

We might also need to trace ourselves back to the underlying causes of our deepest feelings. Has there been a figurative 'tectonic shift' in our own lives at some stage that has caused us to create a lake of our emotional state. This may be that we felt the need to bury own feelings deeply, preferring instead the apparent calm of those nearer the surface. Should this be the case we may need to remind ourselves of the tendency of lakes to include a wave motion, reminding us that what lies beneath will still have an effect at the surface.

Lakes are of course, surrounded by land. So it follows that the water of our feelings will slowly lap away at the everyday land of our own lives. Here we are counselled to take note of the effect of deep feelings that spill out, however gently, on to the everyday nature of our lives. We may need to consider how our behaviour is coloured and affected by our deep emotional conditioning when this card and its energy appear in our readings and so our lives.

In turn we know that at the bottom of the lake there lies silt, sand and accumulated decaying organic matter that is symbolic of the past efforts that too have been shaped and discarded by our deep feelings. We may need with this card to assess the impact of our feelings from our past and consider what we might need to discard now and leave behind, whether as unfilled fantasy or unrealistic longing.

So it is that the Lake is shaped and its behaviour and character moulded by its environs and the habitat in which it find itself. This inflow and outflow tell us to look now at what we allow our emotional to be influence by and consider whether this is conducive to our well-being and wholeness.

Lakes are generally held to be beautiful things we long to admire, as we can see from the example on the card. What is not so easily discerned is what may lurk within and the effect this can have and it is this energy that calls us to explore.

BACKGROUND

From the Lake we move into the next biggest expanse of
water, that if the Sea. A Sea is distinct from an Ocean in that it
is partly landlocked. Seas are recognised as being smaller
bodies of water than the Oceans.

For millions of years the Earth was surrounded by a heavy
blanket of rain, many miles in thickness. This would endlessly
condense, fall as rain, then be boiled by the rock it fell onto
and return as vapour in the sky. When eventually the rock
cooled enough, all the rain that had gathered fell in a torrent
for hundreds if not thousands of years. This rainfall levelled
mountain ranges and cur valets into the landscape. When the
rain finally stopped, we had the first sea in these lower levels.

We all know that sea water is salty. This comes from the
minerals in the silt and sediment carried to them from rivers.
As the water vaporises it leaves behind its mineral content.
Much of this is absorbed by the seas plant and animal life. Salt
however, is not used and so continually gathers.

We also know of the tides of the Seas and their daily ebb and
flow. At these times the water level can rise between 10 and
20 feet, although this does vary in certain places, then
receding to leave the beach exposed. The tides are caused by
the gravitational pull of the Sun and Moon. It is of note that at
the New and Full Moons, when the Sun, Moon and Earth are
in alignment, higher tides result, known as spring tides.
Conversely, Neap or lower tides are formed when the Moon is
in its first and third quarter phase. Then it forms a right angle
to the Sun, so the pull between Sun and Moon is offset,
creating smaller tidal flow.

Although we may imagine it to be so, the floor of the sea is
not flat. It is composed of vast basins, some broader and

deeper than others. In these basins the water flows back and forth, disturbed or pulled by the Sun and Moon and the deeper the basin, the greater the disturbance and flow.

Waves are produced by wind that blows across the surface of the sea, which break when they reach shallower water. Wind will predominately blow in one place in the same direction, forming a surface current; therefore, the stronger the wind, the greater the current. The temperature of the sea water is dependent on the amount of solar radiation falling on its surface. This can range from below freezing in polar areas to over 30 centigrade.

The sea of course also supports a huge range of life, from plant and algae to the myriad and wonderful creatures of the deep. The Sea has long fascinated humanity since we first began exploring and plays a vital role in travel and trade across the world. It is also a source of food as well as leisure on its many wonderful coastlines.

DESCRIPTION

In the image here we gaze out to sea at a seemingly endless horizon, far away from our vantage point on the shore. At our feet the waves break gently before us, slipping effortlessly onto the sand.

In the mid-ground we can see the white water as the waves break, contrasting with the darker blue of the deeper waters beyond. Above the clouds form, reminding us of the cyclical nature of this Element. Above we see the glare from the Sun, reminding us again of the quest on which we continue.

ENERGY

In the Lake we saw the importance of looking to the depths to deal with what we find there. Now with the Sea much can

287

come to the surface and again, it is about how we respond to this emotionally that takes prime importance.

We have seen that the Sea is subject to influence by the wind and that this creates the currents that can carry us, literally and physically as well as on an emotional level, where they will. This tells us that when this card appears for us, its energy is one of 'going with the flow'. For us to achieve this, we need to determine where the current or the flow is going.

To do this, we need to look to the effect our thoughts are having upon us first. This is the realm of Air, as we shall see in the next suit, and we first receive energy mentally before we respond emotionally, like the wind blowing on the surface of the sea. Once we have observed our response here, it is for us to make the choice of whether we wish to go with that particular flow or choose to swim against it. We can choose here whether we move onwards on our emotional path or leave what we have outgrown or no longer have heart for, behind.

We know that the salt content of Sea water comes from the sediment produced from the rivers flowing into it. This tells us our emotions are rarely things that we can leave behind fully and totally in one moment. Rather, we carry something of their debris with us, until we reach a point of being able to float on them, such as the opportunity the Dead Sea offers us.

The reason that we cannot drink sea water is that our kidneys cannot cope with the overload from the high salt content and shut down, killing us. So from the Sea we can learn that we carry deep within us and as part of our inherent being, the emotional effects of our previous experience – they can be absorbed into us. However if we do not do what is required and release hat is not productive and positive for us, it can pollute ad even kill us.

The necessity in working with the energy of this card is then to look to see what is the content of your metaphorical and emotional salt amongst the purity of your being? What is it within you that may be poisoning your system and dragging you down? What it is that may be required so that you can rise again to the surface and seek then to go with where the natural current will take, by your determination and choice?

Of course the Seas break in beautiful formation on its shore. From here we can learn whether we are on the outside looking in at our emotional state or perhaps trying to avoid plunging into those apparently cold depths. It is as if the energy here calls to us 'come on in, the waters lovely'! In order the move beyond emotional conditioning that may detract from our well-being, we first have to feel the full depth of it, again in order to rise to the surface to find an easier current.

This cards' energy may well come in tides, rather than a flood that threatens us. It is no less powerful because of this however. It can benefit is now to observe the times when we may feel up or down, or when certain feelings seek to overwhelm us or retreat. Looking at our emotional tides can allow us to work with our hearts to bring us to a more productive place in ourselves.

9 - OCEAN
BACKGROUND

Moving on in the Water cycle from the Sea to the Ocean takes us of course to a larger expanse and greater depth, which as we shall see is mirrored in this cards' energy and its effect upon us.

Oceans cover approximately two-thirds of the Earth's surface, roughly equivalent to the percentage of water content in the human body. The Oceans provide us with about 97% of our water supply. Due to their size and enormity, the Oceans moderate the Earth's temperature by absorbing incoming solar radiation. This heat in then distributed around the globe by the Oceans current, heating land and air during winter and cooling it in summer. In this way they have a direct impact on our climate and through the process of evaporation, are the source of our rainfall.

The Oceans of the Earth are all connected and are in fact, one body of water we delineate separately. There are five recognised oceans, although we cannot truly mark a point where one stops and another begins. These are the Pacific, Atlantic, Indian, Southern and Arctic, in descending order of size. Like sea water, the oceans contain salt water, with those nearer the Poles and so cooler having higher salinity levels. The total volume of the water of the Oceans is approximately 1.3 billion cubic kilometres and the average depth is 3,682 meters, reaching its greatest depth at almost 11,000 metres. Their total area covers 361 million square kilometres.

The oceans are integral to all known life on Earth. They form part of the carbon cycle and influence our climate and weather patterns. Over 2 million marine species are estimated to live within their domain. The mostly blue colour of the Ocean's water is a composite of several contributing agents, such as dissolved organic matter and chlorophyll. This blue colour is least absorbed by seawater; the same shade of blue is most absorbed by microscopic plants, called phytoplankton, drifting in seawater.

Oceans are divided into three zones of density – the surface, pycnocline, and deep zones. In the surface or mixed layer, the least dense level of the ocean, the temperature and salinity level is relatively constant with depth, due to the current and wave action. In the next pycnocline zone, the density increasing substantially due to decreases in temperature. The most dense, deep zone contains colder and relatively stable water and accounts for approximately 80% of the total water volume. It is noteworthy that the top ten feet of the ocean contains as much heat as our entire atmosphere.

The largest single feature on Earth occurs within the ocean. This is a mountain range that is the ocean ridge. This is almost 40,000 miles long and weaves its way throughout all five oceans. We have currently explored less than 10% of our oceans. The deepest point of the oceans is more than one mile greater than the height of Mount Everest.

DESCRIPTION

The image here is taken from the Atlantic Ocean, but we must remind ourselves here that in reality there is just one Ocean on our planet. As we gaze at the image we can get a sense of the huge expanse of this area of water, as it disappears into the distance and on over the horizon.

We can of course see nothing of what lies below the surface. The appearance of the rays and energy of the Sun in the picture remind us of the impact of the Ocean on our climate and of the action of the waves which we see in the foreground. This is further confirmed by the appearance of clouds, forming from the vaporization of the water in the heat.

ENERGY

In the Tarot Therapy approach, the number Nine of each suit represents its' apex, its highest and most potent energy formation. In the case of Water this is represented by the biggest and deepest volume of Water on the planet – this being of course, the Ocean.

Here we refer to in the singular as reminder that all the ocean are interconnected and are in fact, one body of Water. This tells us that when this card appears in our readings, we need to look at the impact of our feelings and emotions not just on the other levels of our being – their physical, mental and spiritual effect, but also on how we are affecting the whole of ourselves, both inwardly and outwardly. This interconnectedness tells us that we need now to realise that our emotions and feelings cannot stand alone from the other levels of ourselves and have a vital impact upon the course of our whole self and life. The appearance of this card is asking us to see what this effect is and ask what if nay response is required to this.

We might also like to remind ourselves here of the Ocean covering two-thirds of our planet, symbolically meaning that perhaps this same percentage of our beings come from our emotional responses. When we look at ourselves and our individual history we can usually see that in the end, we do what we *want* to, regardless of whether this may be the 'right' thing or not. We have a tendency to follow the promptings of our hearts and how we feel. This cards' energy is then one that prompts us to question this, to finally come to terms with this knowledge and seek to see a true wisdom.

It can be all too easy for a true feeling to become buried so deep as never to be looked and felt, reminding us of the small percentage of the Ocean that humanity has explored. Here we may need to look at what we have not explored emotionally. What may remain buried in the depths of our being, lying dormant and undiscovered for years but is in fact, still a part of us. Do we need to explore these depths and bring up to the light that which we find?

The Suns appearance on the card also tells us that this may be a time of intensity, when we might feel the full force and power of our emotional make-up. This may be experienced in emotional peaks and troughs, great up and downs rather like the canyons and valleys that exist on the Ocean floor. The energy here is the Nine which can be one of extreme feelings and the most powerful feelings. It may be that we are called at this time to connect with what we feel most strongly, deeply and powerfully about. Here the need might be to assess the impact and effect of this, not only on ourselves abut others also and determine the most appropriate response.

10 - VAPOUR
BACKGROUND

Following the massive expanse of water that is the Ocean, we come now to the last stage of the Water Cycle, that of its return to its origins. This is the Vapour as the water is lifted from the surface of the Earth due to heat, to rise into the atmosphere, form clouds, coagulate as droplets and begin again as rain. This process is called Evaporation.

Water Vapour is actually water in a gas form that is held in the air until it changes back into water. We can feel this in the humidity or 'stickiness' we can feel in the air – this is water held in the air. The water condenses into fine droplets, which form clouds and then it rains.

The change in water as it moves between its vapour, liquid and solid form happens due to differences in the arrangement of the water molecules. The molecules in vapour form are more random arranged than in its liquid form. As condensation occurs, meaning the water forms from the vapour, the water molecules become organized less randomly. This causes heat to be released into the atmosphere.

Even though we cannot see it, water is still present in a 'cloud-less' blue sky – in the form of vapour and droplets too small to be seen by the human eye. These water molecules then combine with dust, salt and smoke in the air to form cloud droplets, which grow and develop into clouds, as a form of water we can see. This process occurs higher in the sky where the air is cooler and more condensation thus occurs relative to evaporation. As the water droplets combine, they create larger and heavier drops, which sink to the bottom of the cloud and then fall as rain.

It is known that the surface water of the Earth, from the Ocean, Seas, Lakes,, Rivers and so on provide almost 90% of the moisture in the atmosphere of the Earth (the rest coming from plants). This evaporation is the primary mechanism for this part of the water cycle. The amount of water evaporating is about the same as that which falls as rain. A water molecule will spend on average ten days in the air – fitting nicely with our number and energy here. Furthermore, about 10% of evaporated water returns over the land as rain, the rest falling back over water, mostly the Ocean.

The process of evaporation is reactive mostly to temperature. It is the difference in temperature of water droplets or molecules that causes the change from liquid water to vapour. This occurs as it cools, the heat being taken by the liquid water as it goes. The rate of the loss of water is relative to the rate at which it cools.

So it is that the water cycle is complete and we again have the formation of a single drop of Water, where we began with the One of this suit. From this we can see the cyclic nature of the water processes of our planet, which as we have seen can bear a direct relationship to our emotional well-being.

DESCRIPTION

Water Vapour is of itself, invisible. This of course makes it impossible to show in this pure form in an image. So the image we see could perhaps more accurately be called 'Condensation' rather than Vapour. However we stick with Vapour as this is the product or physical form, rather than the process, which we have followed. It is worth mentioning here that we cannot see our emotions or feelings either.

So the image that we see is more the end product of the process of condensation. We can however see something of the Vapour in the misty area just above the water in the image. We can also determine from the image the way in which the water rises into the air and forms the clouds that we can see.

We can also note something of a beautiful balance between the light (of course from the Sun) on the top half of the image to the deep lustre of the water below. This reminds of the principle of 'As Above, So Below', fitting here in the completion of the Water cycle, as the water returns to the air, apparently disappears, only to return again as rain.

ENERGY

What began as a single drop of Water evolved into the vast depth and expanse of the Ocean. Even this though, is subject to a greater force and disappears from view, as Vapour. Perhaps it is this that tells us much about the nature of our emotional make-up. We all know that we seek to bury or avoid in one way or another painful, hurtful and just plain nasty and unpleasant emotions, but eventually they must rise to the surface.

This reality cannot be avoided and we must take from this that we must face up to our feelings in each moment, whatever they may be. We can however, take comfort in this from the knowledge that they can be released. Once we have brought them up to the surface and expressed them, we know from the process of condensation here, that the natural law means they will evaporate. Once expressed and released, our feelings are then freed to take a different form.

As such they become invisible to us, we have let them go and they are no more. Should they be left unexplored in the depths of the Ocean they can do all manner of harm without us even knowing. If however we are courageous and bold enough to open our hearts, our emotions can find appropriate expression and take on a different form. It is this that the energy of this card gives us.

Of course we have seen that from the water cycle that this same water returns again to us. This tells us that although we may never be fully free of the effects of our emotional responses – especially that which we bury deep in our formative years – we can change the effect they have upon us through expression, understanding and release. The threads may still exist, but the work is done, the feelings complete and so we move onwards and upwards, safe in the knowledge that we have experienced what we were required to do. The water in a different form is them symbolic of that which can refresh and wash us clean, rather than drag us down from within.

We should also note here the relationship between temperature – the Fire / Sun aspect of the human being – and our emotions. This comes from the impact temperature has upon the vapourisation of water. As we will see in that suit, the Fire part of us is closely linked to our will and this interaction between the elements here tells us that we must really want to shift our stuck emotions to succeed – not from an emotional standpoint but from a more powerful, primal level, that of will and motivation.

From this we can also see a direct way in which we create our own reality – if we will and want it enough, all those feelings we thing are bigger than us and that we can never truly come to terms with, accept and free from, can evaporate and disappear. Rue, they return but in a different form, that of understanding, acceptance, and ultimately, love – of the self first and then others.

WATER OF EARTH – MARSH
BACKGROUND

A Marsh, by definition, is a type of wetland where water covers the ground for long periods of time, thereby lending itself perfectly to this combination of Water with Earth. Marshes are usually found at the edges of lakes and streams, again lending themselves to the watery kingdom of this suit. They can also occur in estuaries and low-lying land areas, where a depression or delta, allows water to accumulate.

Usually Marshes are dominated by herbaceous rather than woody plant species, of grasses, rushes and reeds. Any woody plants present tend to be low-growing shrubs. A feature here is that the roots of the herbaceous plants root into the rich, muddy soil, thereby encouraging the marsh to spread, demonstrating the combination of Water and Earth for our purposes.

Marshes provide a habitat for many species that have adapted to flooded conditions. Such life must adapt to a wet mud and low oxygen environment, many having stems that allow air to move from leaves to roots. Marshes are also home to many fish and amphibian species.

Apart from supporting some of the highest levels of biological production, Marshes also improve water quality. This is done by acting as a sink to filter pollutants and sediment from the water that flows through them. During periods of heavy rainfall, Marshes are able to absorb water then release it slowly to waterways, reduce any flooding.

Marshes can form in salt as well as fresh water and tidal conditions, the plant and animal life within them varying greatly due to this. These are the three main recognised types of Marsh and they perform a variety of functions, including buffering stormy seas, slowing shoreline erosion, providing shelter and nesting sites for migratory birds and absorbing excess nutrients that would otherwise lower oxygen level in surrounding waters and harm wildlife.

DESCRIPTION

Perhaps the most well-known area of Marshlands in the world is the Everglades in Florida, USA. This whole are as suitably been described as a 'river of grass' and it is from this area that our chosen image is taken here. This is part of what is called 'Shark River' and illustrates the nature and life of the Marsh perfectly.

We can see the grasses that live amongst the water, rooting into the mud beneath yet protruding above the surface for life. In the distance we can see that the grasses thicken, giving the appearance of solid ground, but once closer it will be found this exists on the same, marshy soil. The beautiful blue reminds that we are still within the suit of Water, yet given form here by Earth, in different life-forms that this combination supports.

ENERGY

We have worked our way through the sometimes deep and seemingly treacherous Waters of this suit. Now we seek our way forward with the workings of the elemental combinations, as they are seen and experienced through the realm of Water. First comes the linking with Earth, producing for us the Marsh.

If we remind ourselves that with the Compound cards in this deck we see them as their essential nature and energy being of the suit to which they belong, expressed by the Element with which they are combined. In the case of this card, our emotional self is here expressed in a more practical and methodical approach.

We have seen how a Marsh has a variety of effects on its surrounding area, from improving the water quality to reducing flooding. From this we can take that this cards energy will enable us to avoid becoming 'drowned' by our emotions and find a level of 'true ground' and stability upon which to express what we are feeling. That the Marsh improves the water quality tells us that our emotions now are more likely to be that which we truly feel, less tainted by others and distortion for outside sources.

For the grasses that inhabit marshlands to do so, they must be able to root into wet soil or mud yet still reach the surface. The energy from this aspect counsels us that although we may still feel 'wet' and 'watery', or emotionally vulnerable, we can still find a means to root ourselves on something approaching solid ground, enabling us to feel more secure with the expression of our feelings. This in turn allows us to 'breathe' a little, as we emerge from the muddy depths of emotional turmoil to reach something approaching stability.

In this way the energy of this card can allow us to feel more comfortable with the nature and expression of whatever emotions are arising for us at the time. It tells us that we can rely on our emotions now not to be distorted but something that if we approach them correctly we can find them of great use in their effect and outworking on the other areas of ourselves and lives.

This can lead us to feel safe now that we are not having to expose our feelings to all and sundry, nor be submerged by emotional tides and turns, but be beginning, at the very least, to integrate our emotional being into our physical and everyday lives, this being the aspect of the Earth suit, as we now know.

WATER OF FIRE – GEYSER
BACKGROUND

A Geyser is an apt depiction of our combination here of Fire with Water. A Geyser occurs when surface water makes its way down to an average depth of 2,000 metres and encounters hot rocks. The pressurised water then boils, resulting in what is called a hydrothermal explosion – the water shots up as a geyser of hot water and steam through a surface vent.

There are over 1,000 geysers across the world, occurs mainly in volcanic areas, the hot rock being caused by the presence of magma. Apart from what is known as the necessary 'plumbing system' (a reservoir to hold the water as it boils and a system of fractures to create the necessary pressure for eruption), it is a combination of intense heat and the water itself that create the geyser.

The heat comes from the magma and this is required near the surface, hence their link to volcanic areas. The boiling point is much higher than normal due to the pressure created.

Prior to the eruption of a geyser, the water at the top of the underground reservoir cools. However due to the narrowness of the channel, normal cooling of the water is prevented. The cooler water then presses down on the hotter water beneath. This allows the reservoir water to become super-heated – it remains liquid at temperatures well above boiling point.

When boiling begins steam bubbles burst through the geyser's vent, reducing the weight of the column of water and the pressure underneath. With this the superheated water erupts into steam, boiling violently as it goes. It is this that gives the spray of steam and hot water that we see. This it is the term geyser is sued, from the Old Norse meaning 'to gush'.

The continued existence of a geyser can be an unpredictable thing, since they are dependent on the delicate balance of the conditions described above. Some geysers are known to become extinct or have periods of dormancy.

The majority of the worlds' geysers occur is just five countries – America, Iceland, Russia, Chile and New Zealand. Most geysers erupt infrequently and irregularly. Eruptions can vary from being every few minutes to several hours apart, as well as lasting from a few minutes to many hours. The height to which the water can reach also varies from just a few feet to over 300, in the case of the tallest, the 'Steamboat Geyser' in Yellowstone National Park in the USA.

DESCRIPTION

The most well-known geyser in the world, although not the tallest or most prolific, is Old Faithful, one of the many housed in Yellowstone National Park in the USA. Our image here is actually that of the lesser-known 'Great Fountain Geyser'. This is also situated in Yellowstone, in the, for our purposes, appropriately named area called Firehole Lake. This geyser erupts every 9 to 15 hours and ranges from 75 to 220 feet high when it does so, usually lasting for about an hour.

The image of the sun behind the erupting geyser creates a striking and beautiful backdrop against which we observe the event. This reminds us of the combination of Fire and Water which as we have seen is necessary for a geyser to exist.

BACKGROUND

From the establishment and grounding of our emotional being that we experienced with the previous card, we see its development and somewhat different expression with our combination here of Fire and Water.

The emotional, feeling nature and energy of this suit is well-known to us now and here we see that essential formation expressed in a fiery way. For a Geyser to form, we now that there must be a store of underground water in a reservoir. This tells us that when this card appears, its energy is signalling to look at what emotions lie beneath our surface and be conscious, at the very least, of what they may be doing to us while they lie there.

We know from the nature of energy itself that nothing can lie dormant forever, just as a Geyser may have a period of dormancy before erupting again. Just as the Water will escape through any channel possible to erupt from its underground source, so our emotions must and will reach for and find expression. The energy here challenges us to find an appropriate and positive expression.

We know that the water forming the Geyser can be much hotter than the normal boiling point. This suggests our emotions are affecting us now and we may be steadily bubbling away beneath the surface. Rest assured however, if we do not release our feelings, this energy will find expression in some fiery manner. As symbolised by the Geyser, this may be in an unpredictable moment, and come when it is least expected, especially so by us.

This may be spectacular and we may well feel the release and freedom in letting out what has been buried, as we in this case, literally, let off steam. The appearance of this card may advise to find an appropriate release before we explode. Of course this can be expressed and experienced in others ways than just our own feelings. It may be through the actions and expression of those around us and indeed by our won and others actions, where we may be caused to show and act with a greater intensity and passion than is the norm for us.

It may be said that the greater the pressure here, the greater the release, as with the height to which the water reaches when the Geyser erupts. In energetic terms this can tell us that if we apply what we feel passionately about to ourselves and our lives, we can indeed achieve a height far greater than we might have previously considered. This cards' appearance counsels us then to let go our inner passion and focus this positively towards our lives, lest we erupt to destructive effect.

WATER OF WATER – WHIRLPOOL
BACKGROUND

A Whirlpool is produced by the meeting of two opposing currents of water, hence it being appropriate for our convergence of water on water here. Whirlpools can also be termed maelstroms or vortexes, usually when they have more power. It is easy to see a small whirlpool in your home – every time you pull the plug on your bath or sink and watch the water disappear.

In the natural world, we can see the build-up of a whirlpool when a river is forced to twist around an object or flow into a narrow riverbed. In an ocean, driving currents can collide and create conflicting tidal flows, depending on the geology of the sea bed. It is this destructive interaction of currents that creates the whirlpool.

In ancient times it was believed that a whirlpool would suck an entire ship into the watery depths beneath. This is akin to our modern view of black holes in space. When a tide does change the current is increased and we do know there can be some danger to boats at these times. Although primarily caused by the collusion of strong tidal currents, whirlpools can also be caused by wind, when they cause the surface current of water to change direction.

The most powerful Whirlpool in the world is the Saltstraumen off the coast of Norway, referred to usually as a maelstrom and which create the strongest tidal currents on the planet. Every six hours the currents can move up to 25 miles per hour, moving over 100,000 gallons of water through the narrow strait where it is located. The Whirlpool itself can be as wide as 33 feet and 16 feet deep. Although the water can appear calm on the surface when the tides turn, beneath the water can be constantly churning and twisting.

Perhaps more famous is the Moskstraumen whirlpool, which has featured in works by Jules Verne ('20,000 Leagues under the Sea') and Edgar Allen Poe ('A Descent into the Maelstrom'), as well as gaining a mention of Herman Melville's 'Moby Dick'.

DESCRIPTION

Our image is that of the Saltstraumen Whirlpool or Maelstrom, mentioned above as the most powerful in the world. This is located 10 kilometres south-east of the town of Bode in Norway and is actually the name of the small strait that gives rise to the whirlpool itself. Nowadays, the whirlpool can be viewed by a bridge that crosses the strait. It is actually a very popular angling spot, the currents giving rise to a high number of fish. There is evidence of a 10,000 year old fishing community there.

As we gaze at the image we can easily see the interaction of the twin and opposing forces if water. They seem to spiral into the centre, sucking everything into it with tremendous force. Once there, the whirling dervish like motion of the water spirals down to greater depths, ensuring the consumption of all it encounters.

ENERGY

We now from our previous studies that Water equates to our feelings and emotions, so it is no surprise that with a meeting of tidal currents in this cards energy that we can experience an apparently overwhelming flow of feeling.

What we have seen from the above study of the Whirlpool is that they are caused by opposing currents. This may tell us that we need to look at what we may be feeling that is in opposition to our natural flow. We may need to question whether we are allowing others to influence the way we feel and if this is in conflict to our true feelings.

Of course the danger with the energy of this card, as with the Whirlpool, is that we can be drawn down and into dangerous territory because of these feelings. Here the need is to straighten out and remain true to our original feeling. This card asks us 'what is our true feeling'?

All this emotions can also create a sense within us that allows us to experience a very deep and powerful sensitivity. We may be over-emotional and find ourselves weeping when we would normally not, and upset by trivial things in ourselves and lives.

This energy can also give rise to a strong empathic ability. This is something that must be managed careful, lest again we become drowned in the current of emotion and dragged down by it. Applied with care however, we can allow this empathy to guide us through the apparent maelstrom of others feelings and their impact upon us. This energy can also bring a huge sense of compassion and love to all and sundry. This again can be easily used if we allow it.

The essential message to accompany the energy that this card brings is to observe our emotional tides, be observant of their source and remain true to our own. Handled carefully and sensibly these feelings can produce a great depth, understanding and love.

WATER OF AIR – SNOW
BACKGROUND

The combination here of Air and Water leads us, perhaps surprisingly, to Snow. Snow is actually precipitation, or rain, that falls due to the upward movement of Air, showing us how the combination here comes into force.

Snow itself forms when water vapour in the atmosphere freezes into ice crystals. When the temperature in the air is low and there is moisture in the air in the form of tiny ice crystals, these collide and stick together in the cloud to form snowflakes. Eventually the ice crystals become heavy enough to fall to the ground as snow.

The temperature needs to be 2 degrees Centigrade or below for snow to fall, the heaviest snowfall occurring when it is below 0 and 2 degrees. Although the snow will begin to melt as soon as the temperature is above 0, this in turn cools the air around it. Where the air warmer than 2 it will fall as sleet then back to rain as the temperature rises. From this we can see that the very existence of snow is dependent on the air and its temperature.

Since it is formed of small ice crystals, snow is a granular material. Its structure, as we know, is soft and open, unless it is subject to external pressure, when it can form into a ball and fall as hail. Snowflakes can come in a variety of shapes and sizes. Although it appears to us as such, snow is not actually white. The complex structure of snow crystals results in countless tiny surfaces that reflect visible light. The small amount of sunlight absorbed by the crystal is done so uniformly over the wavelengths of visible light. It is this that gives snow its white appearance. Due to its chemical make-up, every snowflake has 6 sides.

Over 80% of the Earth's freshwater is frozen as ice or snow and covers 12% of the surface of the planet. When it melts however, one inch of snow can produce less than a tenth of an inch of water. On average a snowflake falls at 3 miles per hour and has 180 billion molecules of water. Snow can appear blue due to its tendency to absorb the red light in the colour spectrum, this being more so if the snow is deep.

A layer of snow on the ground can also damped sound, due to its capacity to absorb sound waves, especially when it is thick and freshly fallen. The crunching sound made as you walk on snow is caused by the air between the ice crystals being crushed as you tread on them. Since fresh snow is cause by a high percentage of air between the crystals, which can barely move, heat transfer is greatly reduced. This means that snow becomes a great insulator and some animals even dig snow caves in which to hibernate through the winter.

DESCRIPTION

The image here is a beautiful rendition of the combination of Air with Water that gives us the often longed for snow fall. There are a great many landscapes of decorative and seasonal snowfall, sitting prettily atop previously green hills. Here however, we are more interested in the snowfall itself and this is what we view on this card.

The different size of snowflakes is perceivable, along with the manner in which they reflect light in order to create their white appearance. The snow that we see falling is of course in the air and it is this rising current hat we know causes the snow to be present. The snow covered hills are also a reminder of the requirement of the air and altitude that coupled with the moisture in it creates this lovely scene.

ENERGY

From the manner in which snow is formed, we know that it is the Water part that is first created, as the ice crystals form from the moisture in the air and stick together to form snowflakes. This tells us that we must first connect to what we are feeling, identify with these emotions but without becoming lost in them, for they as yet have not fallen.

It is only when they interact with the air rising from below that this happens. This tells us that we must apply at least a modicum of thought and rationality to ourselves and lives now. Only when this is done can we afford or find it appropriate to allow what we are feeling to be expressed. Given that snow can tend to deaden sound and bury what it lies on, we may find we need to monitor that which we express and the effect it is having, not just upon our selves and our lives, but also that of others.

The combination here of Water with Air can create either a conflict or a harmony between head and heart with the appearance of this cards energy. We know that the Element to which the cards suit belong, in this case Water, is the essential, basic and foundational level of the energy we encounter here. This, as we know, is emotional and connects us to our feelings. The Element to which the card rather than the suit belongs, is the manner in which this energy flows or is expressed. Air, as we shall shortly see, belongs to the mental level of the human being and our capacity to think.

In this way, the energy of this card is one that can enable us to achieve a balance between heart and head respectively, when those twin, 'complementary opposite' energies are allowed to work in tandem and partnership. The energy here will first connect us to what we are feeling but the message of this card is not to allow ourselves to be led solely by this, in our self and life now. Rather there is a need we can benefit from if we then respond to those feelings with our thoughts.

We may find we need now to take a step back from following the heart and doing what we want and instead looking objectively at this before we act.

This can allow us to achieve the real boon and benefit from the energy this card brings to us – that of connecting us to our intuition. When we balance our both our feelings and our thoughts we can then arrive at a deeper and more complete, or whole truth from within ourselves, which we can call intuition, as 'inner knowing', or even clairsentience. This cannot be forced or calculated but must instead be allowed. It is this combination that we are given the gift of with the energy of this card.

AIR ELEMENT

The Element of Air is linked to the mental level of our being and our thinking processes. The cards of this suit show us the mental energy we are being influenced by and the effect this can have upon us and our rationality.

Our thought processes relate closely to our ability to assimilate what we perceive instinctively and is where we seek to understand, calculate and work out what is going on and why. Once we have 'got our heads around' whatever it is, we can then gain a semblance of control over why we are the way we are and apply some of that understanding to ourselves and lives. The cards here show us this through the symbolism and processes of the element of Air.

As we shall, the cards follow the process of the Element of Air through from its beginnings, as the atmosphere itself, and then through its various stages, until it symbolically blows itself out with the Zephyr of the last card. Just as with all the Elements, we are dependent on Air for our lives and it is the absence of this Element that extinguishes life most swiftly of all, such is our dependency on air.

It is easy to feel the effects of this upon ourselves just by holding our breath and realising how this causes us to feel. Similarly, we can easily step outside for 'a breath of fresh air' and immediately feel the life-affirming effects of this. It is noticeable and significant that this clears our head and how refreshing it is to walk to the top of a hill and allow the wind to blow the cobwebs away.

The Breath has been linked in many health and spiritual practices to the mind. To still and quieten the breath is to do the same to the mind. The energy of the Air Element and its conscious use and control can go a long way to help our spiritual growth and overall health. So often we forget or neglect to breathe properly, breathing only from our chest. Instead, we can quite easily acquire the habit of breathing from below our diaphragm, breathing from the belly. This allows the lungs to inflate more fully, increasing our intake of oxygen, along with the life-force and energy we receive as a result. This has so many benefits, apart from the immediate physical effect upon the mind.

The cards here and the energy they represent, can help us with coming to terms with the working of our minds and allow us to establish firstly an awareness of our thinking and our natural tendencies of thinking pattern. Secondly we can learn to establish an objectivity that allows us to see things more clearly, understanding why things are the way they are and how and why we think about them the way we do. As we shall see from the different types and classifications given to the manifestations of Air, we can be threatened as well as benefit from its use in ourselves and lives as we continue our quest to integrated wholeness.

AIR

1 - ATMOSPHERE
BACKGROUND

We begin our journey through the element of Air with the very thing that gives us our ability to live – the atmosphere itself. At the present time, the Earth is the only planet we know of that is capable of sustaining life. This is due to the level of oxygen within the atmosphere of the Earth, which we need every time we breathe.

It is thought that our atmosphere evolved in three stages. Firstly the atmosphere consisted of hydrogen and helium, which moved so fast they escaped the Earth's gravity and floated into space. Secondly, as the Earth's crust formed the many volcanoes on the surface gave off a mixture of carbon dioxide, steam and ammonia. Lastly, as the carbon dioxide dissolved into the oceans, bacteria living off energy from the Sun developed and gave off oxygen as a waste product. As the oxygen levels grew the ammonia was broken by sunlight, leaving nitrogen and hydrogen, which floated into space, being the lightest. Thus our current atmosphere, enabling life, was created from life itself. Breath really is the stuff of life.

The air in our atmosphere is roughly 78% nitrogen, 21% oxygen and 1% a composition of other gases, which is what we inhale on every breath. When we exhale however, the oxygen is effectively exchanged for carbon dioxide and we breathe out about 18% oxygen, 78% nitrogen and 3% carbon dioxide (CO_2). Plants use this CO_2 to make sugar, illustrating beautifully the inter-dependency of life.

The exact composition of the atmosphere is continually changing and depends on the season, weather and time of day, also latitude, longitude, elevation, and geography.

Earth's atmosphere is typically divided into five layers, from the thickest at the bottom to the thinnest at the top –

1 - the troposphere, the region of rising and falling pockets of air, up to 14 kilometres above the surface
2 – the stratosphere - up to 50 km above the planet. Air flow here is mostly horizontal (where jets fly for stability). Also here is ozone - a thin layer, responsible for absorbing ultra-violet radiation from the Sun, harmful to the existence of life if not done
3 – the mesosphere – meteors or rock fragments burn up at this level, about 80 km above
4 – the thermosphere - with auroras. It is also where the space shuttle orbits, up to 700 km
5 – the exosphere – where our atmosphere merges into space, higher than 700 km above us.

DESCRIPTION

Taken from above our wonderful little planet, the image here shows us something of the visible aspect of the atmosphere in and on which we live. In the foreground of the card we can see the cloudscape and above this the blue of the sky. It appears blue to us because the molecules of air and one wavelength of blue light are approximately equal.

Molecules are actually scattered above and below from this point. Red, orange and yellow move downwards towards the Earth, while the faster blue, indigo and violet wavelengths travel upwards into space. We can see something of this on the image here, with the deep orange turning almost to red as the sun rises here above the curve of the Earth, rising through yellow to the hint of violet visible in the clouds.

ENERGY

Our journey through the element of Air begins with the very breath of life, personified and symbolised in the card by the atmosphere in which we live. As we have seen and know, without this, there can be no life on Earth. Equally, the removal of this element, of all the four our suits are based is the quickest to result in the end of our life.

We have seen that out atmosphere is about 21% oxygen and in the human body 65% of its mass is also oxygen. Since we link the element of air, and so oxygen, to the mental level and its function in our beings, this easily tells us how important this is. This applies both to our breath and to our thinking.

The energy of this card first tells us then to breathe. This is obvious of course, but it can be incredibly easy to revert to an unnatural mode of breathing, whereby we breathe and inhale with only the top half or less, of our lungs. When we breathe by thinking about our breath, we automatically inhale more deeply and fully. We inhale from below our diaphragm, as if we breathe form the belly. This allows for a greater intake of oxygen, along with the life-force, or energy, that accompanies it. If we do not, we effectively deprive our brains of oxygen and we cannot think clearly.

The energy here then challenges and asks us to become mindful, first of our breath and then of our thinking. The question to ask ourselves here is simply 'what are you thinking'? We then need to see the effect of these thoughts upon ourselves and lives.

It is well-known adage in spiritual fields now that 'energy follows thought, illustrating with this principle the way in which we create our own reality. This card is an object lesson in this. We need to realise now that the principle of 'I think therefore I am' applies quite literally. The energy that we apply with our thoughts is the prime factor in what we experience.

316

There is a great deal written and practised on the subject of mindfulness now, in both yogic and Buddhist traditions, along with the practices of yogic breathing or pranayama techniques and we can do well to immerse ourselves in these somewhat, when this card appears in our readings. The breath is central to our overall well-being and the effectiveness of our minds, and the energy coming to us now affords us the opportunity to benefit from this to the maximum degree possible.

2 – CONVERGENCE
BACKGROUND

Given its full title, we concern ourselves now with the Inter-Tropical, or Equatorial, Convergence Zone. This is a band of clouds that encircles the globe near the equator, which consists of showers and sometimes thunderstorms. These clouds can extend for many hundreds of miles and extend to approximately 10 degrees north and south of the equator. The Convergence Zone follows the Sun in that it moves seasonally. It moves north in the northern summer and south in its winter. It is this that creates the wet and dry seasons in the tropics.

This convergence exists due to the trade winds. These move in a south westerly direction in the northern hemisphere and north westerly in the southern hemisphere. The point at which they meet forces the air up into the atmosphere and this is known as the Convergence Zone. As the air rises in expands and cools. This results in huge bands of clouds and thunderstorms over the ocean.

The storms that can result from this movement of Air create the wet and dry seasons in each of the Northern and Southern Hemispheres. The Convergence Zone can therefore have a drastic effect on rainfall in many equatorial areas. Over a period of time this can result in either periods of drought or flooding.

Although specifically referred to here as the area around the equator, a Convergence Zone can exist at any point where two prevailing flows of Air meet and interact, which usually results in distinctive weather conditions. This can often be above mountain ranges where the wind is split by them. An example here is the area above Seattle in the US, where the

Puget Sound Convergence Zone can create extreme weather conditions and is created by the Olympic Mountains.

To further illustrate the duality inherent in the Convergence Zone, fitting it for our numerological value here, there is often a cycle in the rainfall produced that is diurnal, meaning that the clouds formed occur twice daily. We shall also meet some of the effects produced by the Convergence Zone in other cards as we journey through this element.

DESCRIPTION

It is clear to see the principle of the Convergence Zone here and the dualistic nature of this card in the almost back and white split in the clouds here. The image here is in the area of the above-mentioned Puget Sound Convergence Zone.

We saw above that at the Convergence Zone the air is forced upwards where it then cools and collects moisture and produces rain and storms. Clearly this is what we see occurring in this image. The heavier, moisture-filled rain clouds sit beneath the now lighter and drier white, sparse cloud formation. It is clear that a storm is coming and so we need to take action, as we shall see now.

ENERGY

We began with the essence of the element of Air, as the whole of the Atmosphere in which live and breathe. From there we come down to Earth, or at least to a little way above it and in its centre. Here we explore the nature of the element focussed on its behaviour around the Equator, which as we have seen draws together two winds moving in opposing directions.

The duality in nature of the Convergence is easy to see from the above background. Firstly we have the Convergence Zone itself as the result of the above 'meeting of minds' as we

319

could effectively describe it here. Then we have the collusion of cold and warm air, along with the diurnal or twice daily occurrence of this meeting. This all fits with the numerological energy of this card as the Two which perhaps obviously carries the energy of duality, requires balance. This tells us that with the appearance of this card we need to look a little objectively at our thought processes, rather than just making an assumption that what comes into our heads is as it should be.

In other words we need now to start to think! With the One of Air we encounter and learn to deal with the first thoughts we have and here we learn to look at these as it were from the outside. We begin to question what we know. This can sometimes manifest in those around us pointing out an opposite point of view. This does not necessarily mean we experience it in the form of a disagreement or argument – although that is not ruled out – but that if we are open to receiving it we can arrive at a more complete holistic view of a situation but embracing and understanding another's point of view.

The energy of this card then illustrates the principle of the need to look within and question our mode of thinking and what we may believe to be the truth. Just as we know there can be good and bad in all things, so we can see this in the warm and cold air that rises and then falls in the Convergence zone. This may be telling us when this card appears in our readings that we need to realise that we can operate a choice in our thinking. There is very often two different ways of looking at a situation and we may need now to see both before we make a decision on how to see or understand something.

Indeed it may be that this cards' energy is telling us that we need to make a decision, lest it be made for us. We know from our study of the Convergence Zone that the movement of air is natural and will continue to happen, come what may. So it is with our minds. Our thinking has a need to develop and we cannot stay stuck with the same parameters. There is a need now to avoid the 'my minds made up' approach in our heads of stuck and limited thinking and instead make a choice as to how we will approach a situation, person and so on.

3 – PRESSURE

BACKGROUND

From the gentle Breeze we now come to manner in which essentially Wind as we know and feel it, is created. This is due to the pressure of Air exerted by the atmosphere. This is the force exerted upon us and the surface of the Earth by the weight of tiny particles or molecules of Air. Although these are invisible, they still have weight and take up space.

Air Pressure is basically the weight of the Air pressing down on the Earth, the Oceans and the air below. Air Pressure is related to its density, which in turn is related to the temperature of the Air and the height above the Earth's surface. We can see from this the tree factors instrumental in determining Air Pressure, aligning it with our Numerological value here.

The higher we are above the Earth's surface, the more Air Pressure decreases and the greater difficulty we have in breathing. Areas of both high and low air pressure have a great effect on creating the wind and the weather that we experience. A High pressure area comes when the air pressure is greater than the pressure of the air around it, the opposite when it is low.

Low pressures are usually associated with high winds and warm air, often resulting in clouds and rainfall. High pressure areas are created by the air cooling and becoming denser as it moved towards the ground. This evaporates the water vapour in the air, resulting in clear skies and warmer temperatures.

So it is we can see that the pressure of the Air is directly related to the conditions we experience. The majority of the time we simply do not notice the air pressure all around us. This is basically because the air forces on all sides of us balance each other out. All things being equal, air particles will disperse evenly in an area so that there is equal air density at every point. There is however, a vital, third factor to take into account – that of Gravity.

With no other forces at work, everything would be completely balanced in a mass of Air, with equal pressure on all sides. Air particles have mass and so are pulled towards the Earth, which creates the gradual increase in air pressure. Pressure in the Air however, creates an upward force, which creates the differences we can feel in our breath at different heights.

Essentially, the air pressure is greater below things than it is above things, so air pushes up more than it pushes down. But this buoyant force is weak compared to the force of gravity -- it is only as strong as the weight of the air displaced by an object. This is why things do not float off from the Earth' surface as this force can only move things that are lighter than the air above it. This is alos why we float, in space, above the Earth's atmosphere.

DESCRIPTION

In an area of low pressure that brings rain, clouds known as cumulonimbus are created. These generally appear as the dense, fluffy clouds which grow dark when filled with moisture, before they become heavy enough for it to rain. When the air pressure rises however, gaps are created in the clouds and the sky begins to clear. The clouds thin and disperse.

It is this process that we see in our image here. Of course the energy in this card is not about the Air pressure either rising or falling, it is about the air pressure itself and how we respond to it. It is a necessary and ongoing process of change and creation and it is our response to this matters.

ENERGY

From a numerological standpoint, three is the number that carries the energy of creativity and productivity. So it is that with this card we see the creative principle of Pressure at work as being the prime force that determines or creates the weather and conditions that we experience.

Since we relate the workings of the energy of this suit to the mental level of the human being, the energy that this card presents to us concerns the creativity of the mind. In other words, this is about how we respond to what we receive in our minds. We could arguably define this as our level of understanding.

We have seen that the weather conditions are primarily created by either the rise or fall of air pressure. In terms of the Mind, this can relate the manner in which we process and express the thoughts that come to us, and whether we do this or not. As we have seen, pressure is never a constant in this regard and is always subject to a process of change, or creativity.

In this way we may need to detach ourselves a little from our mental processes now and look objectively at the way we are thinking, to consider how may use this more productively or creatively. Just as we have seen that the air pressure goes a long way to creating our weather conditions, so it is the way we think goes an equal length in the reality we create for ourselves.

It has become something of a spiritual maim nowadays that 'energy follows thought' – expressed a number of different ways. This does illustrate effectively that what we think, we experience. The energy of this card can then offer us a powerful opportunity to learn to create our own reality, the way we think it should be.

If we harness the energy of this card positively, we can learn to see how we are instinctively affected, or responding to the thoughts we have and gain some insight as to why these happen. Once this has become known, we can then learn that we can control our thoughts and so shape the reality that we experience and ultimately create, for ourselves.

The energy of this card can then teach us that rather than being taken up or down, made high or low, by external force or pressure, we can become the determining factor ourselves. This powerful awareness can create a state of mind that allows us some dominion and positive response to thought processes that may hitherto have caused us a great deal of anguish in our minds and so as a consequence, in our hearts.

4 – DOLDRUMS
BACKGROUND

As we will see, the Convergence Zone we have previously travelled through has some results and consequences in the Element of Air. One of these is the Doldrums. This area of perpetual low pressure around the Equator, as we have seen, can result in calm period when the wind subsides altogether, often prior to squalls and severe thunderstorms.

Historically and today as well, sailors view these areas of stillness and apparent calm with trepidation as they know what may be to come and this can be life-threatening in its severity. The term Doldrums itself seems to have arisen in the 18th Century when cross-equator voyages became more common. In more colloquial terms this can now be taken as meaning someone who is suffering from a state of listlessness, mild depression, stagnation and inactivity, the significance of which we will see below in the energy of this card.

In the natural world the Doldrums are not a continuous occurrence throughout the year and they do not form an uninterrupted belt around the equatorial region. In the Pacific area, the Doldrums tend to only appear near the continental shores, but in the Atlantic can vary in width and position. This is due to the movement and flow of warm and cooler air in these regions.

More specifically the Doldrums, or the conditions given this name, are created by the Trade Winds, which will meet soon in this suit, These are themselves a result of the Convergence Zone and cancel each other out. The result of the meeting of Trade Winds is that there is no, or very little surface wind. This is then labelled the Doldrums.

The term Doldrums itself is thought to have originated from the old English term 'dold' meaning stupid, with the suffix 'rum', linking it with the word tantrum. It could also have come from the 19th Century term of dullard, meaning a dull or sluggish person and was used in this context to define a general state of low spirits. This could give rise to the tantrum, reflecting what could happen in the natural world, as we have seen.

DESCRIPTION

Our image here depicts a typical scene of calm still ness and inactivity in the air. We can gain a sense of these conditions as we look at the image. The very light, wispy cloud formations are also reflected in the slight movement of the water. From this we can see and indeed sense this stillness and the lack of movement resulting in the whole area of what we see.

It is also possible to see and sense, from the slight rise in the water that we see, that there may be more to come. Hurricanes have been known to begin in the Doldrums and the apparent calm can give rise to a squall which can turn even the biggest ship on its head.

ENERGY

With this card we encounter the numerological energy of the Four. As we know, this is a state of limitation, foundation and boundaries. Since we are dealing here with our minds and their workings, we can see how the energy here can give us cause to pause, turn within and find a stillness and calm.

It may be that this cards' appearance is telling us we need to seek withdrawal from the turbulence of our mind and perhaps practice meditation, breastwork and such like in order to create, or more correctly, allow, that calm, still state of mind which is required at this time.

Whether our minds require this calm and period of inactivity will show itself with surrounding cards and how we are at the time I t appears for us. It may be the other way round of course and that the client at this time is finding that their thinking is tuck, they are going round and round with the same line of thinking or mode of thought and indeed need a release from this – the calm before th storm so to speak, as we have seen can result as a consequence.

Either way, it is likely that the client is not expressing what is in their minds. The limitation of their thinking can come to the fore now and result in the lethargy and inactivity that we have seen happens in the Doldrums. We should be clear, since the usage of the term these days tends to denote an emotional condition that we are here dealing with this as it is in the mind, not the heart. That said we can also see from the image of this card, that there is a natural tendency for one to affect the other.

It is unusual for our thinking not to affect the way we feel. It is a well-known spiritual maxim that 'energy follow thought, which follow emotion'. As we have seen it is likely now that the client is experiencing a period where their thinking is stuck or simply limited. They may not be able to open their mind to new concepts or ideas or a different way of seeing what they are experiencing and 'just can't get past' their thoughts.

Where this is the case meditation can certainly help, the stillness created enabling an opening to new ideas, thoughts and suggestions. They may also need to look at their hearts and consider what they are feeling at this time and whether this is causing their current limitation or listlessness of state of mind. The heart and head are intrinsically linked at an energetic level and here we need to become calm, still and allow the resultant energy, at whichever or both levels to rise.

5 – GUST
BACKGROUND

From the apparent clam and subdues peace of the Doldrums we are abruptly awakened by the Gust now. A Gust of wind is defined as a sudden, brief increase in the speed of the wind, followed by a lull. Numerologically, five is linked to the energy of sudden and unexpected change, hence the placing of this card at this stage of the journey through the Element of Air.

More specifically, a gust is logged as such, when the wind speed reaches 18 miles per hour, the lull being at least 10 miles per hour. Gusts can however, exceed this top speed by a great degree, giving us the unpredictability linked to this energy.

There are three mechanisms that can cause a sudden and strong gust of wind to occur. These are turbulence due to friction, wind shear or heating from the ground. A Gust can herald a change in wind direction, as well as its speed.

In the case of friction, this is caused as the wind comes up against an obstacle, such as trees and in towns and cities, buildings. Interestingly, gusts of this nature are at their least over large bodies of water. Wind Shear however, is a change in the wind over a distance and so can happen over water. Rising air currents created by warmth from the Sun can also cause a Gust as the ground is heated. A thermal of warm air rises causing the air above to sink, which creates a Gust.

In general, winds at ground level are slower than those just a few feet above. By a height of between 30 and 40 feet, the wind can be twice as fast. Some conditions, such as a canopy of trees can then slow the wind speed above, up to several hundred feet. It is then, relatively close to ground level that the Gust is at its strongest.

For a Gust to occur there has to be an unstable air mass, meaning that there needs to be heated, rising air present, mixing with smoother flowing air above. With the friction created by the wind flow in these conditions, the air effectively sticks as it flows along, tumbling over itself and suddenly directing the faster winds at a higher level, towards the ground. When they do so, they come in the form of a buffeting gust, often lasting just a few seconds. When the friction above ceases, the Gust ends, only to begin again a few seconds or more later.

Gusts only occur when there is a strong wind blowing. Of itself this is an indication that weather conditions are changing, this being our watchword here. Essentially, Gusts indicate that the weather is getting more active and this mean a change to the present conditions.

DESCRIPTION

We have all felt a Gust of Wind and often it can have rather annoying consequences for us – destroying the new air-do, and the umbrella along with it. There is also the well-known Aesop's Fable' The North Wind and the Sun' where there ensues a challenge from the Sun to get a man to remove his coat. This comes after the Sun sees the chaos created by the gusts of wind.

It is perhaps in the autumn that we can most directly see a gust of wind however, or at least its consequences. Whilst many of us delight with child-like abandon to run and kick in the fallen leaves, the Gusts that dislodge those leaves can create the whirling dervish of leaves about us, along with inevitable grit that gets in our eye. This swirl and tumult of leaves is depicted for us here as the Gust.

ENERGY

From the stillness within that was the successful response to the Doldrums, we now find that we have to deal with unexpected rise of the Gust. In terms of our mental process this can mean both a sudden change of mind and the need for a new, alternative way of looking at things.

We have seen the unpredictable, sudden nature of the Gust, along with its potential to herald a change in both speed and direction. This can tell us that when this card appears, we need to be open to new views and opinions, either coming to us from others, or from within our own heads. That the Gust can appear seemingly out of nowhere without warning tells us that this change may strike at any time, just as the flashes of insight and understanding can click in our heads with the correct word, thought or observation. We may think we are in control of our minds but perhaps it is the other way around. The energy of this card tells us to be open to this and embrace it.

We have also seen that friction is a prime motivator when it comes to the formation of a Gust. The energy of this card can bring about a friction within the mind. This may be something we disagree with but struggle to come to terms with, a truth we do not like but must admit to or being told a cold, hard truth of something which we know within is correct. Either way, the energy here is often brought to us from external factors but has an impact within our minds.

Gusts tend not to happen by themselves. They usually appear is groups, one following another in their unexpected, topsy-turvy existence. This tells us that the process of change this card energy brings may be something that will take many twists and turns before we are able to see progress and arrive at some sort of conclusion.

Another noticeable factor of a Gust is that it tends to be at its strongest when it is relatively close to the ground, at a height of 30 to 40 feet. This tells us that we may need to ensure we are not prone to a flight of fancy in our mind now, for when we are thinking hard and trying to work things out, as this energy can cause us to do - to get a grip on and understand what is happening – it can be easy to lose a grip on reality. We need to keep the ground in sight now – to keep things real – and then we can allow this either forced or welcome change in our thinking and minds to lead us to progress.

6 – FRONT

BACKGROUND

The classification for this card is that of a Weather Front. This is the boundary layer between two air masses of different temperature and so applicable to our working through the Element of Air. Weather Fronts form from an air of low pressure and acquire movement as they flow across a land mass. As the Front moves across a region, the wind will shift in a clockwise direction. Whether the front is classed as warm or cold can determine the direction of the wind flow – East and Northeast for warm, South, Southeast and Southwest for cold.

As the Front travels, the wind direction shifts clockwise, creating the circular motion so prevalent in so many forms of nature. As the Front moves, so the wind can increase in velocity, though its consistency, strength and gustiness can vary.

It is the difference in the density of the air masses that is the principal cause of a Front, along with difference in temperature and humidity. Cold Fronts can feature thunderstorms and severe weather, whilst warm fronts can bring rain and fog. After the Front has moved on, the weather will usually clear swiftly.

Cold Fronts usually move across the globe from west to east, while warm fronts travel pole wards from their position. It is noteworthy that factors such as mountains and warm bodies of water can slow the movement of a Front. Should a Front cease moving, the density contrast disappears and the Front disintegrates into a line which separates regions of different win speed, known as a shear line. This occurs most commonly over an ocean.

The main difference here is whether the Front is warm or cold. Cold Fronts can move twice as quickly as warm, and produce sharper changes in weather conditions. A Cold Front is located at the leading edge of an area of temperature drop. The Warm Front sits at the edge of a warm air mass and these tend to be broader in scale than Cold Fronts.

In the 'changeover region' that defines a cold weather front, the air behind it is drier and cooler than the air in front, making a marked a noticeable drop in temperature possible. The air behind a warm front is warmer and moister than the air in front and here the temperature can rise and become more humid. The greater the difference in temperature can be an indication of the strength of the front being experienced.

DESCRIPTION

We have seen that a weather Front may be warm or cold but for our purposes in this Tarot deck we are concerned with the nature of a Front itself, rather than its temperature! The Front, which we can see unusually well-defined in this image, is a warm front.

Here we can observe how the warm air is moving in, replacing and warming the cool air ahead of it. It is this that produces the somewhat ominous gathering of cloud overhead and the drop in brightness observable here. Those more sensitive to such things can tend to 'feel' when it is about to rain from these effects and a certain 'rush' in the air as nature prepares for the downfall.

ENERGY

The essential ingredient of the weather Front applicable to the energy of this card is its movement. The nature of the weather Front is that it is moving and it is a progression from one state to another. In Numerology we work with the energy of six as a progression that results from a harmonious flow, which we see here echoed in the Front, as the natural movement of the air as it rises and cools in temperature.

In terms of the energy that comes to us with this cards appearance, the movement of the Front can guide us in our thinking. Now is the time that we need to develop our thoughts. We have seen that the instinctual nature of the Front is to move. Like energy itself, it cannot stay still and is forever travelling where it is bound, in whatever direction this may be. In this it follows its natural tendency, be it equatorial or polar. Similarly, our thinking can never stay still and we must forever seek to learn, develop and grow our minds, both in terms of knowledge and our capacity to 'understand'.

This understanding may be of others viewpoints as well as concepts, ideas and opinions of others. Here we may be challenged and required to take on board new and as yet unexplored areas of information and knowledge, to further our thinking and develop our minds.

One of the principal methods of doing this is through information. We have already seen the propensity of this so-called 'Information Age' and so this need never be a problem. Communication may be one of the key energies of this card. We may need to look at ourselves now and question whether we are preventing a development of our minds and the subsequent consequences in our lives, through a lack of communication.

Communication must, of course, be a two way process, alluding in this to the dual nature of the Front, be it warm or cold. With communication, we need to both give and receive. We may need to talk as well as to listen. We may do well to question now whether these two energies are in balance –

are we tending to do all the talking and no listening or perhaps the reverse?

We have seen that the effect of a Front coming into our lives is a change in temperature and consequent weather conditions around this. This can suggest for us when this card appears in our readings that change is literally, in the air, and we would do well to learn to perceive and determine the way in which this change is coming and 'go with the flow' of it. It is time now to think a little and see what we can see, in terms of the way in which are communicating to others, how they are communicating to us and what this tells us and respond accordingly. If we get this front, great progress and forward movement can be achieved.

7 – TRADE WIND

BACKGROUND

With the seventh card in the Air Element, we encounter the Trade winds. Numerologically, the energy of seven is concerned with establishing progress on our intended path. This fits with the Trade winds, which is the term given to the prevailing pattern of air flow found in the tropics in the lower region of our atmosphere. A Trade wind is determined from the direction from which the wind blows. In the Northern Hemisphere these blow from the northwest and from the southwest in the Southern Hemisphere.

Trade winds blow at approximately 11 to 13 miles per hour in a steady flow. In the Northern Hemisphere, as the warm air around the equator rises, it flows north towards the pole. As it does so, the Coriolis Effect defects it to the right. As it cools, at about 30 degrees, it descends and blows back towards the equator. In the Southern Hemisphere the same situation occurs, but in the opposite direction. These are the Trade winds. The Coriolis Effect is caused by the rotation of the Earth relative to the inertia of its mass, which creates this sideways trend in the air. It is because of this that the Trade winds are a steady and consistent flow.

The Trade winds have been used for centuries by sailors, utilising their momentum and propulsion to cross the oceans. In our weather systems, Trade winds act as the steering flow for tropical storms that form in the Pacific, Atlantic and Indian oceans, making landfall in each of their surrounding areas.

The origin of the term Trade wind comes from the 14th century Middle English use of the word trade, meaning path or track. The link with our understanding of the term 'trade' came from the establishment of merchant fleets undertaking commerce in other lands, having followed the routes the Trade winds took them.

Trade winds form shallow cumulus clouds which are prevented from becoming taller by inversion, which is an increase in temperature with height. At approximately 30 degrees above and below the equator, air begins to descend towards the Earth's surface in high pressure belts known as subtropical ridges. This air is relatively dry because as it sinks the temperature increases but the humidity remains constant, which in turn lowers the relative humidity of the air mass. This is known as a superior air mass. A temperature increase here is the inversion.

DESCRIPTION

The typical feature accompanying the Trade winds is the cumulus clouds, the only area of the Earth not experiencing them being the northern Indian Ocean. Cumulus clouds are low-lying and as can be seen, can have well-defined edges. A feature of cumulus clouds is their vertical development, as can also be seen, 'cumulo' meaning heap or pile, in Latin.

It is these clouds that are often referred to as 'cotton-wool' clouds because of their puffy appearance along with the flat bases they tend to have. These clouds appear along the route of the Trade winds, which we see here, enabling merchant seamen to establish trading routes across the oceans. Here that directive flow is symbolised in the wisps of cloud that seem to stem from the cumuli formations, pointing the way ahead.

ENERGY

The energy of the Seven is commonly to do with movement and flow and here this is no exception. Given that we are dealing with the mental level of the human being and our

338

thinking, this means that here we are receiving an energy that can cause and need us to direct and develop our mode of thought.

This may mean that in a particular situation there can be many different and possibly opposing viewpoints. It may be that we have a need now to take these into consideration. This does not immediately mean that we are wrong with what we have been thinking, only that we may need to widen and expands our viewpoint from its current position. We may need to ask ourselves when this card brings into energy into our life, whether we are limited or restrained in our thinking and we need to move it forwards by seeing a different perspective.

The Seven of Air energy is one that can also herald a time of teaching and learning. This may require us again to open our mind to new concepts, ideas and formulae that we have bene hitherto unaware of. With this new and open-minded approach, we can make great progress in our self-understanding and awareness of others.

It is a common phrase in our etymology to 'go with the flow' and here that can be applied in terms of our mental consideration of a subject or situation. It can be easy now to mentally 'see which way the wind is blowing' and adjust our views, thinking and communication to agree with the majority. The energy here can challenge us to be individual in our thinking and to stick to our opinion, no matter what the current trend or belief is. We may need to ask ourselves now whether we are changing what we are saying or thinking so as to not stand out or avoid a confrontation, argument or even a simple disagreement.

How clear we are in our thinking now can also come to the fore. We know that the Trade winds are a predictable flow and in what direction and approximate speed they will travel.

From this we can learn that there is always a need to be open to additional information, ideas and learning to add to what we already know. This energy will always seek to propel our thinking forwards and tells us that we need to steadily acquire new knowledge, rather than thinking or believing we know it all immediately, or that we have fully mastered a subject. Most things worth knowing about take many, many years to fully come to grips with and this energy reminds us that we do now perhaps know as much as we might like to believe. If we follow the wind however, we can always learn more and grow a little more complete and knowledgeable in the process.

8 – GALE
BACKGROUND

As we continue our journey through the Element of Air, so the wind gets stronger. They are now at Gale force, defined as a very strong wind, blowing in a sustained way at or near the surface of the Earth. The origin of the word Gale is thought to derive from the Norse term galinn, meaning frantic or mad.

In the UK's marine weather and shipping forecast, warnings of gale force winds are issued for any winds measured at Force 8 or more on the Beaufort scale, which is a speed of 34 -40 knots or 39 to 46 miles per hour. This gives our credence to the numerological placing here. Gale force winds are usually associated with deep, low pressure areas although gales can occur in other conditions too. For a gale to occur there is usually a movement of the air from an area of high to low pressure.

On the Beaufort scale a gale is recognised by twigs and branches breaking off from trees and people experiencing difficulty walking against its force. On the sea, moderate and long waves can result with spray blown for their crest. In the direction of the wind bands of foam will lie in strips on the surface of the water. Gale force winds are generally seen as impeding progress if we are walking into the wind, but can 'sweep us off our feet' if it is behind us, when we find we have to step quickly to keep up with the force.

In terms of a definition of the word, a gale is also associated with a loud or noisy outburst, especially of laughter, which does tell us something of the energy linked with this card. It is perhaps for this reason gales are often described as 'howling'. Once in a gale we usually find we need to shout in order to make ourselves heard.

As most of us know, warm air rises and cool air sinks. Therefore air flowing from high pressure to low pressure creates a wind and the greater the difference in pressure, the stronger the wind. For a gale to blow there is therefore a large difference in pressure. When this occurs speedily an even greater force to the wind is created and is therefore sustained, creating the gale force.

DESCRIPTION

As we saw above, as air cools it sinks. As it does so it creates a wind and a water vapour is formed, which creates a cloud, which then causes rain to fall when the droplets of vapour become too big and heavy to stay aloft.

It is this process we see occurring here as a gale force wind gathers and is about to blow. Along with this dramatic and in its own way beautiful cloud formation we can see and even sense the storm about to break and the winds take their toll on all that lies beneath.

ENERGY

Eight in terms of numerology and the energetic influence of numbers, is seen as two times four. The four gives us our foundation and eight thereby gives it another layer and level. In other terms, it increases or doubles its force and this is the case with the energy we experience here.

With the Four of this suit, the Doldrums we found a need to withdraw our minds and seek peace in a certain solitude and inner repose. Now we may well find the opposite and a need to blow ourselves out strongly. This is not as a reaction or unconsidered blast at someone, even if we find we are experiencing anger. Rather, it is a required and necessary expression of our thoughts and mind. We may find we need to release what we have been thinking but has remained unexpressed, for whatever reason.

We do need to ensure we do this in a non-destructive way, since gales obviously have the potential to cause damage. What we need to remember here is that as the air pressure moves from high to low, this will create a wind and an expression of its' experience, in this case a gale. This tells us that we may have held on to our thoughts or way of thinking and now is the time to release this, let it go and allow something new to be blown along.

We can of cause be in a certain danger now of being 'swept off our feet' with the force of this release and new thoughts. We may find we need to take good care with what we say and how we say it, along with the possible and potential consequences of these thoughts and words. As we know, energy follows thought and when our thoughts are this strong, we need to exercise caution, lest destruction occur.

Gales, as we saw above, are often described as 'howling winds', colloquially accompanied by a gale of laughter'. This can show us that two different aspects of what we may find ourselves thinking and expressing when we receive this card. Its' energy can wreak a certain amount of havoc but it can also generate a spontaneous and much-needed release of 'hot-air', with the accompanying relief that this can bring. We need to ensure ours does not hurt others and that we gather the positive energy of the numerical Eight here, that pushes us along the windy path to progress and mental power.

9 – JET STREAM
BACKGROUND

From the onslaught of the Gale we now rise up to the heights of the Jet Stream. The Jet Stream consists of ribbons of very strong winds that are able to move complete weather systems around the globe. The Jet Streams are found between 7 and 16 kilometres above the surface of the Earth and the winds there can reach up to 250 miles per hour.

The actual location of a jet stream will vary with natural fluctuations and changes in the environment. Jet Stream are caused by the differences between tropical air masses and polar air masses .i.e. whereabouts on the globe they are – near the poles or lower/higher down/up. This illustrates the inter-connectedness of our weather systems as it shows us that what happens in one part of the world is dependent on what is happening elsewhere.

The major Jet Streams on our planet flow from west to east (Westerly's), allowing us flights from the UK to be quicker than the opposite direction. The Jet Stream was discovered and is utilised by pilots of aircraft, allowing them to effectively piggy back on these air flows. Somewhat like the Convergence Zones, the Jet Streams are created by a combination of the rotation of the planet and the heating of the atmosphere (by solar radiation).

Jet Streams typically follow a meandering path and may start, stop, split into two or more paths and flow in many different directions. To understand the scale and force of a jet stream, and so the placing of it here and the highest single value and energy in numerology, it is helpful to consider that its width covers several hundred miles and its height approximately five miles. The meandering path Jet Streams take around the globe is created by interruption of its flow by encountering land masses and the previously introduced Coriolis Effect.

The height above the planet is another cause of their being accorded this high numerical value. Jet Streams are found at the level of the tropopause in our atmosphere, the point between the troposphere and the stratosphere. It is here where the temperature increases with the altitude. It is the gradient of the temperature rising or falling that creates the speed of the wind in the Jet Stream. As with the Gale, the greater the gradient, the faster the wind speed; and so put in its simplest terms, the Jet Streams are a result of the fact that the Equator is warmer than the Poles, which creates this wind flow.

A continued study of the pattern, force, direction and path taken by the Jet Stream can go a long way in determining the type of weather that we may experience on the ground. This is usually determined as either above or below average temperatures, as well generally wetter or drier conditions, along with cold or warm air and its direction and strength.

DESCRIPTION

Here we can see the Cirrus cloud formation that typifies the Jet Stream. From our vantage point way below, we can see the direction and flow the Jet Stream is taking, the curvature of the clouds reminding us of the meandering, rather than straight path it follows.

We are also reminded of the great height above the planet the Jet Stream exists at from the top of the mountain range we can see in the foreground. The wispy nature and formation also seems to confirm the height of the Jet Stream, the snow on the ground below reminding us its impact on our weather.

ENERGY

As mentioned above, here we experience the energy of the highest single digit numerically. So it is we rise above the lower levels to the Jet Stream. Here we find winds of excessive force and we must determine now how we are going to deal with the powerful directional flow and force of this energy mentally.

That is essentially a summary of the energy of this card. The Jet Stream represents a need in us to modify and straighten out our thinking, when it all becomes too much for us to cope with in our own heads. Now we need to focus on where our thinking is taking us, what it is leading us to conclude and so where it is taking us on the ground level of our life. This is rather like the weather the Jet Stream causes us to experience. We need now to become grounded in our thinking and observe more objectively what it is doing to us and those around us.

The height the Jet Stream exists at reminds us when this cards energy comes into our lives that in our minds now we may have reached a great height, but at what cost/ It can often be the case that we have become too reliant on our thinking now and so detached from our hearts what we are feeling and from action too. The power, force and flow of our thinking may have overtaken us a little and we may think that we know it all, about whatever our situation is. We may need to look at ourselves and ask if we are perhaps being a little too clever for our own good, or at least thinking that we are.

That the Jet Stream has the impact we have seen it has on our weather and what we experience, tells us that our thinking may be creating our reality, but at the expense of feeling and inspiration. It is rather like an overdose of thought. This can manifest in sleepless nights, strange dreams and nightmares. Now we need to stem the flow of that primal power of our mind, take time out to breathe and perhaps listen to others too.

The overthinking indicated here can be seen in the meandering path of the Jet Stream. This tells us we can at times become so lost in the complexity of our thoughts that there is a need simply to stop! We may need to apply a more direct mode of thinking to our situation or problem and one that is uncomplicated and clear, rather like the cloud formation in the card.

We should also not underestimate the cleverness possible with the energy this card brings. Again the height of the Jet Stream, plus its breadth and depth can tell us we can be capable of grasping and realising great truths now and our insight can also increase dramatically. Along with this potential increase in our mental capacity comes intellectual achievement and focussed communication. If we avoid the easy temptation to go over the top mentally at this stage, in whatever way we could, much can be achieved.

10 – ZEPHYR
BACKGROUND

From our sojourn in the atmosphere and its attendant workings, gust and gales, we must now come down to Earth a little, as we encounter the last stage in the Air cycle. We began metaphorically with a breath, defined as the essence of our Atmosphere. Now we can almost see the extension of the expelling of that breath as a breeze, or more correctly as it is known, a Zephyr!

More correctly though, a Zephyr is defined as a light or gentle wind, or a light current of air. This is from the Greek God of the west wind, Zephyrus. In this we can see how it takes the essence of Air itself, in our atmosphere and blows or expresses it a little, thereby creating the Zephyr or breeze, we have here.

A land breeze is actually formed when at night the land becomes cooler than the ocean, or sea. The cool air then sinks over the land while the ocean air rises due to its warmth, which causes a wind to blow from the land to the ocean. The cool air from the land then pushes the warm ocean air upward. Essentially then, a breeze is created due to a difference in the air pressure.

Often forming over the sea or large expanse of water, we can see this when we notice a ripple effect on the surface of the water as the breeze forms and blows across it. It is of course only when it reaches us that we can feel it, but it is there nonetheless. The 'sea breeze' as it is known is formed when the opposite of the above description occurs.

It is most common for a sea breeze to occur in the morning, as the solar radiation heats the land more quickly than the water. In the evening the opposite occurs, as the land calls and we experience a land breeze. This is rather like the daily breathing in and out, the inhalation and exhalation, of the planet itself and illustrates beautifully the relationship between land, earth and water.

The effect of a breeze is also determined there as 'small wavelets' appearing on water, leaves rustling, and the wind being felt on the skin. The air of a breeze is classed as moving between 4 and 7 miles per hour.

DESCRIPTION

We have seen above the effects of a Zephyr, and we can also surmise that a sea or land breeze will cause light grass to bend and wave. It is this that we see in the image for this card. Whilst we can see the effect of the breeze on the grass we can also see the expanse of sea beyond. This reminds of the dualistic nature described above, whereby a breeze can either come in from the sea or water, or blow out to it. The expanse of sky and the light cloud formation here remind us we are however, in the element of Air.

ENERGY

We saw that the energy of the Atmosphere guided us to breathe, which is very good advice! The effect of the breath can be paramount to our state of mind and what we take in we must also let out.

Like the breeze being defined as a 'gentle wind' however, we go gently, exploring the content of our minds with caution and paying heed to what we encounter as we go. The inner thoughts of our minds are not things to take lightly and neither are they things to ignore. The energy of this card, as it connects us gently to our inner thoughts, guides us to observe what goes on within our minds, but without getting too involved in it and becoming over-analytical.

The energy of the Zephyr also tells us to look at the relationship between what we are inhaling and what we exhale. In terms of the contents of our minds, with which we are concerned in this element and suit, this means we need now to be aware of the source of our thoughts – where do we get our information, learning and thinking from and what do we do with it.

Like the nature of energy our thoughts need expression or they can become stuck in the mind and become a pollutant, blocking our evolution and progress. The energy here guides us to let these things go and find release from nay mental torture and holding on to outmoded ways or patterns of thinking we may be doing.

Once we have become aware of this we may need to look at whether or thoughts now are healthy, positive and productive for us or not. In this so-called 'Information Age' of the internet and all it brings, there is every imaginable (and some unimaginable) source of every kind of information. We may need to assess this now and select what is best, or better, for us.

Having looked at and perhaps adjusted to the intake of our information and stimulus for our thinking, we may also need to look at what we are expressing, if indeed we are. The Zephyr is just a gentle movement of wind, nothing more. This can tell us that need to express our truth, quietly and gently, without excessive force or clamour. The truth is the truth no matter what, and here we can relax in that knowledge and wisdom.

We saw that the Zephyr blows into and out from the sea and can occur in mornings and evenings. This tells us of its dualistic nature, like our need for inhalation and exhalation and the need to study, learn and listen then express what we are thinking. So it is that as we inhale we must exhale. What we think we must express and here the energy tells us to do this quietly and calmly. Essentially the energy of the Zephyr tells us that what we receive on a mental level needs to be equal to what we give. It is in this that we find peace of mind at the end of this journey through the Element of Air.

AIR OF EARTH – DUST DEVIL
BACKGROUND

The first of the Compound Cards foe this Element is the combination of Earth with our host, Air. This we experience as a Dust Devil. A Dust Devil is a strong, defined whirlwind in which dust and debris are caught up, giving us the requisite combination of Earth with Air here. In the correct conditions, the air picks up particles from the Earth of debris and soil, which rise vertically and are carried over a distance.

A Dust Devil is much smaller than a tornado, usually being between 10 and 50 feet wide and rarely more than 100 feet tall. They normally appear in dry conditions, when sunlight heats the surface and the wind is relatively light. This energy is absorbed by the atmosphere to produce a highly unstable layer near the ground.

As this energy is released parcels of hot air are created, rising from the surface. With a light wind these parcels of air then rotate and collect loose debris, particles and dust on the surface of the Earth. The parcels of pockets of air are created when there is a difference in the temperature of the air, creating a change in the pressure. It is for this reason that most dust devils occur in the early afternoon, when temperatures are at their peak. However, any process that produces an unstable surface layer can give rise to thermal plumes and to dust devils.

Dust Devils also often appear in groups or series. Sometimes there is primary Dust Devil, followed by several smaller whirls. These secondary ones are sometimes called Dancing Devils. Although they have been known to last for several hours, most Dust Devils last for less than five minutes. The more vigorous the whirl, the longer its lifespan and the wind speed in the core of a vortex of air that is a Dust Devil is usually between 25 and 50 miles per hour.

The shape of a Dust Devil is usually a cylindrical column or an inverted cone. They have a central column of air but the actual diameter of swirling dust can be five to ten times the diameter of the core. Dust Devils are rarely seen as posing a danger or as a threat; although small objects can be picked up as they travel.

Dust Devils are often electrically charged. As the particles of dust and debris swirl around they bump into and scrape against each other and this creates an electrical charge. These particles also create a magnetic field that is continually fluctuating.

As a Dust Devil continues, the hot air near the surface is channelled up into its vortex. Eventually, cooler air around it is also sucked in, which happens once the speed of the Dust Devil reduces. Once this occurs the Dust Devil collapses in a few seconds and no longer exists.

DESCRIPTION

Here we can see a Dust Devil in its prime, illustrating this combination of the elements of Air with the Earth. We can see the overall shape of the Dust Devil and from the plume that it leaves in its wake we can determine its movement and motion.

We are reminded of the temperature required for the formation of the Dust Devil from the blue skies, along with the dryness of the Earth which we can see from the dusty conditions beneath the Dust Devil and around it.

ENERGY

With the energy of this combination of Elements we have the mental, thinking aspect of the human being combined with the grounded, practical nature of Earth. As we know, the essential nature of this is of the mind, and this is expressed in a down to earth, logical and practical manner.

What we can take from the energy of this card when its energy appears in our readings is basically that we need to act upon our thoughts. It may be that the energy here is calling us to act, that the time of thinking is now over and we may have need to look at what we know for sure and determine and take a course of action in accordance with this.

The essential need here is to ground our thinking with action. We may well need to make plans if none exist as yet and then do something about them. This can give rise to a logical, rational way of thinking, since there is a tendency for this to be more 'grounded' in nature, being the way in which the Earth element seeps into the Air here. The immediate response to what we are experiencing, or a difficulty we may be faced with needs to be first one of thought. This then needs to be responded to through the Earth nature, meaning we need to do something.

The Air element can also be expressed through communication and correspondence of some kind, so we may need to look at what we are being told and what we are receiving into our head and mind. Once this becomes clear, the need is to take action. This action needs to be understood in its scope and kept real, not be along some line of a flight of fancy or unknown factors. The benefit here is that our thinking, under the influence of the energy of this card, should not lead us that way, but serve to keep us grounded and in the mode of reality that we need to exist in.

We may also need to guard against a tendency now to delay and question what we wish to do. The Dust Devil appears only when conditions are right for its existence, so here we can see that our thinking should lead us down the correct course of action. As the Dust Devil collects what is strewn about it we may also need to look at what is around us that can be of practical use to us. There is an analogy here with 'leaving no stone unturned' in our planning.

Given that the Dust Devil has a central core within its overall being, we may also find that we need to keep our plans and ideas o ourselves. Sharing them with all and sundry may not be a sensible thing here, since we need to place ourselves first and act to follow what is right for us to do and continue on our path. With the right balance of these elemental forces great progress can be made on our life's path now.

AIR OF FIRE – HEAT HAZE
BACKGROUND

The interaction of Air with Fire produces the Heat Haze, sometimes called a heat shimmer. When these occur, it is the process of convection that causes the temperature of the air to vary. The variation between the temperature of the air at the surface and the cooler, denser air above creates a gradient in the air. This produces a blurred image and the shimmering effect we term a Heat Haze. From this we can see the interaction of Fire, as the heat, with the Air itself.

When we observe an object at a distance, the air between the object and ourselves, when it is hot, is subject to tiny areas of different temperature. Each area of different temperature sets up interference patterns in the light reflected by the object we are looking at. The result is that the object being observed is no longer clearly defined, but can appear to be shimmering or distorted.

A Heat Haze can then only occur when the surface of the Earth is hotter than the air above it, again showing the emphasis of Fire with Air in this card. As this hotter air rises from the ground it can bend and distort the light rays passing through it. It is this that creates the hazy appearance of objects at a distance. We are essentially seeing, or looking through, these distorted light rays. In this way the hotter air acts like a lens.

It is worth noting here that air pollution can add to the Heat Haze. Warmer, drier weather can result in previously invisible air pollutants becoming visible in the light rays described above. Interestingly, the 'mirage' effect created by this process can often resemble water; hence the mirage often depicted in films as the exhausted traveller sees a pool of water ahead of them in the desert.

Although more common in hot and dry climates of course, it is possible to see or experience a heat haze in cooler areas and even the Arctic. Intense solar radiation here during April and May can cause any exposed rocks to heat up and with the drastically cooler above it, a heat haze can soon appear.

Due to the process of refraction it is common for images seen within, or more correctly, beyond a heat haze, or the mirage itself, to be inverted, i.e. upside-down. This is caused by a layer of dense, cool air, which bends the rays of light over the horizon and back to Earth, thereby inverting objects in its path. Alternatively, an objects image can appear 'looming', meaning closer than it actually is. This is caused by the same process as above, except that the image is not inverted. Instead the density variation in the light rays acts like a lens or magnifying glass.

DESCRIPTION

Here we have a clear image, if that is the right description for something that is inherently hazy or unclear! The blend of Fire with Air can be seen at once from the distinct colouring of the image. In the foreground the yellows, browns and oranges of the recently harvested cornfield remind us of the colours of Fire, contrasted with the deep blue of the sky above. We are further reminded of the heat in this image by the notion of harvest and its associations with the long, hot days of summer.

We can see the heat haze itself as we gaze at this image, almost having to fight the urge to squint in an attempt to see it more clearly, as we do when we see a mirage. Rising to the right of centre of the image we can see dust particles drawn upwards by the hotter air, from the debris left on the ground following the harvest.

ENERGY

357

The combination here of Fire with our host element of Air produces a more combustible effect to our way of thinking. We know that Air relates to the mind and Fire to the spiritual level of the human being. This means that under the energy of this card we can turn a focus of our thinking to higher matters, to moments of inspiration and creative thoughts.

The Fire aspects effectively 'turns up the heat' in our heads and it may be that there is a degree of intensity now to our thoughts. This can create a pressure within that we need to respond to and focus on the positive outcomes that we desire and can go a long way to create from our thoughts now. The energy of this elemental combination can illustrate for us very well and directly the principle of creating our own reality. As energy follows thought we can direct the focus with the heat of the Fire to the creation of a positive reality that can surpass our previously held or believed limits.

This energy can then call us to look beyond what we may already know as fact and allow ourselves to believe in higher causes and principles, bringing this in to our ordinary, everyday reality. The flip side to this is that we may need to guard against certain impatience in our minds and thinking. The heat and intensity of the Fire can allow us to see, or think, things that are not really there, just like the mirage or effect of the haze here.

Keeping a grip on reality but also allowing ourselves to be creatively inspired can be a delicate balance, but as with all the Compound Cards, when we achieve a balance between the forces at play, great progress is possible. This can be rather like the creative process, where we can become carried away by a great idea and believe it to be the best thing since sliced bread, but get lost in the distortion of our own ego. With the energy of this card we are called to keep a grip on reality and see things as they truly are.

Equally what we communicate now can be direct and to the point, due to the power and fire of the heat and the clarity of mind that we can receive. The question we may need to ask ourselves now is whether we are being too direct or too impatient with our own mind. We may need time to allow distorted thinking to come to ground. We may need to cool off a little and literally, le the dust settle on our situation or mode of thinking, in order for a truer picture to emerge. Once this is seen, we can know things as they truly are and express this accordingly, for the greater good of all concerned.

AIR OF WATER – FOG
BACKGROUND

We come now to the Compound Card that is Water combined with Air. This as we can see is experienced in the natural world as Fog. Essentially, Fog is a cloud on the ground. For it to be determined as such it has to reduce visibility to less than one kilometre. The basic requirement for Fog to form is moisture in the Air, hence the combination here as Water with Air.

Fog is then a collection of droplets of water or ice crystals suspended in the air close to the surface of the Earth. Fog most commonly collects in areas where there is a nearby body of water, or most ground. Further to this, the foggiest place in the world is regarded as the Brent Oil Field, in the North Sea. This is where the cold Labrador Current (of air) from the North meets the warmer Gulf Stream from the South.

Fog forms when the difference in the temperature and the dew point is generally less than 2.5% Centigrade. A Fog rises, or begins to form when water vapour condenses into liquid droplets in the air. This can happen when wind convergence forces an upward motion of air, heat evaporating water from the surface of a body of water or cool or dry air moving over warmer air. Fog is a stable cloud which forms when a cool, stable air mass is trapped beneath a warmer air mass.

Fog can form suddenly and disappear just as swiftly, being termed flash fog. Fog commonly produces precipitation in the form of light drizzle or very light snow. This happens when the humidity reaches 100% and the air can no longer contain the moisture.

The thickness of a formation of Fog is determined by the height of the 'inversion boundary', the location of the different temperature of the air. This varies according to the weight of the air above it, in terms of atmospheric pressure. The lower this is, the thicker the fog.

Fog, of course, acts as hazard to visibility, the extent of which depends on its thickness and how large it is. Fog can be a permanent fixture through the day or night, creating a somewhat eerie atmosphere. Mist is often associated with Fog and correctly so, since the only difference in their definition is the limitation to visibility they create – above one kilometre it is mist, below it becomes Fog. When you exhale on a cold day and can see your breath, this is a form of mist.

DESCRIPTION

Much as a Fog can create a very real hazard for many of us, especially so if we are travelling, it can also create an ethereal beauty unlike anything else. It is perhaps this air of mystery and a certain unreality that strikes such a deep and strong cord with us and that we are attracted to.

As we gaze at the image here, we can perhaps feel ourselves being drawn into that mystery. There is something in us that seems to want to look deep into the Fog before us, journey across the expanse of water we see and reveal what is hidden within.

ENERGY

Just as with its equal and opposite counterpart in the Compound Cards (Air of Water) the energy of this card can also direct us to our intuition, through its combination of head and heart energies. The manner in which this is done and hence the workings and energy of this card are opposite however to Air of Water.

As we have seen previously, the suit to which a Compound Card belongs is its essential, basic or outer nature. In this case, this means that the first response we have to the energy of this card when it appears in our readings and lives, is one of Air – i.e. it impacts in our minds. Once we have looked at and assimilated our thinking in this way we then respond with what is in our hearts. Put simply, the energy of this card means that we think first, then feel after.

This process can allow us to gain a great deal of self-awareness and power if we learn to detach and observe it and so gain a degree of mastery over it. The challenge and opportunity the energy here brings us is to look at what our thinking is causing us to feel. By observing from a detached viewpoint we can establish a means whereby we can bring these two different aspects together in unity and so arrive at an inner impression, or an intuition, as to what is the right path or decision in our situation or problem we may be faced with.

Of course the nature of Fog is to obscure our vision and distort what we see. This is another pointer to us to turn inwards and connect with our intuition. If we cannot see clearly on the outside the logical course of action is to turn within and learn to trust what our inner senses are telling us. The combination of elemental energies here affords us this opportunity.

It may be that our thinking, as the Air elemental influence, has become foggy. We may find that we seem unable to think clearly now. Should this be the case we can try to metaphorically shine a light on what we are looking at. This means that we may have a need to see and accept things as they truly and really are, rather than a distorted perception of how we might want them to be in our hearts, from the water elemental influence. By looking at this truth we can then find our way to acceptance which our intuition or our inner voice, our conscience, will confirm for us is correct.

With perseverance and an adherence to the truth as we know it to be we can then find our way through the Fog. This will inevitably lead us within to that 'still, small voice' that is always accurate and never lets us down. We need to ensure we are not distorted either by following only our heads or a predominance of our hearts desire now. Once blended and balanced we can absorb the energy here to guide us forward in our selves and lives and gain the full measure of our intuitive knowing.

AIR OF AIR – GAS
BACKGROUND

The combination of Air with Air gives us Gas, as one of the four fundamental states of matter (the others being solid, liquid and plasma – which we shall meet in Fire). Much like Air itself, a mixture of Gases contains pure gases of different atoms. Individual gas particles, also like Air, are invisible to the human eye. It is these similarities that align this Compound Card with Air of Air.

Because is difficult to observe, it is classified through the use of four physical properties – pressure, volume, number of particles (or moles) and temperature, further strengthening its links to the Air, which is much the same. Compared to the other three states of matter listed above, gases have low density and viscosity (the rate at which particles stick together). Pressure and temperature will influence its particles.

Perhaps the most common form of Gas in Nature as we know it is Natural Gas. This is a fossil fuel formed when layers of buried plants, animals and other gases are exposed to hear and pressure over thousands of years. The energy they originally obtained from the Sun is stored in the form of chemical bonds in natural gas. It is this that we use in cooking and heating and lighting. Natural gas is also found in deep underground rock formations and in undergrou8nd reservoirs. This Gas is distinct from the petroleum fluid used to fuel cars.

Use of natural Gas can be traced back to China in about 500 BC, where, using bamboo pipes gas was extracted to boil sea water to remove the salt. Although the industrial use of gas did not begin until 1825, its supply will run out in approximately 250 years.

Prior to Gas being able to be used as a fuel it must first go through a process to remove its impurities, including water. This process produces a number of by-products, including carbon dioxide and water vapour. Natural Gas is actually a hydrocarbon gas mixture consisting mainly of methane, with varying levels of alkanes (gas compounds) and other gases, although its composition can vary quite widely.

In its pure from, natural Gas is colourless, odourless and shapeless. It is seen today as one of the most clean, safe and useful of all energy sources. Natural gas is considered 'dry' when it almost pure methane, having had fluids removed.

DESCRIPTION

The image here is of the ominously named 'The Door to Hell. This is a crater of natural gas in the Karakum Desert, in Turkmenistan, north of Iran. This was formed over 40 years ago when there was a collapse as geologists were digging. This opened a cavern, over 70 metres wide, filled with natural gas. It was feared this would release poisonous gases, so the gas was ignited. Although the burning was expected to last only a few days it has now been burning for over 40 years.

Looking at the image it is easy to see why it has been dubbed 'The Door to Hell'. More appropriate for our use here we can see the gas being released from the flames in the orange colouring that appears as a fine smoke, riding from the hole as it burns the natural gas within.

ENERGY

Here we experience the heady mixture that is the combination of Air with Air. It is easy to see with the energy of this card that we connect most definitely, and if we are not careful, too much so, to what is happening in our heads and what we are thinking.

The danger we must first encounter and guard against is that of over-thinking and becoming something of an air-head'. This can cause us to become ungrounded and lose a grip on everyday reality and the necessity for practicality. The energy here can cause us to focus so much on our heads that we can tend to spend so long thinking about doing something, the best and most efficient and effective way of doing it and pondering on the likely outcomes that by the time we make up our minds to act, it is too late.

We need to ensure now we do not lose ourselves in procrastination and indecision. These two maladies can result in even the most cocksure of souls when given exposure to the energy of this card. Similarly, we may find that whilst we think we are very clever, intellectual and intelligent, we can lose out in the acquisition and achievement of these equalities to a lack in the area of practicality. Put another way, we may be wonderful at arguing over which came first, the chicken or the egg, but could be at a total loss if asked to fry the product of that proverbial conundrum!

The blessing of this energy can however be experienced in an ability of great insight, adherence to absolute truth and honesty. As well as the cleverness that can be gifted with this cards' energy, we can also experience a heightened ability to communicate. This can be both in our ability to listen and perceive what others are saying, whether they use the words or not. We can find we notice body language and unconscious behavioural patterns more so than normal for us.

It may be that when we see this card in our readings that we are being asked to use our heads, to stop and think a little before we act. Air of Air is an excellent energy to engage your brain and it may be telling us that we need to stop in order to see what is right in front of us, something all too easy to miss.

We have seen how water is removed from the processing of natural gas in order for it to be used. Here this may show us that we have a need to detach from our feelings for a time now, to focus on our head rather than our heart. Whilst we need both to be balanced and whole, it may be that just for a time we have a need to be more led by what we know to be true rather than what we feel.

The truth, whilst it may be a relative thing, is still the truth, as it applies to each individual. Here this card can tell us that, just as natural gas occurs deep within the Earth, we may have a need to think a bit, to dig deep within our minds, to uncover half-forgotten and half remembered principles and agreement we determined to live by. It may that we need to recover our principles, to stick to our truth now and allow these things to come forward from the back of our mind. This card essentially asks us, what is in our mind?

FIRE ELEMENT

Fire has been an important aspect of cultures across the globe since pre-history and has been vital to the development of civilisation. As with each of the four Elements, we are dependent on it for life, in the form of the Sun but also for warmth. From Greek myth comes the tale of how Prometheus stole Fire from the gods in order to protect the helpless humans.

From Greek philosophy, Fire is one of the four classical Elements, with which we concern ourselves in this deck. From then and still, it is associated with passion, energy, ambition, drive, motivation, assertiveness and energy. As we shall as we journey through this Element this can affect us in many ways, all of course leading to our development and wholeness as human beings. Fire has been described as giving rise to the other three Elements as of being the 'upward-downward path' as well as the 'hidden harmony' (Heraclitus 535 BCE – 475 BCE).

Fire has forever been linked with heat, both in terms of the 'four humours' of early and late mediaeval medicine. Identified with the Sun of course, the Element of Fire is (in the Northern Hemisphere) associated with the season of summer. Symbolically, this can lead us to an intense energy that may lead to amplify what we are experiencing.

We saw in the introduction to this book how the manner in which we can receive pure energy from the Universe comes first to us through our soul, and then descends into our individual consciousness through the spirit. This spiritual level is linked to the Fire element. Hence it can also connect us to our aspiration and inspiration. It helps us in this way to be the best we can be and to exceed the limitations of our emotional and/or mental beliefs and supposed limits.

Fire also brings us a connection to our ability of leadership, more personally experienced here with our need and requirement for progress, for striving forward and achieving more. In the human being Fire develops our enthusiasm and allows our inner personality out to shine and be expressed. Whilst the qualities of courage, bravery and passion may help this process this can also lead to a certain rebelliousness, along with a tendency to ill-temper and anger, if we allow that inner Fire to burn uncontrolled.

This is much like the nature of energy itself, which as we know, simply is. What changes and transforms it is how we respond to it and the choices we make, at whatever level of our being, in this response. It is this that the Fire element connects us to, through that instinctual response we make at that spiritual level of our awareness and being.

Fire can bring the fire of creation to us, in our ability to transcend our limits, exceed our expectations and forever develop. It can also bring the power of destruction, purifying or destroying what it encounters. In this it echoes the principle of life itself, in terms of birth, life, death and decay.

FIRE

ONE – SPARK
BACKGROUND

Having seen that Fire is one of the four primal states of being, we come now to its beginning, as aa Spark. Fire itself has been defined as 'a rapid and persistent chemical reaction that releases heat and light'. Fire is not then a substance at all, but a process – that of oxidation. This is the result of combining oxygen with another substance. This sudden release of energy causes the temperature to rise. This creates the ignition that is the Spark of our card.

The Spark of Fire is then the combination of oxygen, heat and a source of fuel, the essential triangle for any Fire to occur. In the process of oxidation if the heat cannot be released faster than it is created, combustion occurs and we have our spark. So it is that the Spark, as the beginnings of the process, of Fire, is a chain reaction between three constituents.

The spark is the source for the flame. The updraft or rise, in the current of air produced by the heat which carry particles of the burning fuel whatever this may be. As these sparks then fall, the Fire is created and spread. In this respect a spark is a tiny version of a lightning bolt and is essentially visible energy.

We should also note here that the spark necessary for the flame can also be created by friction. As any good boy scout at least used to know, two sticks rubbed together with enough vigour and patience will give us our esteemed and cherished spark. With the addition of air, i.e. blowing on this, we can create a fire, as if from nothing. Interestingly, the wood used for this magical process must be completely absent of the one other Element not essential for our purposes – Water. The wood must be bone dry to give us Fire.

We should also mention here that humanity's intervention is not necessary for a fire to start. There are always fires occurring naturally across the globe and here we are experiencing one of the primal, motivating forces in the natural world and in ourselves.

DESCRIPTION

We have seen how a spark is required for a Fire to occur. That Spark is what we see here. This is seen as small incandescent particles that can then ignite the fire. This will usually be some carbon based material, i.e. the fuel for the fire. Once the Spark is ignited, then we have the beginnings of our Fire.

What we see here are Sparks in close-up view. From this it is possible to observe not only the Spark itself, being the fuel, but also the light it gives off. This is momentary of course and will be gone as a soon as we observe it. We can also see light and different colours, from the spectrum of heat created by the different temperatures in the ignition process. We are also able to gain a sense of movement and direction from the trail of light left by the spark.

ENERGY

Just as with the other first, or initial cards of their respective suits, we have in this card the essence and essential energy of the Element of Fire, here symbolised as a Spark. This can immediately bring to mind the term and knowledge that you cannot start a Fire without a Spark.

We are immediately and primarily guided when this card appears to look at our own Spark. We may first need to define what this is. We may have a need now to ask ourselves what is 'sparking off' within us. What is motivating us and what are the reasons we wish to do as we do. This is not what is in our hearts or our minds, but deeper within if you will, the prime force of causal motivation. We may have a need to get really honest with ourselves and admit to ourselves why it is are the way we are or doing what we are doing.

The energy of the Spark can also bring to us a new energy, given that this is exactly what it is. We may have found ourselves lacking in motivation or energy, zest for life and so on prior to the appearance of this card, but now we have the promise of a new surge of enthusiasm with. It may be that if need to dig a little deeper within ourselves and find this spirit, or indeed, spark, within that will carry us through our current situation or dilemmas.

The energy of this card brings with it the primal energy of the Fire itself. As we have seen this can manifest as a sudden thing and there may perhaps need to be a little trust that this will appear when the time is right for it to do so. It may be that this card is guiding us to look within to our core to know when the time is right to set off the spark and act that will begin the process we require.

We may well be aware of the idiom of the 'bright spark' and this cards energy challenges us to be our own bright spark. With the energy it brings into ourselves and lives we are promised that we have the necessary quality and motivation to be just that at this time. From here we can see what our Spark within will ignite in our outer world as well as those around us who we encounter.

Many spiritual systems herald the existence of a 'spark of the divine' within us. It is perhaps to this that we can turn now, that point of faith, trust, belief that we shall overcome any and all opposition that may be rallied against us, that we can overthrow even the biggest enemy and odds stacked against us. The spark within, although small and momentary is also assured and bright enough to be seen from afar. From his humble beginning great things are possible now and all we must do is ignite it.

2 – FLAME
BACKGROUND

As we have seen, you cannot start a Fire without a Spark. We now have our Spark and here we create the Flame from that humble beginning. With the majority of naturally occurring Fires, such as Forest and Wildfires, the initial spark heats a substance, causing it to burn. Once the spark travels, it has the other sources it requires – oxygen and fuel – to further ignite and we have our flame. The initial spark is hereby turned into a self-propagating and self-sustaining fire.

The initial 'pulse' of heat that is the spark results into a furtherance of itself and a bigger version of itself is effectively created, which is the Flame. For any Flame to continue it still requires the triangle of requirements for its continuance – oxygen, heat and fuel.

Once the source of fuel for a fire reaches its ignition point this is an indication its volatile gases are hot enough for the compound molecules to break apart. These atoms recombine with the oxygen and they burn. This stage is what gives us the flames of a Fire. As they heat up, the rising atoms emit light, this process being known as incandescence. It is this that gives us the visible flame.

The colour of the flame depends on the fuel source that is burning. The different colours within a single flame are caused by temperature variations as it burns and consumes the fuel. Usually the hottest part of a flame is at its base and this glows blue. The cooler parts are at the top of the flame and these are typically orange or yellow in colour.

The continued existence of the Flame, the fact that it is self-perpetuating is caused by the Flame itself. The heat of the Flame is enough to maintain the required ignition temperature of the fuel it is burning, so the Flame will continue so long as it has a fuel source and there is oxygen around it. Obviously, this is what causes a fire to spread. Removal of any of these three sources kills the Fire.

Gravity plays a role in how a fire burns. All the gases in a flame are hotter and less dense than the air surrounding it. This causes the flame to move upwards towards the lower pressure. It is for this reason why flames have the shape they do, being pointed at the top.

DESCRIPTION

Here we focus on the Flame itself, as the subject of our card, rather than any other aspect of the triangle that we know a Fire requires to exist. The origins of a fire, as also the Flame itself, is with the spark and once ignited this creates the Flame we see here. We are reminded of the progression from the Spark in those that shower from the Flame. We are reminded of the progression from the Spark in those that shower from the Flame.

Although we cannot see it, every Flame requires fuel which we can assume is beneath the flame. We can be reminded of the requirement of Oxygen from the bend of the flame, or the direction in which it appears to be burning. We are also reminded of temperature variations in the differing colours visible in the flame, including orange, yellow and white.

ENERGY

From the initial Spark comes the Flame. The motivational energy we inherited must now develop to its next stage and we must allow this to develop within us. We need now to fan the flames, so to speak.

Once we have received the beginnings of an idea or been ignited with enthusiasm and motivation for a project or to solve a dilemma in ourselves or our lives, we must take this

375

impulse to another level. This cards energy provides that, in that it can bring us an urge to respond to what we are feeling within. So it is that this card can often be about how we choose to respond to our inner impulse.

It may be an easy thing for many people to simply react to this urge and inner fire. However with the numerological influence and the wisdom of the Tarot, we can be called to look a little further than this. The appearance of this card can advise to respond, rather than react to what we are presented with in ourselves and lives, or what we are sensing within.

The counsel of this cards energy is then to consider alternatives before action blindly. Rather than rushing in we can be well advised now to look for what may be an equal and opposite response to the reaction we may be initially tempted to take. We saw above how gravity plays a part in how a flame burns and we can see now that this card is rather like the force of gravity itself. If we take a simple approach to what the force of gravity is in the expression 'what goes up must come down', we can see that this cards energy tells us to take this principle into account before we surge ahead.

Put another way we need now to consider Newton's Third Law of Motion, that 'for every action there is an equal and opposite reaction'. In this we can see the requirement of the numerological energy of Two to balance out our instinct to act without thinking, speak without consideration or jump to a conclusion. If we are able to catch hold of that Spark of energy from within ourselves, however it may be manifesting, we can arrive at a fuller appreciation of the facts and see things from a more balanced perspective.

This is not to suggest that we remain in limbo forever and a day and we could equally need to guard against this. The somewhat calming influence of this energy to some people may result in such a balanced state as to create an equilibrium that seems to manifest in total inertia. Whilst it may be the right thing not to react to what we are initially caused to do, the energy of this card is showing us a need to have some kind of response, once we have come to a state of balance to do so.

Once this has been done we can then be assured that if we turn within, or indeed upwards to the prompting of our spirit, being the realm of this Element in the human being, we will know, sense or simply fathom the correct course of response for us in that moment. This card then harkens us to turn to that still, small voice within, possibly that of our conscience, as the guiding and balanced, unbiased principle from which to go further.

3 – FLARE
BACKGROUND

Flares have been used for centuries, by artificial means, as a method of signalling and illumination. They can also occur naturally in fires, most notably on the Sun, as a Solar Flare. This is usually when a fire has apparently subsided, only to 'flare up' again. This terminology is often used in our language when tempers flare or a situation reaches a point when something reaches a tension point and control can be lost.

Those of us lucky enough to have a 'real fire' source of heating in or homes or simply a fireplace for pleasure will know that when the fire burns down is needs more fuel to continue burning. Here it is easy to see a Flare happening. Once the newly added source of fuel, such as a new log, heats up it reaches a point of combustion and the heat produced causes the flame to take hold and we see the fire suddenly flare up.

When this occurs may be scientifically explainable but when it actually happens as a fire burns is unexpected and can catch us by surprise. It is unpredictable in nature in this sense and its effect are immediate. The colour is immediately brighter, along with the heat, or warmth produced. For a time, it seems as if the log or fuel source will be consumed swiftly, but then the fire settles down once more and the fire burns steadily once more.

A Solar Flare represents a large release of energy and is observed from Earth as a sudden flash of brightness from the surface of the Sun. This can also happen on some stars, where they are known as Stellar Flares. Solar Flares produce radiation across the electromagnetic spectrum and affect all layers of the atmosphere. Most of the effect is not seen by the naked eye as most of the energy is spread outside of the visible spectrum. Solar Flares are powered by the sudden release of magnetic energy stored in the Sun's corona. Just as with natural fires, Solar Flares are unpredictable.

A Flare is defined as a 'bright, wavering light' or a 'burst into intense, sudden flame', telling us much about the nature of the Flare for our purposes in nature. It is expressed as a expansion outwards in shape and brightness. The nature of flames in a flare is described as 'unsteady'. In summary, the Flare is the point in the burning cycle of Fire we it becomes more intense, suddenly and without warning.

DESCRIPTION

Here we see the point at which a Flame, from our previous card, has 'caught alight' another source of fuel and has 'flared up'. It is easy to realise from the image here that this is single, captured moment in a sudden burst of activity that itself does not last long.

We can also see the lack of a defined shape and notice that, as with the characteristics described above, we can see the flames reaching outwards and upwards. It is almost as if the fire is using the release of energy it has experienced to push itself onwards in its quest, in this case to keep itself alive and burning. Its natural energy and nature is to find more fuel for its continued development.

ENERGY

The energy we receive with this card can be unpredictable in its nature and timing, just as with the nature of when a fire will flare. This does not mean however that it should e something we do not want to happen. Indeed we can find that it is usually necessary if we are to progress in our endeavours and with what are aiming to achieve at this point.

The energy of 'odd' numbers is always basically looked at as active, with even numbers being passive. As the Three then, we know that this energy will provoke a response in us to respond in some way, to be active. Since we are dealing with the Fire or 'being' level in the human being, we can see that the energy of this card will perhaps come when we least expect it.

When and however it does occur, there may well be a need for us to welcome it, despite any misgivings we may sense within. The nature of this card, like the Flare, is progression and as such us to cause us to progress, with whatever it is we are engaged with in life at the time it appears. We can be prone to procrastination, possibly from fear of what might happen and this cards' energy may just be the antidote we need. Traditionally this card can often be seen as time of planning our future and here we can see that along with those plans we may need to 'expect the unexpected'.

It may be that in the midst of our planning we have neglected to identify the need for allowing for the unforeseen. The energy here may then test us a little to see if we can be open to new ideas, new impulses and things arising from within we did not expect. If we can allow ourselves to respond favourably to these, with optimism and expectation, we can find we can achieve a level of stability and progress we may not have realised we were capable of.

A further aspect of the energy here is shown in the brightness of the flare from our fire. This energy can give rise to a sudden and irresistible force of energy, a rush of enthusiasm for a project, person or simply life itself. It may be that we need to take heed of this and do what we can to build on this, to aspire to greater heights, and continue to give fuel to that fire.

This energy needs a response, whatever we may choose for this to be. Should we make the choice to dampen down the flare or ignore it, it will, we can be sure, shine brightly for a short time but then die down and even extinguish altogether. We may have a need now to question if we are about to miss an opportunity through lack of motivation or inertia. Should this aspect be the case, we can find if we look and dig within a little deeper, the resources we need can flare up and spur us on towards our goal.

4 – FIRE WHIRLS
BACKGROUND

Fire Whirls can also be known as a Fire Tornado or a Fire Devil, or more pleasingly a firenado. They are essentially a whirlwind induced by fire and consist of flames. Fire Whirls occur when intense, rising heat and turbulent wind conditions combine to form these whirling eddies of air. These can tighten up to form a flaming structure that can suck in burning debris along with combustible gases.

It is the core of the Fire Whirl that is actually on fire. This core is fed oxygen, one of the triangle of requirements for a fire to exist, by the rotating pocket of air around it. On average this core is 1 to 3 feet in width and between 50 and 100 feet high, reaching a temperature of up to 2,000 Fahrenheit. This is hot enough to re-ignite ashes it can suck up from the ground.

Fire Whirls commonly move slowly at about walking speed of the average person. This is in keeping with the energy of the number Four, which is a stable, steady one. As they move however they can obviously set object in their path alight as well as throwing burning debris into the area around them. The winds created by a Fire Whirl can be strong – up to 100 mph, which can be strong enough to blow down trees. They can exist for up to an hour and cannot be directly extinguished.

A Fire Whirl gets its fuel from combustible, carbon-rich gases that are released by burning vegetation on the ground. These are sucked up by the whirling air which travels up the core of the Fire Whirl, where it reaches an area of fresh and heated oxygen, which allows it to burn. It is this that causes the tall and thin shape of a Fire Whirl.

Fire Whirls are given three classifications. These are all either 'steady' or 'stable', emphasising the numerological energy of the Four, which shares these qualities. The other aspect of the classification is focussed on its movement and where it burns, whether this over a specific area, moving with a wind or in an open area with wind.

Fire Whirls tend to be more common in desert regions or in drought conditions, the drier climate leading to more rapid combustion and energy release. It is of note that a Fire Whirl is really created by an established Fire itself, as it interacts with the air around it.

The nature of a Fire Whirl has poetically been described as performing like an ice-skater pulling their arms in as they spin and sounding like a jet plane flying. Sometimes Fire Whirls can come and go as a larger fire burns around them, being described as shape-shifters in this respect.

DESCRIPTION

Here we see a typical Fire Whirl in action. It is possible to see the manner in which debris is sucked up from the ground and taken inwards and upwards from the wider area at its base. The spiralling movement of the vortex is also discernible from the manner of the flame, along with the shape it creates as it burns and rises.

As we have seen above, a Fire Whirl interacts with the air around it and we are reminded of this as we observe the smoke it produces and the ghost-like appearance of the heat from the central column of flame that is the Fire-Whirl itself.

ENERGY

Traditionally this card is often seen as one representing the security and pleasure from the path of 'hearth and home'. This is seen as stemming from the stabilisation of energy that this card brings in terms of the Tarot Therapy approach.

We have seen the slow movement of the Fire Whirl which blends with the numerological energy of the Four. At the spiritual level of 'being' that the Fire suits represents within the individual, this cards' energy brings a stability that comes from a steady approach taken to where we are focussed in life. We are reminded in this of the walking pace the Fire Whirl moves at.

We know also that the Fire Whirl draws fuel up from the ground for its source of life. This tells us we may need at this time to look at the resources available to us to help us in our quest, whatever this may be at this time. This card may come to us to tell us that we have what we need either without or within us or perhaps both.

That the Fire Whirl takes its fuel from what it finds and what it encounters as it goes and that it then interacts with this in the air around it tells us too that this may be a time for not going it alone. We may need to guard against becoming too stable now and risk the potential of our fire or light going out. Fire Whirls as we know do not last long in the grand scheme of things and if we seek to be overly independent now we may find that we cannot continue as we were. This can be a good time where we can seek the input of others either to establish, maintain or develop our stability and what we need for our steady evolution.

We know that Fire Whirls prefer a dry environment in which to operate. This may tell us that we need to look for where we are becoming dry or stale inside ourselves and what we may need to be introduced or re-ignited in ourselves and our lives. Is there a need at this point for an injection of some excitement and to do what is necessary to create a metaphorical Fire Whirl, again either within or without ourselves?

We should also take note that the Fire Whirl cannot be directly extinguished. From this we can take comfort in the knowledge that whatever it is we can and do bring to stability now – whatever it is that we are motivated to focus on and pour our efforts into – we can manifest a stable foundation with that may last us a good long time. It may be that we need to look at what our source for stability is and whether this likely to serve our purposes for the time to come or consider if what we place our belief and being into now is likely to burn brightly for just a short time and then burn out. It is now we need to consider what we are within ourselves and nurture this for our long-term stability and so growth.

5 – LIGHTNING
BACKGROUND

Lightning is a powerful electrical discharge that occurs during a storm and is accompanied by thunder. Distant lighting can be heard without the sound of thunder, but this is simply because it is too far away to be heard. There are three types of lightning – from a cloud to itself, from one cloud to another and from a cloud to the ground. The charged regions within the atmosphere are temporarily equalised by the lightning.

The first two types of lightning listed above are actually the most common, although we know more about lightning that hits the ground, since it affects us more. Cloud to ground lightning is about 25% of all lighting. Lightning frequency is approximately 40-50 times per second and its average duration is 30 microseconds. Lightning is affected by wind conditions, relative humidity, latitude and proximity to warm or cold bodies of mass.

A typical cloud to ground lightning flash culminates in the formation of a plasma charge that conducts electricity, hence its placing here with the element of Fire. The discharge that we see is actually the culmination of the process of lightning formation. The prime factor in this process is the mix of warm and cold air masses, hence it being heat as the vital factor, again placing it in Fire.

Most lightning originates at the base of a cloud, at the point where freezing occurs within it. Ice crystals that form here collide their positive charge with the negative charge of the base of the cloud, resulting in lightning. The closer to the ground the cloud is, the greater the number of lightning flashes occur. Lighting is basically caused by two oppositely charged bodies moving in opposite directions.

Most of us know the phrase 'lightning never strikes in the same place twice'. Although not technically accurate, this does serve to illustrate our purpose here and its' placing with the energy of the Five numerically, gives its energy of unpredictability and disruption, two characteristics certainly belonging to lightning.

The main streak of lightning that we see is known as a 'leader'. This often splits, forming tree-like branches of visible electricity that form an apparently random direction, making it impossible to predict where they will impact the ground.

Objects struck by lightning experience extreme heat as well as magnetic forces of great magnitude. The heat can be enough to vaporize the sap in a tree, causing an explosion of steam that bursts the trunk.

Apart from the well-used term 'bolt' to describe lightning, terms such as 'bell', 'bead', 'forked', 'ribbon', 'rocket' and 'sheet' have also been used in describing its different formations.

DESCRIPTION

Here we see a typical burst of lightning, if there is such a thing, since no two strikes are ever quite the same. What we can observe as we view this image is the random nature of the dispersal of the lightning. From the 'leader' bolt we can see the many other threads branching off in their crackling formations, drawn variously to and from each other as they go.

We can also see at the top of the image the base of the cloud that has created the lightning that we see. This dark expanse is the area from which the movement of oppositely charged particles that cause the lightning to strike originates. Apart from the lightning itself, we are reminded of the heat and light aspects of this example of Fire in the colours we can see here.

ENERGY

We have seen from previous Fives in this deck that the numerical energy can be a chaotic, unpredictable and seemingly random one. Consequently and as is immediately apparent from the title of this card, this Five is no exception.

The Fives can general can bring up an energy control, the pertinent point being who has it? With the Five of Fire we are pushed to consider whether what we are engaged in and focussing our being on is contributing to the smooth flow of ourselves and our life or causing chaos. We should be clear here that we are not seeking through the energy of this card to establish suppressive control over all that comes within us, but on that allows us to establish a responsive approach to what we encounter that aligns itself with where our motivation and ambitions lie.

This card can herald unexpected forces arising from within us, unforeseen aspects of ourselves coming to the fore and creating a seemingly random flow of knock-on effects. It may be that these sudden and sometimes unwanted energies spill out to those around us and effect our direction in life. We are well advised when this card appears to ground ourselves, lest the force of what comes threatens to burn us.

We know that lighting appears because of two charged masses moving in opposite directions with an opposing charge. This can tell us to examine ourselves to see if our motivation is working with our natural flow or if in some way we may be opposing ourselves, or others involved in our lives. This is a time when we need to seek unity rather than opposition, building and co-operation rather than destruction and challenge.

We may need to accept now that we do not know the likely outcome of our inner striving and driving. What we are responding to from within us may need to be enough at this stage, without knowing the outcome of our intended direction, just as we cannot predict where lightning may strike.

We do know however that where it strikes there is extreme heat and often explosive results. We may need to prepare ourselves for any potential 'fallout' from the consequences of our action as we proceed with following our inner motivation. This does not necessarily mean in a 'negative' way, but it may be that inner selves and thence our outer lives are in need of 'shaking-up' and experiencing some sudden and unexpected change.

6 – BRUSH FIRE
BACKGROUND

In the natural world 'brush' is defined as an area of dense growth of bushes and/or shrubs and small trees. A Brush Fire by definition is a small and localised occurrence and can be seen as a relatively minor incident, as opposed to its big brothers, who we shall meet soon. The Brush Fire is characterised by its low growth and it being focussed on an area of scrubby trees, bush and grassland.

It is however, uncontrolled and often naturally occurring, often being ignited and given life by a Lightning strike, hence its' placing here after this has struck in our previous card. A Brush Fire can occur in any place in the world where there is such coverage of greenery.

There can be many and different names for the naturally occurring wildfires, which are dependent o their size, location and often destructive potential. For the purposes of our Brush Fire here, this is not at all in the classification of the more newsworthy relative of the full-grown Wild or Bush Fire. At this stage in its evolution, the Brush Fire is consuming only the local vegetation in its immediate vicinity.

We should remind ourselves here that Fire is seen as a natural phenomenon and a necessary part of many natural habitats. It only becomes a problem when it becomes out of control, and here this has not happened. In this way they are often known as 'natural vegetation fires'.

Whilst we have mentioned the cause of Lightning above, Brush Fires can also be naturally caused by glowing embers of a previous fire and high winds around such an area. Brush Fires often begin with the ignition of hay or straw as well as wood chips and shavings and sawdust.

The nature and definition of a Brush Fire tells us that it is not uncontrolled. Rather, it burns steadily, making progress only by virtue of the path of fuel it must follow, rather than simply consuming everything it encounters. Here the Brush Fire follows the numerological influence of the Six at which it is placed, the energy at this stage being in part one of steady and appropriate progress rather than rapid, unfocussed advancement.

DESCRIPTION

The chosen image for our Brush Fire is of course just that – a brush Fire in its natural flow. We can see in the foreground of the image the grass in the path of the Fire, yet to be consumed. It is easy to see the dryness of this grass which will of course ignite on contact with the flames.

Elsewhere and just behind the flame we can see the tress, the top of which appear not to have been burned, reminding us of the low level operation of the natural Brush Fire. We can also observe the smoke that rises from the Fire, alerting all in view to its progress and operation.

ENERGY

Once we have processed and chosen to respond how we will to the perhaps enforced change of the Five of Fire we meet the energy of the Six in this Element. Here we find we can channel that energy and focus on forward progress, if we learn to approach and expect steady progress using the tools at hand, rather than giving way to greed and expected sudden advancement.

In one sense the energy of this card can help us to gain a certain dominion and control over lower motives and inner impulses. Instead we can gain a victory over ourselves and what may threaten us. Control is required here, rather than suppression, there being perhaps a subtle but important difference. The energy here, if utilised to work with what we are and have within us, rather than trying to force or subdue it, can propel us forward towards our chosen goals.

In this way we can expect to make steady progress and evolution to what we are focussed upon. Of course this may mean that we need to re-examine and look again at what it is we are focussed upon and question if these goals and targets are still appropriate for us now, in the light of what we have learned so far and the changes we have no adapted to.

Should it be the case that we still feel within that we are headed in the right direction in our lives and that we remain true to hose inner drives, then this is a time for best foot forward, remaining resolute and buoyed by the confidence we should be feeling from this now. If however, we find that what motivated us previously is no longer the case we can still see a victory here, in that we have gained control over the inner self and can re-align ourselves to our new target, still confident and sure in that we are following the right direction.

We can see then that the energy of this card is an example of the principle of 'as within, so without'. The energy here calls us to look within, ensure we are being true to ourselves and what we find there and move steadily and surely onwards, focussed, determined and certain in the knowledge of who we now are and where we are headed in life.

The Brush Fire tells us that at this stage we can only go so far and that if we try and reach beyond our possible, realistic and likely goals, we may well reach burn out and find we lack the fuel and drive to achieve all we ultimately long for. With a more steady consummation of what we have available, we can however keep going for much longer. It is perhaps a time for patience, but without sitting still.

We have seen that Brush Fires occur naturally, being regarded as a natural phenomenon and often a useful and necessary one. This tells us that the energy here is a necessary part of our progress through life, so long as we are aligned with our inner quality, whatever this might be. If we can allow ourselves to respond honestly and positively to our inner selves, good advances and progress can now be made.

7 – WILDFIRE
BACKGROUND

A Wildfire is one looked upon as unplanned and occurring in 'undeveloped' forest or shrub land. Wildfire are generally given three classifications. First, a surface fire, being the most common type of Wildfire and which burns along the forest floor. Second, a ground fire, often caused by lightning and burn the dead organic matter on the ground, such as leaves and so on. Third, a crown or canopy fire, which spread along the tops of trees blown by the wind and have a high intensity.

The ignition source of naturally occurring wildfires is usually lightning. Its fuel consists of the vegetation in its area and path. The direr and more close placed this is, the quicker the fire burns. Resin and oils within some plants also burn more easily and intensely. The topography of the land can cause an end to a wildfire by providing natural breaks in the source of fuel, such as a lake, canyon or river.

Wildfires occur most frequently in areas of low landscape, which are dry, with low humidity, high temperatures and high winds. Frequent storms also give rise to lightning in these areas, providing the necessary start for the wildfire. Other forms of wildfire ignition are volcanic eruption, sparks from rock fall and even spontaneous combustion.

Over time, ecosystems in these areas and plants that grow there developed different adaptations that allow them to survive and reproduce during a fire. An example of this is Pine cones, which remain closed until heated, then releasing their seeds, thereby creating new trees. Some trees have think, fire-resistant bark, such as the Redwood and Sequoia, also featuring high branches, reducing the chances of their being burned.

A further feature applicable here is that areas prone to natural wildfire can benefit from them. The fire destroys harmful bacteria and fungi on the ground that would otherwise harm seeds prior to germination. The fire can also recycle nutrients in the humus layer (the dead organic matter on the ground). A wildfire also clears the area of dry brush, allowing sunlight to aid the growth of new seedlings.

A wildfire is seen as differing from other fires in that it is largely uncontrolled, because of its extensive size and the speed at which it can spread. It also has potential to change direction suddenly and unexpectedly. Predictably, 'wildfire season' is the tinder-box hottest months of the summer.

DESCRIPTION

Our image here is something of a dualistic one. In the foreground we see the greenery of the trees not yet consumed by the fire, whilst in the background clearly the fire rages. It is easy to remind ourselves of the uncontrolled nature of the wildfire here, along with its size. The apparent inevitability of the trees being about to burn also reminds us of the speed at which the typical wildfire moves.

Although dramatic in appearance and seemingly threatening we should remind ourselves of the difference to the Inferno card of the Major Arcana, which is at another level altogether, bout physically and within us as human beings.

ENERGY

There is often a question that can arise when we look at the image on the traditional Tarot card of Rods Seven. This is whether we are seeing attack or defence. The same can be true here and the energy with this card can prompt us to examine which we need to employ now.

We have seen that naturally occurring wildfires have both a destructive as well as necessary cleansing outcome on their environment. If left to its own devices such areas have a tendency and ability to ensure their own survival and propagation. So it is with the natural advancement that comes with the numerical energy of Seven. Here we need to look at the natural direction we are taking from our inner prompting and determine whether we need to have more of this (attack) or pause and reconsider, seeing what we may need to release (defence).

We have also seen that the Wildfire can change direction quite suddenly. This can tell us we may need to consider a similar change in our direction if life or self, if we are to make the most of what is on offer for us at this time, or with what we are presented with in life. It may be the case that the direction we thought we would take in life has reached a turning point and the environment we now find ourselves in is no longer the best or most applicable one for us. By considering a change in our direction we may be able to make the most of the natural flow that is the typical energy that comes with this card.

Just as wildfires can be caused by unexpected and sometime dramatic events – lightning, volcanoes and so on, it may be that we feel the strong effects of other forces in ourselves and lives when this card appears for us. This being the case we may need to assess how to respond – rather than an uncontrolled outburst or instinctive reaction. It may be that now is the time for examining whether we need to stand firm against such forces and press on with our direction. Equally, it could be that now is the time to beat a retreat, acquiesce to the flow of life and go a different way.

Either way, it is only by turning within, to the area of drive, instinct and prompting that the Fire suit calls us to, that we will be able to determine the direction of the natural flow of our lives now. Once this is known, or perhaps simply 'sensed', then we have only to stick with this knowing and respond accordingly. It is then we can rest in the surety of our focus and movement forward in our self and our life.

8 - FIRESTORM
BACKGROUND

A Firestorm is usually created from a larger Wildfire, its defining characteristic being the storm-force winds it creates from every direction. One of its main features is that it has such intensity that it creates and sustains its own wind system. In this way, a Firestorm has a 'chimney effect' where the heat of the original fire draws in more and more of the air surrounding it. This is known as the 'stack effect'

This can be increased very swiftly if a jet stream wind is above or near the fire. This creates a mushroom effect from the updraft, known as a thermal column. This in turn creates strong and gusty winds which are directed inward to the fire, called radial winds. This creates a tremendous turbulence which can cause these inflowing winds to behave and change direction erratically. As the heat rises so more air and dry debris is drawn in to further fuel the fire.

Firestorms can occur from a brush or forest fire, if the surrounding conditions and environment are right for this. The intense energy of a Firestorm can create its own thunderstorms. The thermal column can also produce its own fiery tornados or Fire Whirls, which we saw with the Four of Fire. The Firestorm is the big brother here.

The top of the thermal column or mushroom cloud of the Firestorm can reach an amazing 6 miles (9 km) above the ground. It is this that is responsible for the power of the Firestorm. In the right weather conditions, the warm air in the thermal column can rise at a speed of 170 miles per hour.

Behind the Firestorm cooler air gusts into the space left by the ascending air. This causes violent winds to blow that can then cause separate fires to merge together into one larger, coalesced force. These winds also feed the fire what it needs to keep burning – oxygen in the form of the air, fuel in the form of wood and other debris and other flammable material to keep it alive and intense.

The intense heat produced by a Firestorm manifests largely as radiated heat, which is infrared radiation. This can cause flammable material to burst into flame ahead of the Fire reaching it. This also serves to expand the area and intensity of the Firestorm. The very high temperatures of the fire continue to ignite anything that might burn until its fuel source is depleted. At this point the Firestorm can break up into separate, smaller conflagrations.

One final feature of the Firestorm can be that it produces black rain. Under the right conditions a Firestorm can produce condensation. This can produce a fire cloud (pyrocumulus). The blackness in the rain is actually soot, obviously caused by the fire. These clouds can grow larger and result in lightning.

DESCRIPTION

Here we see the Firestorm in the act of gathering into itself the air around it, creating the mushroom appearance of the thermal column described above. The central column of this beneath the mushroom gives the suggestion of an enormous firework, reminding us of the speed at which this phenomenon happens.

The trees in the foreground remind us of the source of fuel the Firestorm, like all fires, requires, those on the left of the image appearing incandescent as they are ignited, ahead of the flames reaching them, by the heat the Firestorm produces.

ENERGY

There is a certain spontaneity that comes with the energy of this card. The Firestorm arises spontaneously from other factors, be this a previously exiting Wildfire, Lightning strike or whatever. It appears called into existence from the ethers, then rushes off on its intended cause and path. Here then we may need to bring a little of that spontaneity into ourselves and our own lives.

It may be that the immediacy of which we speak here needs to arise from a deeper place within. This can be like the central column of the Firestorm. This draws into it what it needs instinctively and so it is that we may need to look within to our own sense of gnosis, cognisance or inner knowing. Once we have established this level of certainty within ourselves we can find we need to act, and act without delay. To deny that knowledge and surety is to dent ourselves the truth, whatever this may be for us at this time.

Once that inner fore is released it can seem to take on a life of its own, just like the Firestorm creating its own winds for its continuance. The energy of this card is one of acceleration and so it is we need to move with all due speed and alacrity if we are to seize upon any opportunities afforded us by the unleashing of that force within. As we move forward so it is we can find we magnetically and almost magically draw to us what we need on our journey.

The ignition of materials ahead of the flames of the Firestorm can tell us that now may be a time when we need to project forward and examine the likely consequences of our actions. Indeed such may be the power and ability of foresight afforded us now from this energy that we can see and instinctively know within the outcome in the future we will create by our focus and force in the present. It may be that we need to question of those outcomes are in accordance with our inner knowing, our truth and perhaps above all, our conscience.

His being the case we know that we can move forward with full focus, speed and integrity. Should any of these not be in alignment with our inner self, then we must look again, for destruction and loss may inevitably be the result if we do not.

9 - HEATWAVE
BACKGROUND

A heatwave, as perhaps is stating the obvious is a prolonged period of excessively hot weather, usually accompanied by high humidity. The heatwave is measured against the typical climate and conditions in the area in which it occurs. For a more specific definition, a heatwave is said to be in existence when the daily maximum temperature, over more than 5 consecutive days exceeds the average maximum temperature by 5 degrees centigrade. More lyrically, a heatwave features a period of 'abnormally and uncomfortably hot and humid weather'.

The length of a period can of course vary. Technically speaking it could be just one day but have been known to last for much longer, usually over several weeks. Heatwaves form when high pressure at an altitude of between 10,000 and 25,000 feet strengthens and remains in an area. It is this that determines the length of the heatwave. Often this can occur when the Jet Stream, which we have me before, follows the course of the Sun, creating the pressure required in the air.

The high pressure at those heights serves to trap the air beneath. This subsides towards the surface acting as a dome over the atmosphere, thereby trapping the heat. Without the air being allowed to lift there is no convection (movement of fluid) and hence no formation of cloud possible in order to create rain. This results in the ongoing build-up of heat at the surface, giving us our heatwave.

A Heatwave can be a contributory factor to many other natural weather and fire-related phenomenon, such as an increase in the likelihood of the ignition of Brush and Wild Fires. The heat of course dries out all vegetation, requiring only the merest spark to start a fire.

Those that live in colder climates may initially welcome warmer temperatures, but here, at the highest numerical energy of the suit, we should stress that we are looking at the energy from a more extreme form of heat. Once the novelty of several hot days passed we can begin to experience other effects, individually and collectively.

A heatwave can produce a drought and the many effects of water shortages. The heatwave is typical in this in the nature of Fire. We cannot live without it, but with too much we can soon reach a point of burnout, or worse. A prolonged heatwave can have the effect of draining our energy resources, externally as well as internally. Hyperthermia (heatstroke) and heat exhaustion can become common, even causing premature death in those without the necessary resources of health to sustain themselves.

DESCRIPTION

Here we see an image of the sun in full 'heatwave' mode. We can see the waves of heat emanating from the Sun itself and gain the feel of the long, hot, hazy days we experience during a heatwave as we look at the image.

We can see there is no escape or let –up from the heat. The partly silhouetted trees remind us of the effect on vegetation as it dries completely. The clouds in the mid-ground also remind us of the height the heat is trapped beneath, giving us the dome described above.

ENERGY

The energy of the Nine of Fire, as the highest single digit numerical influence (and so the greatest height we can aspire to) is one of lofty aspiration, as befits the height involved with the formation of a heatwave. We can derive a great strength from the energy here if we allow ourselves to tap into the fire in our blood and veins – our greatest and deepest motivations can come to the fore now and seek to drive us forward in an ongoing, unstoppable force.

Such a powerful force must of course be handled with care. It can be all too easy to suffer under the heatwave and lose our clarity, symbolically becoming dehydrated. This can mean we need to look to our emotions, as a metaphorical need for water, linked as we know to our feelings. The danger of a symbolic and literal burnout is high now. Just as with all cards really, there is both a blessing and a curse from this cards energy; here it can perhaps be more immediately and dramatically felt.

So it is there may be a need for rest and recuperation, amidst a time of great effort. We may find we need to dig deep within to find our will and a supply of ongoing sustenance – again a need for water in this respect. Giving ourselves what we need can serve to enable us to not only survive the intensity of the heatwave but prosper under it.

The Heatwave card does indeed bring an intense energy. Here we can find ourselves under the microscope of our own examination. It can be as if we are cut to the quick and the core of ourselves, our inner motivations exposed. If these are not in alignment with our highest potential, capability and good we could find that the heat is too much for us and we can wither beneath it. It may be that now we need to ensure that we do all we need as it is appropriate to do so, but recognise these limits and respect them, taking rest and lying in any available shade when required. Again we see here the dual nature of energy and it existing just as potentiality, our response to it being what matters and the decisive factor between it being 'good' or 'bad', 'positive' or 'negative'.

In this way we can avoid the trap spoken of above that the heatwave produces, finding instead a way of being within and without that maximises our resources but allows for relaxation and enjoyment, along with the intensity and work that can often accompany this cards' energy. In this way we can follow what is the natural way for us, confident and sure that we strive towards the achievement and fulfilment of our goals and inner ambitions. Much is possible at this time, so long as we do not expect it all, or too much and too soon. The price for this can be great, so now is the time to apply that wisdom from within.

10 - EMBERS
BACKGROUND

Here at the end of our firewalk we come to the embers as the flames die down and rest. Embers are specifically the hot, glowing coals that are made from wood, coal or any carbon-based material that is left after a fire.

Embers can however retain a great heat, still sometimes as hot as the Fire from whence they came. As such they also retain the potential to rekindle a fire from their radiated heat and sparks. Whilst the heat from a burning fire is constantly changing, that from the embers is a more constant form of heat, hence their deployment in cooking with barbecues and so on.

Embers form from the only partially burnt pieces of fuel consumed in a fire. They retain some chemical energy and so are still of use. This is usually in the centre of the object where oxygen cannot reach it so it cannot combust and burn. Combustion is still occurring within the pieces of fuel however, albeit at a miniature scale and this is why embers radiate the heat they do. The light within embers, as the small piece of red, yellow and orange is this combustion happening. There is not enough combustion happening at the same time to create a flame however and so the fire gradually dies out.

Once the embers are completely burned out that are no longer carbon, but other oxidized materials such as calcium and phosphorous. It is then that they take on the form which we recognise and call ashes.

In the case of a wild or forest fire, embers are usually made from burnt leaves. As such they are light and small and so easily transported by any wind. This means they can provide a danger of re-igniting a previously extinguished fire. Given the required conditions, embers can also be blown ahead of an existing, burning fire, starting small 'spot fires' as they are known, which are later collected by the larger, central fire. This can occur hundreds of metres in advance of the main fire itself.

DESCRIPTION

Here we see the Embers burning the wood following the fire. In the foreground we can see the last flames still bright with their yellow light. This turns to orange in the mid-ground after the flames have die out, leaving this hot glowing effect from the unburnt wood. In the background at the top of and left of the image there are sparks produced by the Embers.

This reminds us of the constant possibility of the re-ignition of the fire. The sparks here also remind us of the cyclic and ongoing nature of energy that can never be extinguished. Energy, as we now know, simply is and just as it may leave one form, here the carbon-based wood becoming the Embers, so it takes on another. This produces the spark and so we return again to the One of Fire.

ENERGY

The last numerical card of this Element and indeed the Minor Arcana, is fittingly the Embers, the afterglow of a successful Fire that is here burning its last. Much as this may give us comfort and rest, or at the very least point towards a need for these things, we can gain a sense of the glow of the hearth fire as we look at the image. This can remind us of the need for re-fuelling ourselves when this card appears for us, its energy telling us we may need to put our feet up before the fire and rest awhile.

We should take note too that as the last card of the Element and the outworking of the energy of Fire, we should see this as the earned outcome, the reward for what has been a successful achievement. The hard work we have invested should now have paid its dividends and we have earned what we have achieved. Of course it may be that we have done so much of this that a sense of weariness and even exhaustion may be setting in. This again points towards a need for rest and recuperation, a time when we can bask in the glow we see before us in this cards energy.

We should also be aware of the great heat that can still exist within the Embers. This tells us that we should keep a little back with whatever we are engaged in in life at this time. There is a need to always 'stay in our power' and do whatever is required in order to preserve ourselves. So many times it can be all too easy to expound so much time and energy looking after, helping and giving to others that we take nothing for ourselves. How much better it is to first give to ourselves. This way the quality of what we can then more freely give to others is better, which in truth aids them all the more.

The heat within the Embers also tells us that we are not done yet! Despite whatever feelings of being drained and depleted we may be feeling within, the energy of this card tells us that we have within an unstoppable and immortal storehouse of energy. All that is required from us is to locate and fed from this, rather than giving of ourselves. The energy that we speak of there can be defined as 'Universal' and is freely available to all of us. It is eternal and can never deplete. This cards energy tells us we are part of that and it is part of us. Once we have unlocked this particular secret, the endless flow of energy is ours.

This also gives rise to the sparks that we see in the image and always have potential to pop out from the Embers. Here we can see that cyclical nature that exists within all of nature, of birth, life decay, death and rebirth. This is exemplified in the sparks we see, taking us back to the One of Fire. From out of the ashes the phoenix does indeed arise. We may have need when this card appears to see what it is we need to lay to rest in order to allow for our particular phoenix to arise, in whatever form or quality this may be.

FIRE OF EARTH – CINDER
BACKGROUND

We come to the manner in which the Fire element mixes or blends with the other three and finds its expression. We find this first in an earthly way, with Cinder. This is burned or partly burned substance that has not burned down to ashes but is incapable of further combustion. In this way we have the earthy substance left from the Fire.

Cinder is no longer capable of producing flame, but may still burn. In the metallurgical process, this is known as sinter, being any solid substance left from the process of smelting or refining. Volcanic eruption can result in the production of Cinders, giving us a further direct link to the compound of Fire with Earth. In this method of their production they are a coarse material thrown out by volcanoes. These can take the form of blocks or bombs as they can fly out from the volcano.

There are differing types of volcano on the Earth. One of these is the Stratovolcano, known as Cinder Cone volcanos. These are cone shaped and made from alternating layers of ash, cinders and lava. These are the most common types of volcano on the planet. Due to the formation, during eruption fragments of cinder material can be sprayed into the air from vents in the volcanos surface. These cinders are sometimes called scoria and are melted rock with gas filled pieces. They cool very quickly and generally accumulate near the opening of the vent in the volcano. In this way the Cinder Cone shape of the volcano is maintained and gives it its name and identity.

If we look at the rock Cinder itself, this is an igneous rock (ignis meaning fire), formed from cooling and solidifying magma or lava. Cinder is similar to pumice with a low density and many cavities, which are called vesicles. Its colouring is typically black, brown or red, dependent on its chemical constituents. Cinder often goes under the name of 'lava rock'.

DESCRIPTION

Here we see a landscape of lava rock, or Cinder, formed from past eruptions of volcanic activity, known appropriately as Sunset Crater. We can see here the naturally occurring colouring of the Cinder, being largely either red or black, fading in time to pink.

The trees that we silhouetted on the image will of course have grown after the last eruption and stand here as testimony to the resilient Earth energy that accompanies this card. Our eye seems inevitably drawn however to the crater and the source of that more fiery quality.

ENERGY

The energy of this Compound card of the Fire element is a combination of Earth with the Fire. This gives us a drive and passion from within that needs a grounding followed by action. This results in a progressive energy that needs to move us forwards in our endeavours, but in a slow and steady manner.

That Cinder itself is no longer capable of producing flame or fire in this respect tells us we can no longer be carried away by unfocussed fiery energy. That the Cinder retains its solid form shows us we need not now to lose the need for remaining grounded and realistic in our endeavours but can rest assured we still have enough power to drive within us to carry us forwards.

We have seen that during volcanic eruption Cinder can be projected and thrown out from the cone or centre. From this we can deduce that our targets can still be seen but may not be specific or focussed at this stage. By adding in the more earthy aspect to this form of fiery energy we can be able to make plans for that steady progress, driven from within.

We can also gain a strong creative and inspirational spark from the energy of this card. The strong practical streak within us no can come to the fore and may well need to ensure we retain that focus described above. In this way this energy can cause us to consider the purpose and meaning behind doing what we do. It is not about progress for progress' sake. Rather it is the cause that comes or needs to come, to the fore now.

In this way the deeper level of energy that this card brings with it when it appears for us directs us to our sense of self-worth. It may be that we have been aware of a lack of this and this card reminds us we need to focus on this and reconnect with it, if it has been lost somewhat along the way. It is the direction and purpose of our actions that we need to focus on now.

FIRE OF FIRE – PLASMA
BACKGROUND

Plasma is recognised as one of the four fundamental, or for our purposes, elemental, states of matter, the other being solid, liquid and gas (air). The word Plasma comes from the Greek meaning 'anything formed'. It has properties unlike those of the other states of matter.

Plasma itself is made up of free electrons and ions (positive and negative charged particles) of a particular element. Two examples of naturally occurring types of Plasma are the Auroras and Lightning, both of which we have met before.

The main difference to the other states of matter with Plasma is that the electrons in it are not bound to the nucleus and so are free to move around the system, whatever this might be. In this way they reflect the perpetually moving energy of Fire combined with Fire.

We do see plasma all around in our modern world. Every time we switch on a light bulb, the glow we see is the plasma that results from the free flow of electricity. The same is the case with the ubiquitous neon signs in every town and city.

We can see more naturally occurring and myriad examples of Plasma every time we look at the Stars, or the Firmament, as we have met it before. Stars are basically balls of different gases at extremely high temperatures. These high temperatures have the effect of charging up the atoms and creating Plasma, being another way in which we can see here the Compound of Fire with Fire.

Although the requisite temperature to create a Plasma is not achieved in the flames of a Fire, when combined with another source of heat, such a Fire requires for life as we have seen, it fits the purposes and classification of our card here.

413

Elsewhere in Nature we have Plasma in the form of the Sun itself and Solar Winds and in many different forms in the wider Universe, of which are a part of course. Here it is estimated that 99% of our visible universe consists of Plasmas of different types, life existing in between the remaining percent of particles and matter.

The hotter the temperature of the gas, the faster the atoms and molecules it consists of move. In this way, Fire begets Fire. At such temperatures, collisions between such fast-moving atoms cause violent reactions that can tear off electrons.

DESCRIPTION

We have seen above how different forms of Plasma are surrounding us, in the natural world and out in space. Here we see a combination of perhaps the two most common and easily visible types – the Sun and Lightning, giving us our requisite compound of Fire with Fire.

We see the Sun as it sets, fitting for this last suit of the Minor Arcana journey. The beautiful colours we see demonstrates the fiery nature of the Sun, together with its inestimable heat, without which we cannot survive of course. This reminds us of the temperatures required for Plasma to form. Added to this we have the Lightning, which itself also tells us of the above, albeit in a more sporadic and momentary manner.

ENERGY

The combination of Fire and Fire creates an explosive mixture which we define here as Plasma. We know already that we need each of the four Elements in one form or another or our existence. What we also need to realise now is that each of these ideally need to be balanced and proportionate for our healthy and successful life.

414

What we can perhaps more easily see with this cards' energy, than the other Compound cards is how an excess of Fire energy can become destructive. We do not however focus only what may appear to be a 'negative' influence of the energy here. Rather we remind ourselves of the unpolarised nature of energy itself and the important matter being how we choose to respond to and use the energy we receive here.

Because of this we will look first at the energising and motivating energy we can receive with this card. A double dose of Fire as it were can of course get us 'all fired up' and it may be that this is precisely what we have need of in our self and life. So many people can suffer from a malady of lack of motivation and purpose in life and the energy here can find them igniting this.

Indeed this can be so much the case that we can become impatient and may need to guard against a frustration, with anything and anyone that from our perspective now may appear to be getting in our way or, intentionally or otherwise, holding us up. The energy here can bring a fire in our veins and bellies that spurs us onwards and upwards and suddenly anything and everything is possible.

The temptation is to rush headlong into battle and the energy here tells us we are ready for the fight, in whatever form it is required of us. We have made reference above to the violent outbursts that can occur with Plasma and we need to ensure we do not become prey to this course of action ourselves now. Along with the positive reaction this cards energy can engender, the destructive may follow close at hand too.

Instant inspiration can be something of a watchword (or two!) for this card and its energy can help us to rise above the mundane. It may be that abusive behaviour of some kind, such as drug use or anything that heightens the senses to this level of inspired abandon, may be tempting now. We have seen however that we have this Fire within us naturally and now we can delve into this changeable and sporadic energy and employ it to positive effect.

It may be time to ask ourselves what is the Fire that burns within us and to what effect upon us. If we can apply a modified wisdom to these questions we can truly tap into an energy now that can never leave us. Passion can be lodged within our body, heart and mind and remain there, fuelling us for the rest of our lives. What is required of it most is the correct outer focus for the heat in generates within.

FIRE OF WATER – MAGMA
BACKGROUND

Magma is a mixture (as the name from the Greek means) of molten or semi-molten rock, solids and volatiles. The term 'molten' refers to something made liquid by heat, giving us the combination of Fire and Water here.

Largely found beneath the surface of the Earth (and it is thought on other planets too) may also contain suspended crystals, dissolved gas and gas bubbles. Magma itself is a high-temperature, fluid substance. The main areas it forms are magma chambers that feed volcanos and mid-ocean ridges in the Earths' crust. Magma usually forms in high-temperature, low pressure environments within several kilometres of the Earth's surface.

Essentially melted rock, magma is created when rocks, often of differing types, each reach their melting point. As a rock melts its volume changes. As this happens small globules of melt link together and soften the rock. The pressure within the Earth causes the melt to be squeezed from its source. This may occur in up to 35% of a rock and eventually the melted rock mass becomes a crystal. The percentage of melt is determined from the ratio of compatible and incompatible elements within a rock, which in turn determines the type of magma produced. The greater degree of melting, the more closer the Magma produced resembles its source rock.

There are three main ways in which Magma is naturally formed. First heat transfer, when the rising heat melts the cooler rock around it. Close to melting point already, the additional heat provided is enough to melt these rocks and Magma is formed. Second decompression melting, where two tectonic plates within the Earth are pulled apart and the mantle rises into the gap. As the pressure is reduced the rock begins to melt and we have our Magma. Third, flux melting, where water can enter a body of rock. Descending plates carry the water, sediment and other material into volcanic areas.

Whilst the processes, formation and nature of Magma can be complicated we can basically think of Magma as a much of mineral crystals within a liquid. It is not a stretch of the imagination to think of it also as liquid fire. What we need to be clear about for our purposes here is that magma is dependent on heat, as our form of Fire, for its existence. Like all elements we cannot separate one from the other, this being clear again here.

DESCRIPTION

Here we can see both aspects of the combination of Elements here. We can see the flow from a volcanic eruption in the top left of the image. What follows and leads our eye down into and across the foreground of our image is the magma itself, the liquidised fire that runs its way forwards.

When we examine the flow of Magma itself we can see within the liquid flow the part formed rock formations, which are in actuality partially melted, as we have seen. The colour and the very nature of the Magma itself remind us of the terrific temperatures and heat pivotal to the entire process.

ENERGY

The Compound of Fire with Water gives us an energy of an expressive nature, tempered by feeling and compassion. When under the influence of this energy then we can find ourselves to our lives with a degree of passion and focus that is at once given a devotion and love fuelled by our hearts desire. So it is the energy of this card allow us to make great strides forwards if we have the courage to follow our higher instincts and passions.

We have seen the tremendous temperatures and heat required to melt the rock of our hearts, so allowing our bodies to move more fluidly through life and its challenges. It is when we allow this natural process to evolve that we can find that motion and realise we cannot achieve goals and targets by force alone but by compassion and love, for ourselves and others. It may be at the time this card appears for us we need to examine whether we are pushing blindly forwards and have a need to be more compassionate in our thoughts and actions, both inwardly and outwardly. This is also echoed in the low-pressure environments in which the conditions for Magma formation occur best.

We can also make note here that only a certain percentage of the rock can turn to its liquid state in the Magma process and that this is determined from the compatibility of the elements involved. Being half of water, and so of the emotions, this cards energy will focus on our state of heart and whether this is working for or against us. The energy brought to us here can cause us to become quite self-critical if it turns in on itself and in so doing cause us to feel that we are incompatible with others and even ourselves.

Should this be the case we will need to balance and centre ourselves by delving deeper within and locating the source of the Fire and passion within us. Here we are reminded of the depth within the Earth at which magma can be formed and so it is we may need to dig within ourselves to find the source of our power, courage and drive once again. If we can apply this with love firstly to ourselves then we can allow ourselves to go with flow that we are naturally creating, like the movement of Magma and we can find that all is well in our world once more.

What we aspire to can be highlighted and paramount for us now and in order to achieve or at least make some inroads towards this fulfilment, we must follow our hearts desire and be true to what is within us. It may that a certain toughness is required, a little akin to the policy of 'tough love' required in parenting at times, that we must apply to ourselves. Once a compatible balance between the elements is achieved here we are able to realise we have created the flow we long to go with.

FIRE OF AIR - SMOKE
BACKGROUND

Lastly then, we come to the Compound of Fire with Air, which perhaps predictably, gives us Smoke. Smoke itself is a collection of tiny particles of solids, liquids and gas. The Smoke visible to us is mostly carbon, tar, oils and ash.

Smoke occurs when there is not enough oxygen (our showing of the Air element here) to burn a source of fuel completely, known as incomplete combustion. The Smoke that results is the collection of the unburned particles. Each particle is too small for our visible spectrum but together we see them as Smoke. The exact composition of Smoke produced will obviously therefore depend on the type of fuel remaining unburned.

Smoke can contain flammable compounds, which present a danger of further combustion, or re-ignition. Notably, for our purposes, this occurs with an increase in oxygen. This can cause a backdraught or flashover effect, with a plume of flame billowing outwards from the original fire. Another feature to note for the properties of this card is that Smoke obscures visibility.

As we know by now, there are three substances required for a Fire to exist – fuel, heat and oxygen. If we eliminate any one of those, the Fire cannot exist. As a Fire consumes its fuel, whether this be wood or other material so it increases the heat and fuelled by a supply of oxygen, it burns happily. It is this process that produces the Smoke - hence our classification here of Fire with Air. Once the fuel source has been consumed the Smoke disappears.

Smoke can be seen as an unwanted by-product of a Fire. The particles of materials within Smoke are airborne and its effect can be more destructive than the Fire itself, as these materials and particles burn commensurate with the quantity of air mixed into them. Fires with a high oxygen level burn at a high temperature and a small amount of Smoke produced. Equally Fires burning with less oxygen produce more Smoke, which is often more toxic in its content.

DESCRIPTION

The image here is one that illustrates the combination, or Compound of our two elements. Equally, half the image being filled with flames from a Fire, the other half consisting of the billowing clouds of Smoke produced as it burns.

The fact that the Smoke exists at all reminds us that we are not done burning yet, since as we saw above, there must still be fuel to consume for this to happen. Whilst the image gives the impression of great heat with the flames we can remind ourselves here that for Smoke to appear in the quantity we see it here, in Fire terms the temperature is relatively low. The Fire is therefore fed by the air around, which of course we cannot see.

ENERGY

When we think of a combination of Smoke and Fire, as we have here we tend to immediately think that 'there is no smoke without fire' and also the opposite of this. For our purposes this can tell us that this cards energy tells us that without a force of Fire inside us, perhaps best described as our passion, we can at best only blow hot air, or Smoke.

So it is we can see a need with the appearance of this card for us to be firmly focused on what it is we are responding to within and a need to speak that truth as well as act on it. The energy here requires absolute honesty and truth from us and in our expression. Sometimes this can be hard to admit to, let alone express, but if we turn to that inner strength and power which is our Fire now, we can find that what we do present to the world in our thoughts and our communication can be without equal.

We have seen that the appearance of Smoke with a Fire is dependent on a lack of oxygen. This tells us that we may need to focus our attention on our thoughts and thinking process a little more at this time, to achieve the requisite balance here – all the Compound Cards being and requiring a balance between their two Elements for their successful response and outworking.

Equally an overbalance the other way, with an excessive focus on our thinking rather than following the inner or higher instinct the Fire gives us, can result in a Backdraught or Flashover. This can show us that the result of erring too much on the mental can have effects we may not anticipate, however clever we might think we are. It may be that we need to check we are not likely to leave a trail of chaos in our wake with the plans and ideas in our mind at this time.

Following on from this, we know that Smoke obscures our visibility. From this we can deduce that the energy of this card tells us to look within to our inner and higher sources rather than rely on logic and deduction alone. We may not be able to see where we are heading when this card appears for us, but with our attention on our purpose and inner source, we can allow ourselves to be successfully guided forwards.

We know too that once the source of Fuel has been consumed the Smoke disappears. Here then we need to ensure we preserve the Fire lest it be extinguished. So it is that this cards energy calls us to herald the inner source, available to us all, in whatever form it may be for us. And do what is necessary in order to preserve its continued existence within us and our life.

423

CARD BACKS

The image on the back of the cards is taken from the logo that I first designed and featured on my very first business cards, some 30 years ago! All this time later, it still seems appropriate for use here and set against the parchment style backing to the cards, gives a feel of some ancient esoteric manuscript holding a mystery to be revealed, as each Tarot card can be said to be.

The eight points of the star relate to the eight ancient Festivals of the 'Wheel of the Year' celebrated as marker points of the annual cycle of the natural world. Observed today as the Solstices at midsummer and midwinter, the Spring and Autumn Equinoxes, plus the four 'Fire Festivals' of Imbolc, Beltane, Lughnasadh and Samhain.

The circle that links each of the points of the star symbolises the continuity of life as the cycle turns and turns each year, as well as the links we have with the natural world. The dots between the words around the outside can create a five-pointed star or Pentacle, an ancient symbol representing, amongst other things, the levels of the human being, as physical, emotional, mental and spiritual, plus the topmost level of Soul. Here as you know now, they apply to the four suits of the Minor Arcana, along with the Major Arcana above.

Lastly, the words, explained in full detail in Volume 1 of the Tarot Therapy series, translate to read

THE WHEEL OF TAROT SPEAKS THE LAW OF NATURE

This can also be shown in tabular form, developing the Three Septenaries layout of the Major Arcana that first appeared in Tarot Therapy Volume 1. This shows how the cards of the Major Arcana align naturally with the eight Festivals of the Wheel of the Year. This shows us just one way in which the Tarot speaks the law of Nature as well as how the Tarot is energy and this energy is best expressed through the natural world.

IMBOLC - SOLES OF FEET - CANYON							
FEST IVAL	SPRING EQUIN OX	BELTA NE	SUMM ER SOLSTI CE	LUGHN ASADH	AUT UMN EQUI NOX	SAM HAIN	WINTE R SOLSTI CE
CHA KRA	BASE	SACRA L	SOLAR PLEXU S	HEART	THR OAT	BRO W	CROW N
CAR D	TORNA DO	WATE RFALL	RAINF OREST	DESERT	ECLI PSE	TSUN AMI	AVALA NCHE
CAR D	EARTH QUAKE	AURO RA	HURRI CANE	MOUN TAIN	ICEB ERG	DRO UGH T	RAINB OW

CARD	INFERNO	VOLCANO	FIRMAMENT	MOON	SUN	METEOR	EARTH

CONCLUSION

Although the creation of this deck has taken two years since I began, it evolved over a much longer period of time than that. During this gestation it went through many transformations until it finally settled on its final form, as you see it here.

The one constant throughout the twists and turns it undertook was nature. One of the first inspirations for this deck was to feature the natural imagery I was seeing in many different, beautiful and inspiring ways on the very many decks I acquired over the years. These were always as part of the overall image on the card however and somehow what was for me the best part was relegated or lost amongst the symbolism and people that were featured. This is not to say that that approach is wrong of course, only to offer here a different viewpoint.

As its story unfolded, I eventually settled on the idea that what I wanted to get across was the essential energy of the cards and this is best expressed in the natural world that is all around, beneath and above us, and that we are part of. In my experience it takes a very subdued soul indeed not to be inspired or affected in anyway by the myriad forms of beauty the natural world can present to us.

As well as being an exercise in expressing the energy of the Tarot and bringing it to life, this deck is also a celebration of Nature. One thing that became abundantly clear to me as I researched the 'Background' sections for each card was the amazing workings of this planet we call Earth and the Universe in which we are situated. I hope that something of this has come across to you as you read this book and as you continue to use the cards.

Should this be the case I hope that it will inspire you to learn to live a life more in keeping with a sense of the sacred at its

427

heart, whatever you conceive that to be, as well as one that honours the natural kingdom, in all its varied forms and ways.

I have always felt that the only purpose of our being alive is to grow spiritually and honour that which is sacred to us. For me, this is at the core of everything we do, or should do. This affects every aspect of my being and my life and looming large amongst this is connection to Nature. This can be celebrated in many different ways and one of these for me is to here include an exhortation, not just to help protect nature by supporting organisations such as Friends of the Earth, Greenpeace et al but of looking at your intrinsic and instinctive connection to Nature and realise that you are part of it, 'She' is part of you and you are both inter-dependent on each other, for life, health and well-being.

As this truth is realised so I hope that you will find it necessary to adapt and change your lifestyle so that it is more in keeping with the natural world. There is so much we can do that helps create a better reality for all of us, in the individual acts possible by all of us. If this deck has inspired you in anyway, act on it this way.

FURTHER READING

Steve Hounsome has written three volumes in his previous series on Tarot Therapy. These are –

- *TAROT THERAPY VOLUME 1 – The Theory and Practice of*
- *TAROT THERAPY VOLUME 2 – The Major Arcana: Seekers Quest*
- *TAROT THERAPY VOLUME 3 – The Minor Arcana: The Map of the Quest*

His other published titles are –

- *TAMING THE WOLF: Full Moon Meditations*
- *PRATICAL SPIRITUALITY*
- *PRACTICAL MEDITATION*
- *HOW TO BE A TELEPHONE PSYCHIC*

These titles are available via Steve's website at www.tarottherapy.co.uk

Or from Amazon, using the following link –

http://www.amazon.co.uk/Steve-Hounsome/e/B0084DX386/ref=ntt_dp_epwbk_0

They are available in paperback version or for Kindle and e-book format.

Steve's previous books on Tarot Therapy contain an extensive Bibliography of books on the Tarot.

TAROT THERAPY PRODUCTS
www.tarottherapy.co.uk

Steve Hounsome produces a range of products and services to help you explore and apply Tarot Therapy. These are detailed below –

TAROT THERAPY CARDS

The complete 78 card deck is available, with an optional, unique and hand-made Tarot Therapy bag, imprinted with the Tarot Therapy logo.

TAROT THERAPY TRAINING

There are three courses available, for those wishing to train as a Tarot Therapist –

- **INTRODUCTION** – For the complete beginner
- **CERTIFICATE** – For those wanting to learn how to read the Tarot as Therapy
- **DIPLOMA** - For those wanting to develop their existing knowledge and ability

All these courses are held regularly in Poole, Dorset, UK and are available as distance-learning courses.

TAROT THERAPY, PAST LIVES AND MEDIUMSHIP READINGS

Steve is available for readings either in person in Dorset, England, or by 'phone or email.

PERSONAL, PSYCHIC & SPIRITUAL DEVELOPMENT CD'S

Steve has produced a range of meditations and exercises for personal, psychic and spiritual development. These are available as cd's or as downloads from the website.

TAROT CLUB, MOON MEDITATIONS, SPIRITUAL AND PSYCHIC DEVELOPMENT GROUPS

Steve hosts a guided Meditation each New and Full Moon.

He also runs weekly Spiritual and Development Groups for beginners and the more experienced.

He hosts a fortnightly Tarot Club, to explore, experience and enjoy all things Tarot.

All these meetings take place in Poole, Dorset, UK.

Full details of all the above are available at Steve's website –

www.tarottherapy.co.uk

You can also email Steve at –

steve@tarottherapy.co.uk

Printed in Great Britain
by Amazon